3

Raspberry Delights

A Collection of Raspberry Recipes
Cookbook Delights Series – Book 14

Karen Jean Matsko Hood

Current and Future Cookbooks
By Karen Jean Matsko Hood

DELIGHTS SERIES

Almond Delights
Anchovy Delights
Apple Delights
Apricot Delights
Artichoke Delights
Asparagus Delights
Avocado Delights
Banana Delights
Barley Delights
Basil Delights
Bean Delights
Beef Delights
Beer Delights
Beet Delights
Blackberry Delights
Blueberry Delights
Bok Choy Delights
Boysenberry Delights
Brazil Nut Delights
Broccoli Delights
Brussels Sprouts Delights
Buffalo Berry Delights
Butter Delights
Buttermilk Delights
Cabbage Delights
Calamari Delights
Cantaloupe Delights
Caper Delights
Cardamom Delights
Carrot Delights
Cashew Delights
Cauliflower Delights
Celery Delights
Cheese Delights
Cherry Delights
Chestnut Delights
Chicken Delights
Chili Pepper Delights
Chive Delights
Chocolate Delights
Chokecherry Delights

Cilantro Delights
Cinnamon Delights
Clam Delights
Clementine Delights
Coconut Delights
Coffee Delights
Conch Delights
Corn Delights
Cottage Cheese Delights
Crab Delights
Cranberry Delights
Cucumber Delights
Cumin Delights
Curry Delights
Date Delights
Edamame Delights
Egg Delights
Eggplant Delights
Elderberry Delights
Endive Delights
Fennel Delights
Fig Delights
Filbert (Hazelnut) Delights
Fish Delights
Garlic Delights
Ginger Delights
Ginseng Delights
Goji Berry Delights
Grape Delights
Grapefruit Delights
Grapple Delights
Guava Delights
Ham Delights
Hamburger Delights
Herb Delights
Herbal Tea Delights
Honey Delights
Honeyberry Delights
Honeydew Delights
Horseradish Delights
Huckleberry Delights
Jalapeño Delights

Jerusalem Artichoke Delights
Jicama Delights
Kale Delights
Kiwi Delights
Kohlrabi Delights
Lavender Delights
Leek Delights
Lemon Delights
Lentil Delights
Lettuce Delights
Lime Delights
Lingonberry Delights
Lobster Delights
Loganberry Delights
Macadamia Nut Delights
Mango Delights
Marionberry Delights
Milk Delights
Mint Delights
Miso Delights
Mushroom Delights
Mussel Delights
Nectarine Delights
Oatmeal Delights
Olive Delights
Onion Delights
Orange Delights
Oregon Berry Delights
Oyster Delights
Papaya Delights
Parsley Delights
Parsnip Delights
Pea Delights
Peach Delights
Peanut Delights
Pear Delights
Pecan Delights
Pepper Delights
Persimmon Delights
Pine Nut Delights
Pineapple Delights
Pistachio Delights
Plum Delights
Pomegranate Delights
Pomelo Delights
Popcorn Delights

Poppy Seed Delights
Pork Delights
Potato Delights
Prickly Pear Cactus Delights
Prune Delights
Pumpkin Delights
Quince Delights
Quinoa Delights
Radish Delights
Raisin Delights
Raspberry Delights
Rhubarb Delights
Rice Delights
Rose Delights
Rosemary Delights
Rutabaga Delights
Salmon Delights
Salmonberry Delights
Salsify Delights
Savory Delights
Scallop Delights
Seaweed Delights
Serviceberry Delights
Sesame Delights
Shallot Delights
Shrimp Delights
Soybean Delights
Spinach Delights
Squash Delights
Star Fruit Delights
Strawberry Delights
Sunflower Seed Delights
Sweet Potato Delights
Swiss Chard Delights
Tangerine Delights
Tapioca Delights
Tayberry Delights
Tea Delights
Teaberry Delights
Thimbleberry Delights
Tofu Delights
Tomatillo Delights
Tomato Delights
Trout Delights
Truffle Delights
Tuna Delights

Turkey Delights
Turmeric Delights
Turnip Delights
Vanilla Delights
Walnut Delights
Wasabi Delights
Watermelon Delights
Wheat Delights
Wild Rice Delights
Yam Delights
Yogurt Delights
Zucchini Delights

CITY DELIGHTS
Chicago Delights
Coeur d'Alene Delights
Great Falls Delights
Honolulu Delights
Minneapolis Delights
Phoenix Delights
Portland Delights
Sandpoint Delights
Scottsdale Delights
Seattle Delights
Spokane Delights
St. Cloud Delights

FOSTER CARE
Foster Children Cookbook
   and Activity Book
Foster Children's Favorite
   Recipes
Holiday Cookbook for
   Foster Families

GENERAL THEME
   DELIGHTS
Appetizer Delights
Baby Food Delights
Barbeque Delights
Beer-Making Delights
Beverage Delights
Biscotti Delights
Bisque Delights
Blender Delights
Bread Delights
Bread Maker Delights

Breakfast Delights
Brunch Delights
Cake Delights
Campfire Food Delights
Candy Delights
Canned Food Delights
Cast Iron Delights
Cheesecake Delights
Chili Delights
Chowder Delights
Cocktail Delights
College Cooking Delights
Comfort Food Delights
Cookie Delights
Cooking for One Delights
Cooking for Two Delights
Cracker Delights
Crepe Delights
Crockpot Delights
Dairy Delights
Dehydrated Food Delights
Dessert Delights
Dinner Delights
Dutch Oven Delights
Foil Delights
Fondue Delights
Food Processor Delights
Fried Food Delights
Frozen Food Delights
Fruit Delights
Gelatin Delights
Grilled Delights
Hiking Food Delights
Ice Cream Delights
Juice Delights
Kid's Delights
Kosher Diet Delights
Liqueur-Making Delights
Liqueurs and Spirits Delights
Lunch Delights
Marinade Delights
Microwave Delights
Milk Shake and Malt Delights
Panini Delights
Pasta Delights
Pesto Delights

Phyllo Delights
Pickled Food Delights
Picnic Food Delights
Pizza Delights
Preserved Delights
Pudding and Custard Delights
Quiche Delights
Quick Mix Delights
Rainbow Delights
Salad Delights
Salsa Delights
Sandwich Delights
Sea Vegetable Delights
Seafood Delights
Smoothie Delights
Snack Delights
Soup Delights
Supper Delights
Tart Delights
Torte Delights
Tropical Delights
Vegan Delights
Vegetable Delights
Vegetarian Delights
Vinegar Delights
Wildflower Delights
Wine Delights
Winemaking Delights
Wok Delights

GIFTS-IN-A-JAR SERIES
Beverage Gifts-in-a-Jar
Christmas Gifts-in-a-Jar
Cookie Gifts-in-a-Jar
Gifts-in-a-Jar
Gifts-in-a-Jar Catholic
Gifts-in-a-Jar Christian
Holiday Gifts-in-a-Jar
Soup Gifts-in-a-Jar

HEALTH-RELATED DELIGHTS
Achalasia Diet Delights
Adrenal Health Diet Delights
Anti-Acid Reflux Diet Delights
Anti-Cancer Diet Delights

Anti-Inflammation Diet
   Delights
Anti-Stress Diet Delights
Arthritis Delights
Bone Health Diet Delights
Diabetic Diet Delights
Diet for Pink Delights
Fibromyalgia Diet Delights
Gluten-Free Diet Delights
Healthy Breath Diet Delights
Healthy Digestion Diet
   Delights
Healthy Heart Diet Delights
Healthy Skin Diet Delights
Healthy Teeth Diet Delights
High-Fiber Diet Delights
High-Iodine Diet Delights
High-Protein Diet Delights
Immune Health Diet Delights
Kidney Health Diet Delights
Lactose-Free Diet Delights
Liquid Diet Delights
Liver Health Diet Delights
Low-Calorie Diet Delights
Low-Carb Diet Delights
Low-Fat Diet Delights
Low-Sodium Diet Delights
Low-Sugar Diet Delights
Lymphoma Health Support
   Diet Delights
Multiple Sclerosis Healthy
   Diet Delights
No Flour No Sugar Diet
   Delights
Organic Food Delights
pH-Friendly Diet Delights
Pregnancy Diet Delights
Raw Food Diet Delights
Sjögren's Syndrome Diet
   Delights
Soft Food Diet Delights
Thyroid Health Diet Delights

HOLIDAY DELIGHTS
Christmas Delights
Easter Delights

Father's Day Delights
Fourth of July Delights
Grandparent's Day Delights
Halloween Delights
Hanukkah Delights
Labor Day Weekend Delights
Memorial Day Weekend
  Delights
Mother's Day Delights
New Year's Delights
St. Patrick's Day Delights
Thanksgiving Delights
Valentine Delights

HOOD AND MATSKO
FAMILY FAVORITES
Hood and Matsko Family
  Appetizers Cookbook
Hood and Matsko Family
  Beverages Cookbook
Hood and Matsko Family
  Breads and Rolls Cookbook
Hood and Matsko Family
  Breakfasts Cookbook
Hood and Matsko Family
  Cakes Cookbook
Hood and Matsko Family
  Candies Cookbook
Hood and Matsko Family
  Casseroles Cookbook
Hood and Matsko Family
  Cookies Cookbook
Hood and Matsko Family
  Desserts Cookbook
Hood and Matsko Family
  Dressings, Sauces, and
  Condiments Cookbook
Hood and Matsko Family
  Ethnic Cookbook
Hood and Matsko Family
  Jams, Jellies, Syrups,
  Preserves, and Conserves
Hood and Matsko Family
  Main Dishes Cookbook
Hood and Matsko Family,
  Pies Cookbook

Hood and Matsko Family
  Preserving Cookbook
Hood and Matsko Family
  Salads and Salad Dressings
Hood and Matsko Family
  Side Dishes Cookbook
Hood and Matsko Family
  Vegetable Cookbook
Hood and Matsko Family,
  Aunt Katherine's Recipe
  Collection, Vol. I-II
Hood and Matsko Family,
  Grandma Bert's Recipe
  Collection, Vol. I-IV

HOOD AND MATSKO
FAMILY HOLIDAY
Hood and Matsko Family
  Favorite Birthday Recipes
Hood and Matsko Family
  Favorite Christmas Recipes
Hood and Matsko Family
  Favorite Christmas Sweets
Hood and Matsko Family
  Easter Cookbook
Hood and Matsko Family
  Favorite Thanksgiving Recipes

INTERNATIONAL
DELIGHTS
African Delights
African American Delights
Australian Delights
Austrian Delights
Brazilian Delights
Canadian Delights
Chilean Delights
Chinese Delights
Czechoslovakian Delights
English Delights
Ethiopian Delights
Fijian Delights
French Delights
German Delights
Greek Delights
Hungarian Delights

Icelandic Delights
Indian Delights
Irish Delights
Italian Delights
Korean Delights
Mexican Delights
Native American Delights
Polish Delights
Russian Delights
Scottish Delights
Slovenian Delights
Swedish Delights
Thai Delights
The Netherlands Delights
Yugoslavian Delights
Zambian Delights

REGIONAL DELIGHTS
Glacier National Park Delights
Northwest Regional Delights
Oregon Coast Delights
Schweitzer Mountain Delights
Southwest Regional Delights
Tropical Delights
Washington Wine Country
  Delights
Wine Delights of Walla
  Walla Wineries
Yellowstone National Park
  Delights

SEASONAL DELIGHTS
Autumn Harvest Delights
Spring Harvest Delights
Summer Harvest Delights
Winter Harvest Delights

SPECIAL EVENTS
  DELIGHTS
Birthday Delights
Coffee Klatch Delights
Super Bowl Delights
Tea Time Delights

STATE DELIGHTS
Alaska Delights
Arizona Delights

Georgia Delights
Hawaii Delights
Idaho Delights
Illinois Delights
Iowa Delights
Louisiana Delights
Minnesota Delights
Montana Delights
North Dakota Delights
Oregon Delights
South Dakota Delights
Texas Delights
Washington Delights

U.S. TERRITORIES
  DELIGHTS
Cruzan Delights
U.S. Virgin Island Delights

MISCELLANEOUS
  COOKBOOKS
Getaway Studio Cookbook
The Soup Doctor's Cookbook

BILINGUAL DELIGHTS
  SERIES
Apple Delights, English-
  French Edition
Apple Delights, English-
  Russian Edition
Apple Delights, English-
  Spanish Edition
Huckleberry Delights,
  English-French Edition
Huckleberry Delights,
  English-Russian Edition
Huckleberry Delights,
  English-Spanish Edition

CATHOLIC DELIGHTS
  SERIES
Apple Delights Catholic
Coffee Delights Catholic
Easter Delights Catholic
Huckleberry Delights Catholic
Tea Delights Catholic

CATHOLIC BILINGUAL DELIGHTS SERIES

Apple Delights Catholic, English-French Edition
Apple Delights Catholic, English-Russian Edition
Apple Delights Catholic, English-Spanish Edition
Huckleberry Delights Catholic, English-Spanish Edition

CHRISTIAN DELIGHTS SERIES

Apple Delights Christian
Coffee Delights Christian
Easter Delights Christian
Huckleberry Delights Christian
Tea Delights Christian

CHRISTIAN BILINGUAL DELIGHTS SERIES

Apple Delights Christian, English-French Edition
Apple Delights Christian, English-Russian Edition
Apple Delights Christian, English-Spanish Edition
Huckleberry Delights Christian, English-Spanish Edition

FUNDRAISING COOKBOOKS

Ask about our fundraising cookbooks to help raise funds for your organization.

The above books are also available in bilingual versions. Please contact Whispering Pine Press International, Inc., for details.

Please note that some books are future books and are currently in production. Please contact us for availability date. Prices are subject to change without notice.

The above list of books is not all-inclusive. For a complete list please visit our website or contact us at:

Whispering Pine Press International, Inc.
Your Northwest Book Publishing Company
P.O. Box 214, Spokane Valley, WA 99037-0214 USA
Phone: (509) 928-8700 | Fax: (509) 922-9949
Email: sales@whisperingpinepress.com
Websites: www.WhisperingPinePress.com
www.WhisperingPinePressBookstore.com
Blog: www.WhisperingPinePressBlog.com
SAN 253-200X

Raspberry Delights

A Collection of Raspberry Recipes
Cookbook Delights Series – Book 14

Karen Jean Matsko Hood

Published by:

Whispering Pine Press International, Inc.
Your Northwest Book Publishing Company

P.O. Box 214
Spokane Valley, WA 99037-0214 USA
Phone: (509) 928-8700 | Fax: (509) 922-9949
Email: sales@whisperingpinepress.com
Websites: www.WhisperingPinePress.com
www.WhisperingPinePressBookstore.com
Blog: www.WhisperingPinePressBlog.com
SAN 253-200X
Printed in the U.S.A.

Published by Whispering Pine Press International, Inc.
P.O. Box 214
Spokane Valley, Washington 99037-0214 USA

For sales outside the United States, please contact the Whispering Pine Press International, Inc., International Sales Department.

Manufactured in the United States of America. This paper is acid-free and 100% chlorine free.

Book and Cover Design by Artistic Design Service, Inc.
P.O. Box 1782
Spokane Valley, WA 99037-1782 USA
www.ArtisticDesignService.com

Library of Congress Number (LCCN): 2014900834

Hood, Karen Jean Matsko
    Title: Raspberry Delights Cookbook: A Collection of Raspberry Recipes: Cookbook Delights Series – Book 14

    p.   cm.

ISBN: 978-1-59808-140-4   case bound
ISBN: 978-1-59808-099-5   perfect bound
ISBN: 978-1-59808-100-8   spiral bound
ISBN: 978-1-59808-101-5   comb bound
ISBN: 978-1-59808-103-9   E-PDF
ISBN: 978-1-59210-376-8   E-PUB
ISBN: 978-1-59434-868-6   E-PRC

First Edition: January 2014
1. Cookery (Raspberry Delights Cookbook: A Collection of Raspberry Recipes: Cookbook Delights Series - Book 14)   1. Title

Raspberry Delights Cookbook

A Collection of Raspberry Recipes
Cookbook Delights Series – Book 14

Gift Inscription

To: _____

From: _____

Date: _____

Special Message: _____

_____

_____

_____

_____

_____

_____

_____

_____

*It is always nice to receive a personal note to
create a special memory.*

www.RaspberryDelights.com
www.WhisperingPinePress.com
www.WhisperingPinePressBookstore.com

Dedications

To my husband and best friend, Jim.

To our seventeen children: Gabriel, Brianne Kristina and her husband Moulik Vinodkumar Kothari, Marissa Kimberly and her husband Kevin Matthew Franck, Janelle Karina and her husband Paul Joseph Turcotte, Mikayla Karlene, Kyler James, Kelsey Katrina, Corbin Joel, Caleb Jerome, Keisha Kalani Hiwot, Devontay Joshua, Kianna Karielle Selam, Rosy Kiara, Mercedes Katherine, Jasmine Khalia Wengel, Cheyenne Krystal, and Annalise Kaylee Marie.

To our grandchildren and foster grandchildren: Courtney, Lorenzo, and Leah.

To my brother, Stephen, and his wife, Karen.

To my husband's ten siblings: Gary, Colleen, John, Dan, Mary, Ray, Ann, Teresa, Barbara, Agnes, and their families.

In loving memory of my mom, who passed away in 2007; my dad, who passed away in 1976; and my sister, Sandy, who passed away due to multiple sclerosis in 1999.

To Sandy's three sons: Monte, Bradley, and Derek. To Monte's wife, Sarah, and their children: Liam, Alice, Charlie, and Samuel. To Bradley's wife, Shawnda, and their children: Anton, Isaac, and Isabel.

To our foster children past and present: Krystal, Sara, Rebecca, Janice, Devontay Joshua, Mercedes Katherine, Zha'Nell, Makia, Onna, Cheyenne Krystal, Onna Marie, Nevaeh, and Zada, our future foster children, and all foster children everywhere.

To the Court Appointed Special Advocate (CASA) Volunteer Program in the judicial system which benefits abused and neglected children.

To the Literacy Campaign dedicated to promoting literacy throughout the world.

Acknowledgements

The author would like to acknowledge all those individuals who helped me during my time in writing this book. Appreciation is extended for all their support and effort they put into this project.

Deep gratitude and profound thanks are owed to my husband, Jim, for giving freely of his time and encouragement during this project. Also, thanks are owed to my children Gabriel, Brianne Kristina and her husband Moulik Vinodkumar Kothari, Marissa Kimberly and her husband Kevin Matthew Franck, Janelle Karina and her husband Paul Joseph Turcotte, Mikayla Karlene, Kyler James, Kelsey Katrina, Corbin Joel, Caleb Jerome, Keisha Kalani Hiwot, Devontay Joshua, Kianna Karielle Selam, Rosy Kiara, Mercedes Katherine, Jasmine Khalia Wengel, Cheyenne Krystal, and Annalise Kaylee Marie. All of these persons inspire my writing.

Thanks are due to Carol Spitzer and Sharron Thompson for their assistance in editing and typing this manuscript for publication. Thanks go to Artistic Design Service, Inc. for their assistance in formatting and providing a graphic design of this manuscript for publication. This project could not have been completed without them.

Many thanks are due to members of my family, all of whom were very supportive during the time it took to complete this project. Their patience and support are greatly appreciated.

Raspberry Delights Cookbook

Table of Contents

Raspberry Delights Cookbook
A Collection of Raspberry Recipes
Cookbook Delights Series – Book 14

Introduction

Raspberries have always been one of my favorite berries. They are full of flavor and texture and a popular fruit in all forms of preparation. They are great for cooking and nutritious to eat alone. Their blossoms are beautiful, and the fruit is delicious to eat.

As a poet, I found it enjoyable to color this cookbook with poetry so that readers could savor the metaphorical richness of the raspberry as well as its literal flavor. Also included are some articles on history, cultivation, and botanical information, along with interesting facts about raspberries. Sections that discuss health and nutrition as well as some raspberry folklore are also included in this book.

The *Cookbook Delights Series* would not be complete without *Raspberry Delights Cookbook* since raspberries are such a prized American fruit. We hope you enjoy reading this cookbook as well as trying out all of the delicious recipes that have been gathered together for your culinary adventures.

The cookbook is organized in convenient alphabetical sections to assist you in finding recipes related to the type of cooking you need: appetizers and dips; beverages; breads and rolls; breakfasts; cakes; candies; cookies; desserts; dressings, sauces, and condiments; jams, jellies, and syrups; main dishes; pies; preserving; salads; side dishes; soups; and wines and spirits.

Following is a collection of recipes gathered and modified to bring you *our Raspberry Delights Cookbook: A Collection of Raspberry Recipes, Cookbook Delights Series* by Karen Jean Matsko Hood.

Raspberry Delights Cookbook

A Collection of Raspberry Recipes
Cookbook Delights Series – Book 14

Raspberry Botanical Classification

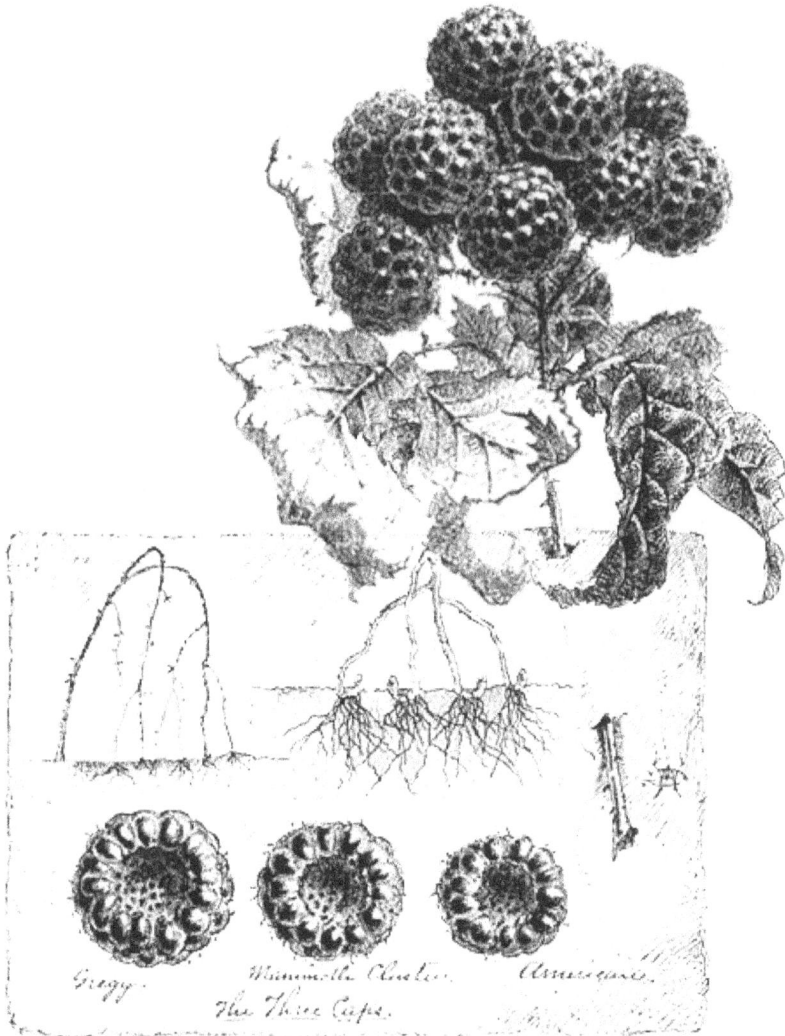

Gregg.

Mammoth Cluster.
The Three Caps.

Americane.

Raspberry Botanical Classification

The red raspberry, in proper botanical language, is not a berry at all but an aggregate fruit of numerous drupelets around a central core. In raspberry and other species of the subgenus *Idaeobatus*, the drupelets separate from the core when picked, leaving a hollow fruit, whereas in blackberry the drupelets stay attached to the core.

Raspberries belong to the genus *Rubus*, which is a part of the Rose family (*N.O. Rosaceae*). Cultivated raspberries have been derived mainly from two species, the wild red raspberry (*Rubus ideaus*) and black raspberry (*Rubus occidentalis*). There is also a purple type which is a cross between the black and the red raspberry. The yellow type is a mutant red raspberry.

Although most of the berries grown in Washington are Meekers, there are a small amount of many other cultivars that are grown. There are more than 20 varieties grown in Washington.

Other *Rubus* species also called raspberries include:
- Arctic raspberry (*Rubus arcticus*)
- Flowering raspberry (*Rubus odoratus*)
- Wine raspberry (*Rubus phoenicolasius*)
- Whitebark raspberry or Western Raspberry (*Rubus leucodermis*)
- Bramble raspberry or Blackberry (*Rubus fruticosus*)

Not all of these are included in the same subgenus.

Did you Know? . . . .
Did you know these helpful raspberry measurements?
1 cup raspberries = about 123 grams
1-1¼ cups raspberries = 10 oz. pkg. frozen berries
1 pint berries = 2 cups = 500 ml. = ¾ lb. = ⅓kg.
2 pints (4 cups) raspberries needed for one 9-inch pie

Did you know you can freeze raspberries that you cannot use right away? Just wash, cut the hulls off, and pop them into a zip lock bag, removing as much air as possible.

Raspberry Cultivation and Gardening

Raspberry Cultivation and Gardening

Site Selection

Raspberries are the most demanding of all small fruits in their preference for well-drained, sandy loam soil at least 24 inches deep. Check the future planting site after a heavy rain for the presence of standing water. On sites slow to drain, install drain tile 24 inches deep, or plant the raspberries on mounds of soil 1 foot high. Excessive soil moisture during late winter when new roots are growing leads to root rot development.

Select a site that receives full sun all day long. Plants grown in the shade often remain small and produce tart fruit. Provide for cultivation on either side of the rows to allow for primocane growth.

Soil Preparation

Control weeds and build up the soil a year before planting. Use a contact, foliar-applied herbicide to kill the sod or native vegetation. Consider seeding a fall crop of cereal rye or barley to the planting site to build up organic matter. Use between 2 and 2.5 pounds of seed for each 1,000 square feet. Do not allow the rye to head out the following spring before planting. Amend the soil pH with lime when the pH is less than 5.5. The ideal pH range is between 6.0 and 6.5. If the soil needs lime, apply the fall before planting.

Cultivation

Dormant plants are usually available in nurseries from mid-January to March in western Washington. From March to early April stock is available for immediate planting. Do not use any planting stock that already has started to bud out appreciably; it generally does not perform well. Purchase virus-free, certified nursery stock, because it lives longer. Sucker plants dug from an established planting during the winter when the plants are dormant often have virus diseases that can survive during transplanting.

The generally accepted planting distance for red raspberries in the Pacific Northwest is 30 inches between plants within the row, in rows spaced 8 to 10 feet apart. This stool method of planting, which maintains canes as discrete bushes, permits more ease in controlling weeds and excess primocane growth. Hand plant the row, then cut down the canes to a handle of three to four buds above ground level. This practice encourages early development of basal shoots without promoting production of fruiting laterals during planting. In subsequent years, allow 10 to 12 primocanes to grow from each original stool. Maintain the row at a width of 12 inches; remove excess primocanes using a hoe or rotatiller. In the English hedgerow planting system, growers set out plants at 30-inch intervals, but allow new primocanes to fill in the row to a width of 8 inches.

Fertilization

Raspberry primocanes normally grow an average of 8 to 9 feet during the spring and summer. Adjust fertilizer rates annually to achieve this amount of growth. Apply fertilizer in the late winter (March) as bud swell begins. Either broadcast fertilizer over the entire row, or band it 1 foot on either side of the row. West of the Cascades, apply 2 to 3 pounds of a 5-10-10 fertilizer to each 100 feet of row. East of the Cascades, in areas of relatively high phosphorous and potassium, use only nitrogen. Consider an application of ¾ to 1 pound of ammonium sulfate per 100 feet of row.

Watering

The raspberry plant is fairly deep rooted but can still suffer from a shortage of summer rainfall. Moisture is critical during the fruit ripening stage in early June and the late August or September period, when flower buds form for the following year's crop. Apply an inch of water per week when rain does not fall. Overhead irrigation during the ripening stage can encourage fruit rot if the weather is cool and cloudy; consider using a trickle or soaker hose irrigation system.

Trellising and Training

Raspberry Canes lack sufficient strength to remain erect. Install a post and wire trellis support. Erect the trellis the first summer the new plants are in the ground. If the newly planted canes grow vigorously the first summer, tie them to a wire support to ensure a crop the second year.

The first step in building a trellis involves placing secure, 6-inch-diameter end posts, preferably ones that have been treated with an environmentally safe wood preservative. Within the row, space 3-inch-diameter wooden posts at 25 to 30 feet, or place metal posts every 20 feet. Use 12-guage or stronger wire to support a heavy fruit-laden canopy. A three-wire trellis is the universally accepted design. Place the top wire 54 inches above the soil line and fix two detachable training wires 30 inches above the soil line. During the late summer renovation process, tie primocanes to the top wire, leaving the lower two wires on the ground. In the Scottish stool system canes are gathered together in upright bundles and tied to the top wire with binder twine. For the English hedgerow system, space the canes along the top wire and tie each cane individually. Leave primocanes long during the fall and early winter, topping canes in early fall makes them more susceptible to cold injury.

In May of the following spring, when new primocanes attain a height of 3 to 4 feet, bring up the training wires to collect the primocanes. Fasten the training wires to bent nails on the sides of the intermediary posts, or hook them together with wire loops. A four-wire trellis has two wires at 54 inches, and two training wires below. Secure primocanes between the top pairs of wires with twine or metal loops of wire every 3 to 10 feet. A four-wire cross arm trellis incorporates an 18 to 36-inch wide wooden cross arm attached at the top of each post within the row. During August, secure primocanes to these wires with twine. During the following spring, allow new primocanes to grow up through the center of the canopies to prevent them from interfering with picking of fruit from the floricanes.

Raspberry Delights Cookbook
A Collection of Raspberry Recipes
Cookbook Delights Series – Book 14

Raspberry Facts

Raspberry Facts

Raspberries typically grow in forest clearings or fields, particularly where fire or wood-cutting has produced open space for colonization by this opportunistic colonizer of disturbed soil. The raspberry flower can be a major nectar source for honeybees. As a cultivated plant in moist temperate regions, it is easy to grow and has a tendency to spread unless cut back.

Two types are commercially available: the wild-type summer bearing, that produces an abundance of fruit on second-year canes within a relatively short period in midsummer, and double- or "ever"-bearing plants, which also bear a few fruit on first-year canes in the autumn, as well as the summer crop on second-year canes. In the United States, raspberries can be cultivated from USDA plant hardiness zones 3 to 9.

Raspberries are very vigorous and can be a little invasive. They propagate using basal shoots (also known as suckers); extended underground shoots that develop roots and individual plants. They can sucker new canes some distance from the main plant. For this reason, raspberries spread well and can take over gardens if left unchecked. In the spring, mark out the boundary of the plant and push a spade straight down the boundary. This will sever the suckers. Then dig out the suckers that grow outside the boundary.

Pick the raspberries when they have turned a deep red and drop off easily from the core when touched. This is when they are the sweetest. Excess fruit can be used by making raspberry jam or can be frozen.

Leaves of the raspberry cane are used fresh or dried in herbal and medicinal teas. The leaves have an astringent flavor and in herbal medicine are reputed to be effective in regulating menses. Leaves are found in groups of three or five and the undersides are silver-white in color. Blackberries have similar looking leaves but the undersides are green.

Raspberries contain significant amounts of polyphenol antioxidants, chemicals linked to promoting endothelial and cardiovascular health. Xylitol, a sugar alcohol alternative sweetener, can be extracted from raspberries.

Raspberry Delights Cookbook

A Collection of Raspberry Recipes
Cookbook Delights Series – Book 14

Raspberry Folklore

Raspberry Folklore

Here is the story that has been passed around. According to legend, it was believed all raspberries were originally white. The nymph Ida went looking for berries to soothe the crying and upset infant Jupiter. While picking berries, Ida pricked her finger on bramble thorns. After that episode, raspberries have since been tinged red with Ida's blood. (The botanical name of the raspberry is *Rubus idaeus. Rubus* means 'red' and *idaeus* means 'belonging to Ida').

Martin Van Buren, while campaigning for the presidency in 1840, was said by his opponents to "wallow in raspberries," which at that time was a shocking extravagance.

Raspberries are mentioned often in Russian novels because of their ruggedness. The toughest and most prolific are the red and yellow varieties. The black and purple varieties, sometimes missed, are more vulnerable to weather and disease, arch and trail. According to folklore, persons who passed under those arches were protected from evil spells. They could also be miraculously healed of such ailments such as hernias, blackheads, boils, and rheumatism.

In Christian art raspberries are seen as a symbol of kindness. The red juice is thought of as blood which runs through the heart, which is also believed to be the place where kindness originates. Their delicate state in transport has led them to symbolize fragility as well. A tribe in the Philippines also believes that raspberry canes, when hung outside a house, protect the family inside from any souls that try to enter by catching them.

English herbalists believed that pregnant women who drank raspberry tea would not experience problems during child birth. Cherokee women drank raspberry juice during labor believing the same thing. Native Americans also believed that it would help with nausea felt during pregnancy.

Gargling with the juice was believed to help relieve sore throats.

Rubbing joints with the canes of the fruit was thought to ease pain.

Raspberry Delights Cookbook
A Collection of Raspberry Recipes
Cookbook Delights Series – Book 14

Raspberry History

Raspberry History

The red raspberry is indigenous to Asia Minor and North America. Fruits were gathered from the wild by the people of Troy in the foothills of Mt. Ida around the time of Christ. Records of domestication were found in 4th century writings of Palladius, a Roman agriculturist, and seeds have been discovered at Roman forts in Britain. Therefore, the Romans are thought to have spread cultivation throughout Europe.

In Medieval Europe, wild berries were considered both medicinal and utilitarian. Their juices were used in paintings and illuminated manuscripts. During this period, only the rich partook of their tasty bounty. King Edward I (1272-1307) is recognized as the first person to call for the cultivation of berries. By the seventeenth century, British gardens were rich with berries and berry bushes. By the eighteenth century, berry cultivation practices had spread throughout Europe.

When settlers from Europe came to America, they found Native Americans already utilizing and eating berries. Due to the nomadic nature of this culture, berries were dried for preservation and ease of transportation. Settlers also brought cultivated raspberries that were native to Europe with them to the new colonies. The first commercial nursery plants were sold by William Price in 1771.

In 1761, George Washington moved to his estate in Mount Vernon where he began to cultivate berries in his extensive gardens.

By 1867 over 40 different varieties were known. After the Civil War, major production areas emerged in the regions of New York, Michigan, Oregon, Washington, Pennsylvania, Ohio, Illinois, and Indiana.

By 1880, approximately 2,000 acres were in cultivation. By 1919, production had risen to 54,000 acres. By 1948, growth had slowed to 60,000 acres.

Today, the leading producing regions for red raspberries are Washington, Oregon, and California. However, Washington accounts for nearly 60% of the U.S. production of red raspberries, at nearly 70,000,000 pounds per year.

Raspberry Nutrition and Health

Raspberry Nutrition and Health

ONE CUP RASPBERRIES PROVIDES:

Vitamins, Minerals, Other	Nutrition Provided
Vitamin C	50% of recommended daily allowance
Folic Acid	10% of recommended daily allowance
Sodium	0
Cholesterol	0
Dietary fiber	8 grams, 32% of recommended daily allowance
*Calories	60
Carbohydrate	15grams
Protein	1gram
Fat	1gram
Fiber	32% of recommended daily allowance
**Folic Acid	6% of recommended daily allowance
***ORAC Value	2789

*   Raspberry calories also show up on "negative calories" lists, claiming to provide fewer food calories than the calories needed to digest them.

**   Folic acid aids in the prevention of birth defects.

***ORAC Value provides anti-cancer and anti-aging benefits.

Other Nutritional Facts

Raspberries are a source of soluble fibers and may lower high blood cholesterol levels and slow release of carbohydrates into the blood stream of diabetics.

Raspberries are also high in potassium, vitamin A, E, B Complex, K, phosphorus, potassium, magnesium, manganese, and calcium.

Raspberries have anti-inflammatory properties.

Raspberries are reported to have strong antioxidant properties. These antioxidants may inhibit collagenase enzymes, which may damage collagen in the skin, causing premature aging.

Raspberries have been shown to have anti-cancer properties.

A homemade wine, brewed from the fermented juice of ripe raspberries, is antiscrofulous, and raspberry syrup dissolves the tarter of the teeth.

Raspberries are reported to have healing capabilities on skin wounds.

The ellagic acid found in raspberries is reported to increase the protective effects of sunscreens.

Ellagic Acid Found in Raspberries and their Anti-carcinogenic Properties

Ellagic acid acts as a scavenger to "bind" cancer-causing chemicals, making them inactive. It inhibits the ability of other chemicals to cause mutations in bacteria. In addition, ellagic acid from red raspberries prevents binding of carcinogens to DNA, and reduces the incidence of cancer in cultured human cells exposed to carcinogens.

Ellagic Acid (milligrams/g dry weight)

Fruit	Seeds	Pulp	Whole
Meeker	8.40	3.36	4.31
Chilliwack	7.78	2.58	3.39
Willamette	8.13	2.05	2.91
Average	8.10	2.66	3.54

Medicinal Action and Uses

Raspberries can be used as a stringent and stimulant. Raspberry leaf tea, made by the infusion of 1 ounce of dried leaves in a pint of boiling water, is employed as a gargle for sore mouths, canker of the throat, and as a wash for wounds and ulcers. The leaves, combined with the powdered bark of slippery elm, make a good poultice for cleansing wounds, burns, and scalds, removing proud flesh and promoting healing.

An infusion of raspberry leaves, taken cold, is a reliable remedy for extreme laxity of the bowels. The infusion alone, or as a component part of injections, never fails to give immediate relief. It is useful in stomach complaints of children.

Raspberry leaf tea is valuable during parturition. It should be taken freely - warm.

General information

Red raspberry has long been established as a female herb. The leaf tea is used by pregnant women to help prevent complications and make delivery easier.

Red raspberry is used to relax uterine and intestinal spasms. It is known to strengthen uterine walls and promote healthy nails, bones, teeth, and skin.

The red raspberry leaf can aid women's immune system as well as facilitate healthy skin and bone development for the baby. Vitamin E serves to promote better circulation in the mother who is dramatically increasing her blood volume during pregnancy.

Red raspberry can diminish the effects of morning sickness, false labor pains, hot flashes, and menstrual cramps. Using red raspberry after childbirth helps decrease uterine swelling and reduces postpartum bleeding.

Red Raspberry Tea	
Ingredients:	1 to 2 teaspoons dried red raspberry leaf 1 cup boiling water
Directions:	Steep for 10 minutes. Sweeten to taste. Drink 2 to 3 cups daily while pregnant.

Small children can drink red raspberry tea for vomiting, dysentery, and diarrhea. Warm raspberry tea also soothes sore throats, mouth ulcers, bleeding gums, and canker sores.

The successful use of red raspberry is based on tradition more than science. Even though it is widely available, safety of use with young children or those with severe liver or kidney disease is unknown.

Raspberry Delights Cookbook

A Collection of Raspberry Recipes
Cookbook Delights Series – Book 14

Poetry

A Collection of Poetry with Raspberry Themes

Table of Contents

Raspberry Blossoms

Blossoms unfold,
fragrance explodes.

Hummingbirds cheep,
awaken my soul.

Chickadees argue,
wrens chatter.

The honeybees scold in
sheer morning mist.

Pine bark breath
permeates my senses.

Taste the fragrance of the
sweet summer day.

෨෨

Karen Jean Matsko Hood ©2014
Published in *Raspberry Delights Cookbook*, 2014
By Whispering Pine Press International, Inc., 2014

Raspberries Sungold

Strands of gold sway in the sun,
succulent with kernels that burst with wheat.
Honeybees soar from jasmine to jonquil to
drip with nectar sweet from creation.

Wheat ground in old stone mills, busy with daylight
Bread bakes in earthen stoves over hot coals
tasty and aromatic. Smooth with fresh, creamy butter, the gold
melts on warm yeasty bread.

Topped with fresh raspberry jam gathered from
golden glen. Hunger is satisfied
with sweet fruit of the land.
And all the sun
Touches, turns to gold.

છ

Karen Jean Matsko Hood ©2014
Published in *Raspberry Delights Cookbook*, 2014
By Whispering Pine Press International, Inc., 2014

Wild Garden

Do you remember the view of
that wild summer garden?
Clusters of red raspberries
hung as tiny ornaments
on the chlorotic bush.

Orchard grass began to brown.
You felt a crunch in clumps
under the soles of your
playful, stumbling tread.

Shasta daisies swayed with
bright yellow centers,
grandstand hues of columbine.
Multi-tasking nectar-makers,
Honeybees gathered pollen.

Yellow velvet
quiet under purple.
Oh, that summer garden,
I do miss.

❧

Karen Jean Matsko Hood ©2014
Published in *Raspberry Delights Cookbook*, 2014
By Whispering Pine Press International, Inc., 2014

Somewhere Between the Spice Bottles

There they are all lined in rows
to stand alphabetically. Parsley,
sage, rosemary, and thyme
should actually be parsley, rosemary
sage, and thyme in proper order,
but it is the musical tone we favor
and the lyrical notes we savor.

Is there room for tarragon or should
we replace the dill?
Can we find
sweetness among the cinnamon sticks,
tartness among the lemon oils?
Is it the smell of vanilla bean
to prize among the bottles or
simply sweet fragrance that
hides the sour?

༒

Karen Jean Matsko Hood ©2014
Published in *Raspberry Delights Cookbook*, 2014
By Whispering Pine Press International, Inc., 2014

Raspberry Syrup

Deep crimson mason jars lined in rows.
Carefully sealed golden lids,
Collect dust on uneven birch shelves
Trimmed with yellow paint that peels.

Old, worn hands cracked with age
Squeeze juice from berries picked before.
Raspberries hide behind olive leaves
Framed in carmine gold in forest clearings.

Search that brings
fond memories,
Bind up our belongings
In the old blue Chevy.

Drive the stick-shift
Down the road,
Up to the foothills
Below Montana's Rocky range.

Right by the road
We stop,
Papa, Mom, and me,
Look through the

Myriad of verdant greens,
To find the tiny crimson berries,
The sweet, scarce,
Unrevealing raspberries.

છ

Karen Jean Matsko Hood ©2014
Published in *Raspberry Delights Cookbook*, 2014
By Whispering Pine Press International, Inc., 2014

Nature's Dance

Hot rays stand above
penetrating canopies of clouds,
ever-greening blades of grass,
while wildflowers wilt
to music of a cricket chorus
harmonizing with the colors
of the sand.

Aspen leaves quake in the wind,
tremble and twirl their own soft-shoe style.
Poplar foliage now ground cover,
goldenrod sways in the distance,
cattails take their last stand.
All becomes still,
to anticipate the next drama.

Boughs of long-needled pine
ripple in the breeze that swirls.
Ice crystals sprout
frosty needles in a glaze.
Pine cones peer through
gossamer-white quills,
waiting for wings to fly.

Blossoms of cherry trees perfume the air,
fragrance delicious to serve a feast.
Hummingbirds ballet on tiny toes
quench their thirst on vernal nectar.
Honeybees jitterbug in frenzied play
delight to the spirit,
sensational to nation.

❦

Karen Jean Matsko Hood ©2014
Published in *Raspberry Delights Cookbook*, 2014
By Whispering Pine Press International, Inc., 2014

June Visitors

I watch tiny orbs,
floral buds swell.
First pea-sized marbles sprout,
then expand to walnut sizing.

All the while the worker ants
snake on these ballooning spheres.
Orbit networks of delight,
feast on sticky treats.

Sweet feed for their families
drip from succulent rounds of green,
distend to the moment they burst
to show off pink petals that unfurl.

Fragrance intoxicates,
beauty musically exquisite,
voracious visitors expose magnificence,
peony ecstasy.

Armies of ants return home
to feed their families
and defend their farm while
singing birds prime summer.

June visitors.

ↀ

Karen Jean Matsko Hood ©2014
Published in *Raspberry Delights Cookbook*, 2014
By Whispering Pine Press International, Inc., 2014

Earth's Natural Ruby

Earth's natural ruby
grows from a vine
firstborn in the original garden,
its fruit never forbidden or cursed.
One taste of this succulent yield
primes a deep desire
for a sweet taste of heaven
never to be starved,
only greedily quenched.
Its seedy firm textured skin yields
to the slightest pressure.
Raspberry's fresh flavor bursts
wild on the tongue,
quenching thirst, to stain
lips a sinful red.
Earth's gift is this precious fruit
should be accepted as grace
for the blessing of the ground.

❧

Karen Jean Matsko Hood ©2014
Published in *Raspberry Delights Cookbook*, 2014
By Whispering Pine Press International, Inc., 2014

Motherly Gardening

My mother
Taught me
To garden
To dig with bare hands
In clay and
Loam,
And crawl with
Montana angleworms,
That shine in dim
Rays that reflect
From Big
Sky. My mind
Wanders
Through the muck,
Reddish heavy,
Muddy ooze.
Intrigued with
Life
And worms,
Those bugs
Slink through
The gumbo,
Slip in its
Heaviness.
Great Falls'
wind
Reminds
Me to
Plant those
Seeds
Before chinook
Winds come
To make
More mud.
Wise old mom
Knew that
Earthen mire
Grounded me
In ways
Earthworms
Inch and
Always
understand.

ev

Karen Jean Matsko Hood ©2014
Published in *Raspberry Delights Cookbook*, 2014
By Whispering Pine Press International, Inc., 2014

Raspberry Delights Cookbook

A Collection of Raspberry Recipes
Cookbook Delights Series – Book 14

Raspberry Types

Raspberry Types

Two types of raspberries are commercially available: the wild-type summer bearing, that produces an abundance of fruit on second-year canes within a relatively short period in midsummer. The second type of raspberry is double- or "ever"-bearing plants, which also bear a few fruit on first-year canes in the autumn, as well as the summer crop on second-year canes. In the United States, raspberries can be cultivated from USDA plant hardiness zones 3 to 9.

Fall Fruiting Red Raspberry Cultivars			
Cultivar	Harvest Season	Fruit Characteristics	Plant Characteristics
Autumn Bliss	Very Early	Larger and firmer than Heritage. Very nice flavor.	Canes short and sturdy needing minimal support.
Fall Gold	Early	Yellow fruited cultivar with mild sweet flavored fruit.	Bushes are only moderately vigorous, average yield.
Heritage	Late	Large, dark fruit, mild flavored.	Vigorous canes need support. Winter-hardy for sheltered areas east of the Cascades.
Summit	Early	Equal in size and firmness to Heritage. Difficult to pick under hot conditions	Plants not as vigorous as Heritage, has resistance to root rot.

Did You Know? . . . .

Did you know that raspberry leaves are found in groups of 3 or 5, and the undersides are silver-white in color? Blackberries have similar looking leaves but the undersides are green.

Raspberry Delights Cookbook
A Collection of Raspberry Recipes
Cookbook Delights Series – Book 14

RECIPES

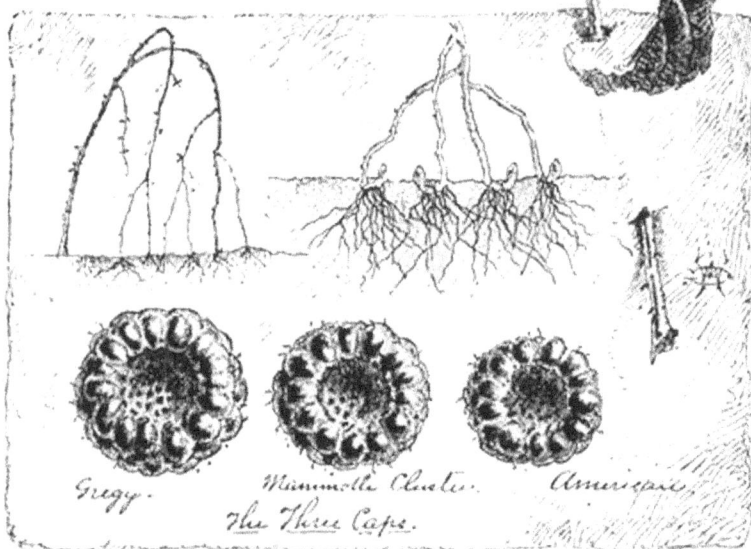

Gregg.   Mammoth Cluster.   Arnicapie.

The Three Caps.

Raspberry Delights Cookbook
A Collection of Raspberry Recipes
Cookbook Delights Series – Book 14

Appetizers and Dips

Table of Contents

Page

Crockpot Little Sausages

This appetizer is so easy to make and great to take to a potluck or buffet.

Ingredients:

2	pkg. little Vienna sausages
½	c. chopped onion
1	c. raspberry jelly
1	c. chili sauce
½	c. ketchup

Directions:

1. In nonstick skillet, brown sausages slightly. Place in 3 to 4 quart slow cooker.
2. Cook onion in skillet over medium heat until crisp tender.
3. Add raspberry jelly, chili sauce, and ketchup to skillet and heat, stirring until blended.
4. Pour over sausages in slow cooker, cover, and cook on low 2 to 3 hours.
5. Serve from crockpot.

Yields: 8 to 10 servings.

Warm Cheese Dip

The raspberries add a pleasant surprise to this cheese dip.

Ingredients:

3	oz. cream cheese, softened
1	c. Cheddar cheese, shredded
1	c. muenster cheese, shredded
2	Tbs. Dijon mustard
1	garlic clove, minced
¼	c. tart fresh raspberries
2	Tbs. chopped parsley
2	Tbs. chopped chives

Directions:

1. Mix all ingredients and place in small baking dish.
2. Bake at 350 degrees F. for 15 to 20 minutes until melted and bubbly.
3. Serve with apple slices, baby carrots, celery sticks, crackers, chunks of bread, warmed meatballs, tiny sausages, and so on!

Yields: 6 servings.

Raspberry Chicken Wings

These chicken wings are easy to make and delicious.

Ingredients:

1½ c. seedless raspberry jam
⅓ c. balsamic vinegar
3 Tbs. soy sauce
1½ tsp. crushed red pepper
1 five-lb. pkg. frozen chicken wings, thawed

Directions:

1. Preheat oven to 400 degrees F.
2. Line baking sheet with aluminum foil.
3. In small saucepan, combine jam, vinegar, soy sauce, and red pepper over medium heat.
4. Stir until smooth.
5. In large bowl, toss chicken wings with half the jam mixture.
6. Place on baking sheet and bake 50 minutes.
7. Brush wings with remaining jam mixture and bake 8 to 10 minutes or until chicken is no longer pink inside and outside is glazed.
8. Serve immediately.

Pastried Raspberry Chipotle Brie

This is a delicious combination of flavors and is great with the puff pastry.

Ingredients:

1   sheet frozen puff pastry, defrosted
6   Tbs. raspberry Chipotlé sauce
1   sm. round brie
1   egg, beaten
5   Tbs. chopped nuts (walnuts, pecans, almonds)

Directions:

1. Butter baking pan and line with aluminum foil.
2. Roll pastry on lightly floured surface and cut one 8-inch and one approximately 4-inch circle (a little larger than the round of brie). Keep remaining dough.
3. Place 8-inch circle on baking pan and center brie on top of dough. Top brie with raspberry sauce and nuts.
4. Bring the dough up the sides of the cheese and press firmly so it will stay.
5. Brush edges of dough with egg. Brush outer rim on the 4-inch dough circle with egg and place over top of cheese with the moistened side down. Press the two edges of the dough together firmly to seal.
6. Brush top and sides with egg.
7. Cut decorative designs from dough scraps and place on top.
8. Brush decorations with egg.
9. Refrigerate 30 minutes (minimum) before baking.
10. Preheat oven to 375 degrees F. Bake 20 to 30 minutes or until golden brown. Let stand 10 minutes before serving.
11. To serve, transfer baked brie to serving dish by carefully lifting the brie with the foil.
12. Trim away excess foil.

Yields: 6 to 8 servings.

Raspberry Chick/Shrimp with Salsa

This is a simple appetizer to make with great flavor. Choose chicken or shrimp.

Ingredients:

1   lb. boneless/skinless chicken breast, cubed, /or/ shrimp (cleaned)
1   Tbs. olive oil
     raspberry salsa, as desired
     shredded coconut, as desired

Directions:

1. Sauté chicken/shrimp in frying pan with olive oil and salsa until thoroughly cooked.
2. Turn into oven-ready casserole dish and sprinkle with shredded coconut.
3. Place under broiler until coconut is golden brown.

Raspberry Cream Cheese Spread

This is an easy-to-make spread on muffins or bagels. Enjoy!

Ingredients:

4   oz. cream cheese, softened
1   c. raspberries
2-3 Tbs. powdered sugar

Directions:

1. Blend powdered sugar and cream cheese.
2. Mix in raspberries.
3. Serve on bagels or English muffins.

Mini Polenta Raspberry Sandwiches

This makes a delicious and unique combination of flavors. The brie contrasts nicely with the tart raspberry and basil flavors.

Ingredients for sandwiches:

    1   tube prepared refrigerated polenta /or/
        home prepared polenta
    ¼   c. olive oil
    1   c. fresh raspberries
    ½   lb. brie cheese, sliced
    16 fresh basil leaves

Ingredients for homemade polenta:

    1   lb. cornmeal, coarsely stone-ground
    2   qt. boiling water
    1   tsp. salt

Directions for sandwiches:

1. Preheat oven to 350 degrees F.
2. Make sandwiches with polenta, fresh raspberries, brie slices, and basil leaves, securing with wooden toothpicks.
3. Place on baking sheet and bake at 350 degrees F. for 7 to 8 minutes until cheese melts and sandwiches are hot.

Directions for polenta:

1. Remove polenta from package and slice ¼ inch thick.
2. Heat oil in heavy nonstick skillet over medium high heat.
3. Add polenta slices for 2 to 4 minutes per side until crisp and light brown.
4. Remove to paper towel to drain.

Directions for homemade polenta:

1. Bring salt and water to boil.
2. Add corn meal in very slow stream.

3. Don't let pot stop boiling, stirring constantly with wooden spoon to keep lumps from forming.
4. Continue stirring as mush thickens, for about ½ hour. The longer you stir the better the polenta.
5. The finished polenta should have the consistency of firm mashed potatoes. Add boiling water as necessary.
6. Polenta is done when it peels easily off sides of pot.
7. Note: If you don't want to stir and stir polenta for ½ hour and can plan ahead, put the recipe in a slow cooker the night before and cook at least 6 hours. In the morning you will have the smoothest, creamiest polenta you only dreamed about.

Yields: 4 servings.

Raspberry Cheese Ball

This makes a great-tasting cheese ball appetizer. The raspberries also add color to make this a very attractive appetizer!

Ingredients:

8   oz. cream cheese, softened
2   Tbs. sherry
½   c. walnuts or pecans, chopped, toasted
¼   c. raspberry preserves, seedless

Directions:

1. Combine cream cheese, sherry, and nuts, mixing until well blended.
2. Chill mixture at least 30 minutes.
3. At serving time, shape into a ball. Make a hollow on top of ball. Spoon raspberry preserves into hollow and around sides of the ball.
4. Serve with crackers.

Raspberry Quesadillas

This recipe makes a tasty appetizer with the delicious combination of raspberries, turkey, and cheese.

Ingredients:

3   Tbs. butter
1   c. fresh raspberries
½   tsp salt
1   tsp. chipotle in adobo, finely chopped, to taste
8   six-inch flour tortillas
1   c. Cheddar cheese or cheese blend
4   oz. smoked turkey or chicken, chopped
2   green onion, thinly sliced
    sour cream
    green onion, finely sliced or slivered

Directions:

1. Heat butter in nonstick skillet until foamy; add raspberries and salt.
2. Cook, stirring, about 3 minutes or until raspberries are crisp-tender.
3. Remove raspberry mixture from skillet and set aside to cool slightly, then wipe skillet with paper towel.
4. Place 4 flour tortillas on work surface.
5. Sprinkle each tortilla with 2 tablespoons cheese, ¼ of the turkey, 3 tablespoons raspberry mixture, ¼ of the green onions, and another 2 tablespoons cheese.
6. Cover each with a tortilla.
7. In dry skillet over medium heat, brown quesadillas, one at a time, about 3 minutes on each side, turning carefully, until cheese is melted and tortillas are crisp and lightly browned.
8. Cut each quesadilla into triangles, place on serving dish.
9. Place a small bowl of sour cream and a small dish of chopped onion on the side for guests to add to their quesadilla wedge.

Sausage and Raspberry Sauce

Your company and family together will enjoy these tasty and flavorful tidbits for a great get together. Raspberry sauce adds a very surprising flavor.

Ingredients:

2   Tbs. butter
1   lg. onion, chopped
½   c. raspberry jelly
½   c. brown sugar, firmly packed
2   lb. smoked sausages, cocktail size
1   c. fresh raspberries
1   Tbs. cornstarch
2   Tbs. warm water

Directions:

1. In large skillet, melt butter over medium high heat.
2. Add onion and sauté, stirring constantly, until onion is golden.
3. Stir in raspberry jelly and brown sugar, add sausages, and reduce heat to medium low.
4. Cook, stirring occasionally, 20 minutes or until mixture begins to thicken.
5. Add raspberries and cook for few minutes or just until berries are crisp tender. Remove and drain on paper towels.
6. Combine the cornstarch with water and stir into mixture in pan; cook until mixture thickens.
7. Arrange raspberries and sausage on serving platter with wooden picks.
8. Place thickened mixture in small bowl along side for dipping.

Yields: 30 appetizers.

Slow Cooker Saucy Meatballs

This makes a colorful, easy-to-make dish while you're getting ready for your party!

Ingredients for dish:

2   lbs. precooked meatballs (Use your favorite recipe, or the one below.)
1   c. raspberry jelly
1   red bell pepper, chopped
8   oz. pineapple chunks, canned
2   c. cocktail sauce (Use your favorite recipe or the one below.)

Ingredients for meatballs:

2   lb. hamburger
6   Tbs. fine dry bread crumbs
4   Tbs. onion, minced
2   lg. eggs, lightly beaten
    salt and pepper to taste

Ingredients for cocktail sauce:

1½ c. tomato ketchup
½   c. horseradish
2   Tbs. lemon juice
    celery salt to taste
    Tabasco sauce to taste

Directions for dish:

1. Place precooked meatballs in 4- to 5-quart slow cooker, and top with jelly and red bell peppers.
2. Drain pineapple, reserving juice; add pineapple to slow cooker.
3. Combine cocktail sauce and ⅓ cup reserved pineapple juice in small bowl.

4. Pour into crockpot, cover, and cook on high for 1 to 2 hours, stirring twice during cooking until meatballs are glazed.
5. Turn heat to low until ready to serve.
6. Stir occasionally during party.

Directions for meatballs:

1. Mix all ingredients together, shape into meatballs.
2. Fry in heavy skillet until done.

Directions for cocktail sauce:

1. Shake all ingredients until well mixed. Add celery salt and tabasco sauce to your taste.
2. Make ahead and chill in refrigerator.

Yields: 10 to 12 servings.

Raspberry Cream Dip

This dip is the perfect complement on your appetizer tray.

Ingredients:

1   c. heavy whipping cream
¼   tsp. salt
1   c. mayonnaise
1   Tbs. balsamic vinegar
⅓   c. raspberries, fresh or frozen
1   Tbs. powdered sugar

Directions:

1. Beat cream and salt on medium until stiff peaks form.
2. Gently fold in mayonnaise, balsamic vinegar, raspberries, and powdered sugar, until thoroughly combined.
3. Pour into a decorative bowl, cover, and refrigerate at least 1 hour.
4. May be kept in refrigerator up to 3 days.

Raspberry Fruit Dip

This is an easy snack recipe for kids to make.

Ingredients:

2   c. raspberries, fresh or frozen (defrosted)
1   c. vanilla yogurt
¼   c. cream cheese

Directions:

1. Combine all ingredients in blender or food processor and mix until smooth.

Yields: 4 servings.

Warm Brie with Raspberry Chutney

Our family loves brie cheese, and this is one of our favorite ways to serve it.

Ingredients:

1   c. raspberries, fresh or frozen
2   Tbs. chopped onion
1½ tsp. ginger root, grated
¼   c. brown sugar, firmly packed
2   Tbs. cider vinegar
1½ tsp. cornstarch
⅛   tsp. salt
1   cinnamon stick
1   brie, 8 or 12 inch round

Directions:

1. In saucepan, combine all ingredients except brie cheese; mix well.

2. Bring to a boil over medium heat, stirring frequently, and boil 1 minute.
3. Remove cinnamon stick, cover, and refrigerate at least 30 minutes.
4. Place brie on microwave safe serving dish.
5. Microwave on high for 2 to 3 minutes or until warm.
6. Remove from oven.
7. Top cheese with cold chutney.
8. Serve with crackers or a sliced baguette.

Deep Fry Camembert with Raspberry Sauce

Our family loves camembert cheese and this is an excellent flavor combination.

Ingredients:

6   oz. camembert cheese
1   egg
½   c. fine bread crumbs
¾   c sesame seeds
3   c. vegetable oil for frying
¾   c. raspberry preserves

Directions:

1. Cut chilled cheese in 8 equal wedges. In shallow bowl, beat egg.
2. On sheet of wax paper, mix bread crumbs and sesame seeds.
3. Dip each cheese wedge in egg and turn to coat. Roll cheese in crumb mixture to coat. (If preparing ahead, cover and refrigerate now until ready to cook.)
4. In heavy saucepan, heat 2 inches oil to 376 degrees F. or until a 1-inch bread cube turns golden brown on all sides.
5. Fry cheese until golden. Drain on paper towels.
6. Melt raspberry preserves for dipping sauce.

Walnut Curried Cheese Spread with Raspberry Hot Mustard Sauce

This is a very flavorful appetizer with a tantalizing mix of flavors.

Ingredients for cheese spread:

8   oz. cream cheese, softened
1½ c. sharp Cheddar cheese
2   Tbs. sherry
¾   tsp. curry powder
½   c. green onion, finely chopped
¾   c. walnuts, finely chopped, toasted

Ingredients for topping:

1   can raspberries, drained, reserving ½ c. syrup
     /or/ 1½ c. frozen raspberries, reserving ½ c. juice
1   Tbs. plus 1 tsp. hot mustard
1   Tbs. cornstarch

Directions for cheese spread:

1. Blend together all but the walnuts (reserving ¼ cup onions for garnish).
2. Shape into round flat disk 1½ inches thick and 8 inches in diameter.

Directions for topping:

1. In saucepan, heat reserved raspberry syrup, cornstarch, and mustard until thickened, stirring often.
2. Gently stir in raspberries and cool.
3. Spread topping on cheese spread in 6-inch circle in the center.
4. Garnish with remaining onions.
5. Serve with crackers.

Raspberry Delights Cookbook
A Collection of Raspberry Recipes
Cookbook Delights Series – Book 14

Beverages

Table of Contents

Berry Healthy Raspberry Smoothies

This soymilk smoothie is easy to make and healthy. Best served cold.

Ingredients:

2   c. soy milk
1   can raspberries, drained
¼   c. sugar
1   tsp. vanilla extract

Directions:

1. Combine all ingredients in blender.
2. Blend until smooth and frothy.
3. Serve immediately.

Citrus Raspberry Mimosas

My daughter enjoys occasional mimosas, and this is a good one.

Ingredients:

6   oz. frozen orange juice concentrate
6   oz. frozen pineapple juice concentrate
2   c. raspberry juice
1   can lemon-lime soda (12 oz.), chilled
     orange slices and raspberries for garnish

Directions:

1. In pitcher or punch bowl, combine all juices.
2. Just before serving, add soda, orange slices, and raspberries.

Yields: 4 servings.

Cranberry-Raspberry Punch

This is an easy-to-make punch to enjoy.

Ingredients:

3½ gal. raspberry sherbet
2½ qt. vanilla ice cream
2   qt. cranberry cocktail
2   qt. sparkling lemon-lime soda

Directions:

1. Soften sherbet and ice cream.
2. Add 1 quart of juice; mix.
3. Add remaining juice; blend well.
4. Just before serving, add sparkling lemon-lime soda.

Raspberry Smoothie

This is an easy-to-make smoothie and very refreshing. I am sure you will enjoy this drink.

Ingredients:

6   oz. raspberries (fresh or frozen)
6   oz. vanilla yogurt
1   Tbs. honey
½   c. ice (3 ice cubes)

Directions:

1. Place all ingredients into an electric blender.
2. Blend well at high speed.
3. Pour into a glass and serve immediately.

Yields: 1 serving.

Creamy Raspberry Punch

Try this creamy raspberry punch for your next party gathering!

Ingredients:

4   c. apple raspberry juice, chilled
1   c. sparkling water, chilled
1   c. milk
1   pt. raspberry sherbet
1   pt. vanilla ice cream
8   oz. frozen raspberries

Directions:

1. Combine apple raspberry juice, sparkling water, and milk in a large pitcher or mixing bowl.
2. Scoop the sherbet and ice cream into a large punch bowl.
3. Pour the apple raspberry liquid over top.
4. Garnish with the frozen raspberries.

Yields: 10 servings.

Creamy Raspberry Sipper

This recipe makes a refreshing, cold drink. Some people do not like raspberry seeds and strain them out. We enjoy the seeds and leave them in the drink. Follow guidelines for your preference.

Ingredients:

1¼ c. raspberries, fresh
1¼ c. white grape juice, unsweetened
1½ c. raspberry sherbet
¼   c. water
1   Tbs. lemon juice
10 ice cubes
    fresh mint sprigs (optional)

Directions:

1. Combine raspberries and grape juice in blender, cover, and process until smooth.
2. Strain mixture through several layers of dampened cheesecloth, reserving liquid.
3. Combine reserved liquid, sherbet, water, and lemon juice in blender.
4. Cover and process until smooth.
5. Add ice cubes; process until frothy.
6. Garnish with fresh mint sprigs and serve.

Yields: 4 one-cup servings.

Minted Raspberry Lemonade

This is one of my favorites, and a delicious twist to the every-day lemonade taste.

Ingredients:

½ c. raspberries, unsweetened
1 c. lemon juice (4 med. lemons)
¾ c. sugar
1 tsp. mint, fresh, minced, /or/ ¼ tsp. dried mint flakes
6 c. water

Directions:

1. Mash and drain raspberries, reserving juice. Discard pulp and seeds.
2. In large container or punch bowl combine lemon juice, sugar, and mint.
3. Stir in water and reserved raspberry juice.
4. Serve over ice.

Yields: 7 servings.

Raspberry Apple Ice Tea

This makes a refreshing tea on a hot day.

Ingredients:

1½ c. raspberry flavored herb tea
½ c. apple juice
½ c. carbonated water
  ice cubes
  sugar to taste (optional)
  raspberries and apple slices for garnish

Directions:

1. Mix tea and juice together and pour over ice in 2 tall glasses.
2. Add carbonated water and sugar, if desired.
3. Garnish with fresh raspberries and slices of apple.

Yields: 3 servings.

Raspberry Café au Lait

Try this recipe for a new variation on a favorite coffee drink.

Ingredients:

⅔ c. coffee
⅓ c. milk
2 Tbs. raspberry syrup
  cinnamon, nutmeg or chocolate powder optional

Directions:

1. Pour coffee into cup.
2. Steam milk and add to coffee, leaving layer of foam on top.
3. Sprinkle cinnamon, nutmeg or chocolate powder on top of the foam, if desired.

Raspberry-Banana Smoothies

This raspberry-banana smoothie is quick, easy, and delicious!

Ingredients:

1   c. milk
1   c. raspberries, fresh or frozen, unsweetened
1   sm. banana, ripe, cut into chunks
½   c. apple juice
½   c. raspberry yogurt

Directions:

1. In blender, combine all ingredients, cover, and process until blended.
2. Pour into chilled glasses.
3. Serve immediately.

Yields: 3 servings.

Raspberry Breakfast Shake

This makes a tasty, colorful, and nutritious shake to be enjoyed at breakfast or any time.

Ingredients:

2   c. plain yogurt
1   c. raspberries, fresh
1   med. banana, ripe
½   c. orange juice

Directions:

1. Combine all ingredients in blender.
2. Blend until smooth and frothy.
3. Pour into glasses and serve.

Raspberry Ice Tea

This is a great flavored tea.

Ingredients:

2   c. raspberries, fresh or thawed frozen
3   Tbs. honey
2   jasmine tea bags /or/ 1½ Tbs. loose jasmine tea
1   lemon, cut into 8 slices for garnish
    zest and juice of 1 orange

Directions:

1. Purée raspberries in a blender.
2. Using wooden spoon, rub the purée through a fine sieve set over a bowl.
3. Put the orange zest, orange juice, honey, and 6 cups water into a saucepan; bring to boil and add the tea.
4. Remove saucepan from heat and let the tea steep for 3 minutes.
5. Strain the tea into the purée, stir mixture, and chill.
6. Serve the drink garnished with the lemon slices.

Yields: 8 servings.

Raspberry Pineapple Smoothie

This recipe makes a refreshing variety of raspberry smoothie. If you enjoy a tropical, fruity drink, then you will enjoy this fresh smoothie.

Ingredients:

½   c. fresh pineapple chunks
1   c. raspberries
1   banana, peeled, sliced into ½-in. pieces

2   c. buttermilk
1-2 Tbs. honey
3-4 mint leaves, fresh
4   ice cubes
    fresh raspberries for garnish

Directions:

1. Place all ingredients except garnish in blender and purée until smooth.
2. Pour into 4 tall glasses and garnish with raspberries.

Yields: 4 servings.

Raspberry Zinger

Citrus juice adds a nice flavor combination to this drink.

Ingredients:

4   c. raspberries, fresh or frozen
½   c. sugar
1   c. orange juice
4   c. vanilla ice cream
2   c. crushed ice
    whole berries for garnish

Directions:

1. Purée berries and strain through a fine sieve to yield approximately 2 cups purée. (If berries are frozen, partially thaw before puréeing.)
2. Combine purée with remaining ingredients.
3. Blend until smooth and pour into chilled glasses.
4. Garnish with 2 or 3 berries.

Yields: 6 servings.

Raspberry Crush

This is a delicious creamy raspberry crush and easy to make.

Ingredients:

- 1   c. raspberry juice
- 1   c. fresh raspberries, frozen
- ½   c. banana, sliced fresh, frozen
- 1   c. plain yogurt, frozen
- ½   c. ice cubes, chopped

Directions:

1. Pour the raspberry juice into blender, add the raspberries, banana, yogurt, and ice cubes.
2. Blend until smooth with a thick consistency.

Yields: 3 cups.

Raspberry-Cider Punch

This is a tasty, clear punch to enjoy.

Ingredients:

- 5   oz. raspberries, fresh
- 4   c. sparkling apple cider, chilled
- 1   Tbs. lime juice

Directions:

1. Purée raspberries; strain through sieve to remove seeds.
2. Combine raspberry purée apple cider, and lime juice in a pitcher and serve.

Yields: 6 servings.

Raspberry Frosty

Try this frosty cold drink. It is very good.

Ingredients:

- 2   c. raspberries, fresh or frozen
- 1½ c. vanilla ice cream
- 3   Tbs. sugar
- 1   lemon, juiced
- 1   lemon-lime soda pop
      whole berries for garnish

Directions:

1. Mix first 4 ingredients in blender until smooth. (If frozen berries are used, partially thaw before blending.)
2. Pour into 4 glasses and slowly add soda to fill each glass.

Raspberry Float

A raspberry beverage that's perfect for a hot summer day.

Ingredients:

- 2   c. raspberries, fresh or frozen
- 1   banana, sliced
- 1   pt. raspberry sherbet
      ginger ale

Directions:

1. Mix raspberries, banana, and ginger ale in a blender.
2. Place a scoop of sherbet in stemmed glasses.
3. Fill glasses with ginger ale; serve with spoons and straws.

Yields: 6 servings.

Red Cactus, No Alcohol Version

Who says this drink has to have alcohol to taste good? This drink is a favorite to both young and old.

Ingredients:

1¼ c. raspberry-cranberry juice, frozen concentrate
3   c. frozen raspberries, whole
¾   c. limeade, frozen concentrate
½   c. orange juice, reconstituted
4   c. crushed ice
1   lime, sliced
     sugar

Directions:

1. Combine all but last two ingredients in blender and blend until slushy, adding more ice if necessary.
2. To prepare glasses, moisten rims with lime slice, and dip in plate of sugar.
3. Fill glasses and garnish with lime wheel slices.
4. Garnish with 2 or 3 berries.

Yields: 4 to 6 servings.

Tea Punch

This is a simple spiced punch with a touch of tea. It is very refreshing on a hot summer day.

Ingredients:

1   c. sugar
1   c. cold water
1½   tsp. whole cloves
1   cinnamon stick
1   Tbs. Jasmine tea
3   c. boiling water

1　orange, juiced
½　c. raspberry juice
½　c. unsweetened pineapple juice

Directions:

1. Combine first 4 ingredients in a small heavy saucepan.
2. Bring to a simmer.
3. Place tea in another pot and add boiling water.
4. Steep 3 minutes.
5. Strain tea and return liquid to pot.
6. Add spice mixture and fruit juices.
7. Simmer 5 to 10 minutes.
8. Serve hot or cold.

Raspberry Chocolate Cream Coffee

Serve this drink in front of a fire on a cold winter's eve.

Ingredients:

¼　c. heavy cream
2　Tbs. raspberry syrup
1　Tbs. chocolate syrup
1　c. coffee
　　ground cinnamon, grated orange peel

Directions:

1. Whip all but 1 tablespoon of cream.
2. Stir reserved tablespoon of cream and raspberry syrup in a saucepan over low heat until mixed.
3. Add coffee gradually, stirring constantly.
4. Pour into a mug and top with whipped cream, cinnamon, and grated orange peel.

Yields: 1 serving.

Creamy Raspberry Slush

You need to enjoy raspberry seeds for this one.

Ingredients:

1½ c. raspberries, fresh
1¼ c. grape juice, unsweetened white
1½ c. raspberry sherbet
¼ c. water
1 Tbs. lemon juice
10 ice cubes
   fresh mint sprigs (optional)

Directions:

1. Blend raspberries and grape juice in blender until smooth.
2. Combine reserved liquid, sherbet, water, and lemon juice in blender; cover and process until smooth.
3. Add ice cubes; process until frothy.

Yield: 4 servings.

Raspberry Cappuccino

If you like coffee, you will love this cappuccino.

Ingredients:

¾ c. chocolate milk
⅓ c. espresso /or/ 1 Tbs. instant coffee dissolved in ⅓ c. water
2 Tbs. chocolate syrup
1½ c. frozen yogurt, coffee or chocolate flavored
1 c. fresh raspberries, frozen
½ c. milk
   unsweetened chocolate powder for garnish

Directions:

1. Combine chocolate milk, espresso, and chocolate syrup.
2. Add frozen yogurt, raspberries, and blend until smooth.
3. Pour into 2 glasses.
4. Blend milk on high speed until frothy, about 15 seconds.
5. Pour onto smoothies and sprinkle with chocolate powder.

Yields: 2 servings.

Raspberry Colada

This is a delicious raspberry colada to enjoy.

Ingredients:

3   c. raspberries, whole, frozen
¼   c. sugar
½   c. orange juice, reconstituted
1   c. pineapple juice
½   c. crème de coconut
2   c. ice, crushed
1   lemon, sliced

Directions:

1. Combine all ingredients except lemon slices in blender and blend until slushy, adding more ice if necessary.
2. Pour into glasses and garnish with lime wheel slices.

Yields: 4 servings.

Raspberry Peach Breakfast Shake

Raspberry and peach nectar make a delicious shake.

Ingredients:

10 oz. raspberries, frozen in light syrup, thawed
1   c. canned peach nectar
½   c. buttermilk
1   Tbs. honey

Directions:

1. Place all ingredients in blender and process until smooth.
2. Pour into glasses and serve.

Yields: 4 servings.

Raspberry-Pineapple Break

This is so quick to make and very refreshing.

Ingredients:

1   c. raspberries; fresh or frozen
1   c. pineapple, fresh
2   c. cold water
    honey; to taste

Directions:

1. Whirl raspberries and pineapple in blender.
2. Add water and honey to taste; whirl again.
3. Strain. Garnish with tiny piece of pineapple.

Yields: 4 servings.

Raspberry Lemonade

This raspberry lemonade is excellent.

Ingredients:

2   cans frozen lemonade concentrate (12 oz. ea.), thawed
2   pkg. frozen sweetened raspberries (10 oz. ea.), partly thawed
2-4 Tbs. sugar
2   liters club soda, chilled
    ice cubes

Directions:

1. In a blender, combine lemonade concentrate, raspberries, and sugar. Cover and process until blended, then strain.
2. In a 4½ quart container, combine raspberry mixture, club soda, and ice cubes; mix well. Serve immediately.

Yields: 3½ quarts.

Raspberry Delights Cookbook

A Collection of Raspberry Recipes
Cookbook Delights Series – Book 14

Breads and Rolls

Table of Contents

Applesauce Raspberry Muffins

These delicious, moist muffins with the apple raspberry combination make great bran muffins.

Ingredients:

1   c. butter
1½ c. all-purpose flour
⅓ c. sugar
3   tsp. baking powder
⅓ c. oil
1   tsp. ground cinnamon
1   c. raspberries, fresh or frozen, no sugar added
¾   c. milk
1   c. applesauce, unsweetened
1¼ c. bran flakes cereal, slightly crushed
2   eggs
      dash of salt

Directions:

1. Coat 12-cup muffin pan with butter.
2. In large bowl, thoroughly mix flour, sugar, baking powder, salt, and cinnamon.
3. In small bowl, mix milk, applesauce, cereal, and egg whites.
4. Gently fold in raspberries.
5. Stir liquid ingredients into dry ingredients until the dry ingredients are just moistened; about 20 strokes.
6. Note: Over mixing will result in poor textured, tough bread.
7. Spoon batter into greased muffin tin, dividing evenly among 12 cups.
8. Bake 20 to 25 minutes at 400 degrees F. until muffins are browned and a toothpick inserted in center comes out clean.
9. Allow muffins to sit 2 minutes in the tin, then transfer to wire rack to cook.

Fresh Raspberry Teacakes

These are easy-to-make, delicious muffins. They are great served warm with butter.

Ingredients:

2   c. flour
¾   tsp. baking soda
¾   tsp. cinnamon
¼   tsp. nutmeg, freshly grated
¼   tsp ginger, ground
¼   tsp. salt
1   c. sugar
2   lg. eggs, room temperature
2   tsp. pure vanilla extract
½   c. oil
4   Tbs. butter, melted, cooled
1   c. fresh raspberries

Directions:

1. Blend together flour, baking soda, cinnamon, nutmeg, ginger, and salt in large mixing bowl; set aside.
2. Whisk together the sugar and eggs in small bowl until light, about 2 minutes.
3. Blend in vanilla, oil, and butter.
4. Make a large well in center of dry ingredients, pour in wet mixture, and combine quickly until a batter is formed.
5. Very gently fold in the raspberries.
6. Spoon batter into 16 buttered and floured 2¼-inch muffin cups, filling them ⅔ full.
7. Bake at 400 degrees F. for 20 minutes or until well risen, firm to the touch, and toothpick inserted in the center of muffin emerges clean and dry.
8. Transfer teacakes to a rack, let cool a few minutes, and then remove from pans to continue cooling.

Yields: 16 teacakes.

Banana Raspberry Muffins

This is a very tasty banana muffin, and the addition of raspberries makes a nice variation.

Ingredients:

3   ripe bananas, mashed
½   c. water
⅓   c. vegetable oil
1   c. raspberries, fresh or frozen
1   egg
2   c. flour
1   tsp. baking soda
2¼ tsp. baking powder
2   tsp. cinnamon

Directions:

1. In large bowl mash bananas well; stir in water, oil, and egg.
2. Mix in flour, cinnamon, baking soda, and baking powder.
3. Beat with a fork 2 minutes.
4. Batter is thick at first, but loosens as you beat it.
5. Gently fold in raspberries.
6. Fill greased muffin tins ¾ full and bake at 350 degrees F. for 20 minutes.

Banana Berry Nut Bran Muffins

The addition of nuts and bran cereal make this a flavorful muffin.

Ingredients:

1½ c. sugar
4   ripe bananas, puréed
1   pkg. frozen raspberries
1   c. walnuts, chopped
2   eggs
3   tsp. baking soda

1½ tsp. vanilla extract
2   c. oat bran
1   qt. buttermilk
4   c. Kellogg's All Bran
2½ c. unsifted flour

Directions:

1. Combine first 8 ingredients. Add remaining ingredients.
2. Fill muffin tins ⅔ full and bake at 375 degrees F. for 30 minutes.

Yields: 2 dozen muffins.

Raspberry Bread

This is tasty bread for a quick snack.

Ingredients:

1¾ c. sugar
3   c. all purpose flour
1½ tsp. baking soda
1   Tbs. cinnamon
¾   tsp. salt
2   c. frozen raspberries, drained
1¼ c. oil
4   eggs, beaten.

Directions:

1. Mix sugar, sifted flour, soda, cinnamon, and salt.
2. Add oil and eggs.
3. Stir until mixed well.
4. Add raspberries.
5. Pour into two bread pans sprayed with non-stick cooking spray and bake 1 hour at 350 degrees F.

Yields: 2 loaves.

Berry Best Raspberry Muffins

The addition of applesauce and raspberries makes this a very moist muffin.

Ingredients:

1   c. all-purpose flour
¾   c. whole wheat pastry flour
¾   c. sugar
1   Tbs. baking powder
1   tsp. lemon peel, finely shredded
2   egg whites
⅔   c. buttermilk
⅓   c. applesauce
1   tsp. vanilla extract
1   c. raspberries, fresh or frozen (don't thaw frozen)

Directions:

1. Preheat oven to 400 degrees F.
2. Grease 6 large, 3-inch muffin cups.
3. Set aside.
4. In large bowl, stir together both flours, sugar, baking powder, and lemon peel.
5. Bend well.
6. Make a well in the center of mixture.
7. In small bowl, beat egg whites until foamy.
8. Stir in buttermilk, applesauce, and vanilla.
9. Add liquid mixture to dry mixture and stir until just moistened.
10. Fold in raspberries.
11. Spoon batter into prepared cups, filling each ¾ full.
12. Bake 22 to 25 minutes, or until toothpick inserted in center comes out clean.
13. For standard sized muffins, bake 18 to 20 minutes.
14. Cool muffins in pan for 5 minutes, then remove and cool on wire rack.

Orange Scones with Raspberry Filling

These are delicious scones with raspberry filling.

Ingredients:

3¼ c. flour
¼   c. sugar
4   tsp. baking powder
½   tsp. salt
7   Tbs. butter
3   eggs, beaten
½   c. whipping cream
1   Tbs. grated orange peel
3   Tbs. raspberry preserves
    powdered sugar

Directions:

1. Mix flour, sugar, baking powder, and salt; cut in butter until mixture resembles coarse crumbs.
2. Beat eggs, cream, and orange peel.
3. Add to flour mixture, mixing just until moistened.
4. Shape dough into ball; knead 10 times on lightly floured surface.
5. Divide dough in half; roll out each half into a 12 x 6 inch rectangle.
6. Spread 1 rectangle with preserves; top with remaining rectangle.
7. Cut into 8 3-inch squares; cut each in half diagonally.
8. Place on lightly greased cookie sheet.
9. Bake 12 to 14 minutes until lightly browned.
10. Sprinkle with powdered sugar.

Did You Know? . . . .

Did you know that sixty to seventy pints of raspberries can be harvested from one 100-foot row?

Raspberry Banana Muffins

These are delicious and moist muffins.

Ingredients:

2   c. flour
½   tsp. baking powder
¾   tsp. baking soda
¼   tsp. salt
¼   lb. butter
1   c. sugar
2   eggs
3   overripe bananas
¼   c. sour cream
1   tsp. vanilla extract
1   pt. raspberries
½   c. chopped toasted almonds

Directions:

1. Sift together flour, baking powder, baking soda, and salt.
2. Cream butter with sugar until fluffy. Beat in eggs.
3. Purée bananas, sour cream, and vanilla.
4. Alternately add dry ingredients in 3 additions, and banana mixture in 2 additions to the egg mixture.
5. Beat enough to incorporate.
6. Fold in raspberries and toasted almonds.
7. Spoon into greased muffin tins and bake in preheated 350 degrees F. oven for 25 minutes, until puffed, browned, and springy.

Yields: 12 muffins.

Did You Know? . . . .

Did you know raspberries are more perishable than most fruit? Make a point of refrigerating them as soon as possible after purchasing or picking.

Raspberry Banana Nut Bread

This is a moist alternative variety of the traditional banana nut bread that is great with raspberries.

Ingredients:

1¾ c. sifted flour
2 tsp. baking powder
¼ tsp. baking soda
⅓ c. butter
⅔ c. sugar
2 eggs
1 c. bananas, mashed
1 c. walnuts, chopped
1½ c. raspberries

Directions:

1. Sift together flour, baking powder, soda, and salt.
2. Set aside.
3. Cream butter.
4. Gradually beat in sugar until light and fluffy.
5. Add eggs, one at a time.
6. Add flour mixture and banana alternately in three parts.
7. Stir in walnuts.
8. Gently stir in raspberries.
9. Pour into oiled 9 x 5 inch loaf pan.
10. Bake at 350 degrees F. for 50 minutes.
11. Take out of pan and set aside to cool.

Did You Know? . . . .

Did you know you should not wash the berries until you are ready to use them? That is because washing makes them more prone to spoiling.

Raspberry Cornbread

Try this raspberry cornbread warm out of the oven with your next meal.

Ingredients:

½ c. butter
1 c. sugar
2 eggs
1 c. yellow corn meal
1½ c. flour
2 Tbs. baking powder
½ tsp. salt
1½ c. milk
½ c. raspberries

Directions:

1. With electric mixer, cream butter with sugar.
2. Add eggs and corn meal.
3. Sift flour, baking powder, and salt onto sheet of waxed paper.
4. Add ⅓ of the flour mixture to the corn meal mixture.
5. Add ½ cup milk.
6. Beat and repeat twice until all milk is used.
7. Coat raspberries with flour and stir into mixture.
8. Pour into 8-inch square pan, greased or lined with waxed paper.
9. Bake at 375 degrees F. for 40 minutes or until toothpick comes out dry.
10. Serve hot.
11. This recipe freezes well.
12. When thawed in a microwave or oven on low heat, tastes freshly baked.

Raspberry Fritters

My mom used to make us warm apple fritters for breakfast as a special treat when I was a kid. This is an alternate version and makes a great special, easy-to-make breakfast. These are delicious served warm.

Ingredients:

1½ c. flour
¾   c. sugar
3   tsp. baking powder
¾   c. fresh raspberries
1   egg, beaten
1   c. milk
    vegetable oil for frying

Directions:

1. Sift together dry ingredients.
2. Add berries.
3. Mix egg and milk, and add to dry mixture.
4. Mix just until moistened.
5. Drop batter by tablespoons into deep hot oil at 375 degrees F.
6. Fry until golden brown 3 to 4 minutes, turning once.
7. Drain on paper towel.
8. Roll in powdered sugar, sugar, or cinnamon and sugar.

Did You Know? . . . .

Did you know that even under ideal conditions, raspberries will only keep for 1 to 2 days in a refrigerator? For best flavor and texture, consume them as soon as possible.

Raspberry Lemon Streusel Muffins

Your family and friends will love these muffins.

Ingredients for streusel topping:

¼ c. butter, melted
½ c. all purpose flour
2 Tbs. sugar
1½ tsp. lemon peel, finely shredded

Ingredients for muffins:

2½ c. all purpose flour
2 tsp. baking powder
1 tsp. baking soda
1⅓ c. sugar
1 Tbs. lemon peel, finely shredded
1 egg
1 c. buttermilk
½ c. butter, melted
1 Tbs. lemon juice
1½ c. frozen raspberries, whole, do not thaw
1 Tbs. flour

Directions for topping:

1. Adjust oven rack to middle position and preheat oven to 400 degrees F.
2. Stir all streusel ingredients together to form soft, crumbly dough. Set aside.

Directions for muffins:

1. Whisk dry muffin ingredients and lemon peel together.
2. In separate bowl, combine all liquid ingredients.
3. Add dry ingredients and stir until almost fully incorporated.
4. Toss frozen raspberries with flour to coat; then gently fold into dough, handling only enough to incorporate berries.

5. Using paper muffin cup liners, fill each cup until ¼ inch from top.
6. Crumble streusel topping over each.
7. Bake 15 minutes; then reduce heat to 350 degrees F. and bake for another 10 minutes, or until lightly browned and muffin springs back when pressed lightly with fingertip.

Yields: 9 to 12 muffins.

Sweet Raspberry Muffins

These are a nice, easy-to-make version of raspberry muffins that are just a touch sweeter.

Ingredients:

1   c. raspberries
½   c. brown sugar
2   c. all purpose flour
½   tsp. baking powder
½   tsp. salt
2   eggs
4   Tbs. butter, melted
1   tsp. vanilla extract
¼   c. milk
¼   c. syrup

Directions:

1. Combine sugar and raspberries.
2. Stir in flour, baking powder, and salt.
3. In separate bowl, beat together eggs, milk, vanilla, butter, and syrup.
4. Combine the 2 mixtures, using a fork to stir.
5. Do no over mix.
6. Fill well-greased muffin tins ¾ full.
7. Bake at 450 degrees F. for 20 to 25 minutes.

Raspberry Oatmeal Rolls

Raspberry jam adds great flavor to these rolls.

Ingredients:

1   pkg. active dry yeast
¼   c. water, warm
⅔   c. milk, scalded
¼   c. sugar
1   tsp. salt
¼   c. butter
2½ c. sifted all-purpose flour
1   egg, beaten
1   Tbs. orange peel, finely grated
1   c. quick oats
2   Tbs. butter, melted
¾   c. red raspberry jam

Directions:

1. Dissolve yeast in ¼ cup warm water.
2. Pour scalded milk over sugar, salt, and ¼ cup butter; cool to lukewarm.
3. Stir in 1 cup flour and beaten egg.
4. Add yeast-water mixture, orange peel, and oats.
5. Stir in enough remaining flour to make a soft dough.
6. Turn dough onto floured surface and knead until smooth.
7. Place in greased bowl, turning to grease top.
8. Cover and let rise in warm, draft-free place until doubled.
9. Punch down and let rest 10 minutes.
10. With half of the dough, form a 9 x 12 inch rectangle. Brush with melted butter and spread evenly with raspberry jam.
11. Roll up as for jelly roll.
12. Cut in 1-inch rounds and place on greased baking sheet.
13. Repeat for other half of dough. Cover and let rise in warm, draft-free place 30 to 45 minutes, until doubled.
14. Bake at 350 degrees for 30 to 35 minutes.
15. Glaze with vanilla icing or glaze, if desired.

Raspberry Poppy Seed Muffins

Raspberry and poppy seeds combine to make excellent flavor and texture. Enjoy.

Ingredients:

1   c. sugar
½   c. butter
4   egg yolks
1   tsp. vanilla extract
1   c. sour cream
½   c. poppy seeds
8½ oz. cake flour
½   tsp. baking powder
1   tsp. baking soda
6   egg whites
¼   tsp. cream of tartar
1   pt. raspberries

Directions:

1. Preheat oven to 315 degrees F.
2. Grease and flour muffin tins.
3. Mix together butter and sugar in mixer on second speed.
4. Add 1 teaspoon vanilla to egg yolks.
5. Slowly add yolks, one at a time, to butter and sugar mixture.
6. Beat until mixture is soft lemon color.
7. Stir in sour cream and poppy seeds.
8. Sift dry ingredients together and add to egg yolk mixture.
9. In separate bowl, beat egg whites, sugar, and cream of tartar until stiff. Fold into egg yolk mixture.
10. Gently stir in 1 pint of fresh raspberries.
11. Bake in greased muffin tins 20 to 25 minutes.

Yields: 12 to 18 muffins.

Cornbread Sticks with Raspberries

These are very tasty corn bread sticks, with the added taste of raspberry.

Ingredients:

1   c. milk
1   egg
1   c. yellow cornmeal
1   c. flour
2   Tbs. sugar
1   Tbs. baking powder
½   tsp. salt
1¼ c. raspberries

Directions:

1. Preheat oven and cast iron pans to 425 degrees F.
2. Beat milk and egg until blended.
3. Sift together cornmeal, flour sugar, baking powder, and salt.
4. Add raspberries to dry ingredients.
5. Combine liquid and dry ingredients, stirring quickly.
6. Remove pans from oven and brush or spray with oil or baking spray.
7. Pour batter into iron pans.
8. Return to oven and bake 15 to 20 minutes.

Did You Know? . . . .

Did you know that leaves of the raspberry cane are used fresh or dried in herbal and medicinal teas? The leaves have an astringent flavor and in herbal medicine are reputed to be effective in regulating menses.

Did you know the raspberry flower can be a major nectar source for honeybees?

Old-Fashioned Raspberry Buns

These are delicious raspberry buns.

Ingredients:

8 oz. flour
3 oz. caster sugar
4 oz. butter
1 egg, beaten
2 dashes milk
   raspberry jam

Directions:

1. Set oven to 425 degrees F.
2. Grease and flour baking sheets.
3. Sift flour into bowl and rub in the butter.
4. Add sugar and beaten egg with enough milk to make fairly stiff consistency.
5. Divide mixture into walnut-size balls and place on baking sheet, allowing space for them to spread slightly during cooking.
6. Make small hole in center of each ball and spoon in a little raspberry jam.
7. Dust lightly with caster sugar.
8. Bake 10 minutes then reduce heat to 350 degrees F. and bake 5 minutes more, until golden in color.
9. Cool on wire rack.

Did You Know? . . . .

Did you know you should not use soap on fruit stains? It will set stains. Soak the garment immediately in cool water. Wash. If stain remains, cover area with a paste made of oxygen-type bleach, a few drops of hot water, and a few drops of ammonia. Wait 15 to 30 minutes. Wash. For old stains: sponge with white vinegar. Rinse. Repeat procedure for fresh stains.

Raspberry Spice Muffins

These make a nice treat for a weekend breakfast or brunch.

Ingredients:

1½ lbs. cake flour
2   Tbs. baking powder
2   tsp. baking soda
1   Tbs. ground cinnamon
1   tsp. ground allspice
1   tsp. ground nutmeg
½   tsp. ground cloves
½   tsp. salt
1   c. applesauce, chunky
2   c. brown sugar
1½ c. egg substitute /or/ use eggs
½   c. canola oil
1½ lbs. raspberries
⅔   c. quick oatmeal
⅓   c. brown sugar
2   Tbs. canola oil
1   tsp. ground cinnamon

Directions:

1. In bowl combine flour, baking powder, baking soda, spices, and salt; set aside.
2. In separate bowl combine applesauce, sugar, egg substitute, and oil; mix well.
3. Stir into flour mixture and mix just to blend.
4. Fold in raspberries.
5. Scoop ¼ cup batter into each greased muffin tin.
6. In another bowl mix oatmeal, sugar, oil, and cinnamon.
7. Sprinkle 1 heaping teaspoon over each muffin and bake at 400 degrees F. in conventional oven, or at 375 degrees F. in convection oven, 20 to 24 minutes, until firm to the touch.
8. Serve warm.

Yields: 36 muffins.

Raspberry Delights Cookbook

A Collection of Raspberry Recipes
Cookbook Delights Series – Book 14

Breakfasts

Table of Contents

Orange-Berry French Toast

My daughter loves French toast, and this is a delicious addition of flavor.

Ingredients for sauce:

3   c. cold water
5   Tbs. cornstarch
¼   c. lemon juice, fresh
2   c. sugar
8   c. raspberries, fresh or frozen, no sugar or syrup
2   Tbs. triple sec
2   Tbs. raspberry liqueur

Ingredients for bread:

1   loaf soft French or Italian bread, unsliced
8   oz. cream cheese
⅓   c. powdered sugar
½   c. raspberries, fresh or frozen, no syrup

Ingredients for batter:

4   eggs
½   c. sour cream
1   c. milk
1   c. orange juice
½   c. powdered sugar
1   tsp. vanilla extract
½   tsp. nutmeg

Directions for sauce:

1. In large heavy saucepan, mix cold water, cornstarch, lemon juice, and sugar.
2. Stirring constantly bring to a boil. The mixture will thicken and become smooth and almost clear.

3. Lower heat and add berries.
4. If using frozen berries, cook until berries are defrosted and have released their juices, about 10 to 12 minutes.
5. If using fresh, takes about ½ the time.
6. Add triple sec and raspberry liqueur.
7. Keep warm until serving.
8. Note: Any leftover sauce freezes beautifully. Triple this recipe and freeze in various size containers, as it is great over pancakes, pound cake, and ice cream!

Directions for bread:

1. Place unwrapped cream cheese in microwave bowl.
2. Microwave on high 45 seconds, until soft enough to stir.
3. Mix in powdered sugar and berries. Set aside.
4. Cut thin slices off each end of the loaf of bread, then slice lengthwise…but do not cut all the way through.
5. Spread cream cheese mixture inside the loaf.
6. You can freeze the bread at this time for later use; just slip it back into the plastic wrapper it came in, defrost before cooking, or place in refrigerator to use in the morning.
7. Slice bread crosswise into 1-inch slices.
8. Dip into batter and fry on lightly greased hot griddle until brown on both sides and hot in center, about 3 minutes on each side.

Directions for batter:

1. Combine all ingredients in blender and blend thoroughly.
2. Pour into deep bowl for dipping.

Yields: 6 servings.

Did You Know?....

Did you know the USDA does not recommend inverting jars for sealing? Instead, process in a water bath for 10 minutes.

Raspberry-Almond Coffeecake

My daughter enjoys making coffeecake, and this is a moist cake, rich with raspberry flavor.

Ingredients for coffeecake:

1   c. fresh raspberries
3   Tbs. brown sugar
1   c. flour
⅓   c. sugar
½   tsp. baking powder
¼   tsp. baking soda
⅛   tsp. salt
½   c. yogurt
2   Tbs. butter, melted
1   tsp. vanilla extract
1   lg. egg
3   Tbs. almonds, sliced

Ingredients for icing:

¼   c. powdered sugar, sifted
1   tsp. milk
¼   tsp. vanilla extract

Directions for coffeecake:

1. In small bowl mix raspberries and brown sugar. Set aside.
2. In large bowl combine flour, sugar, baking powder, baking soda, and salt. Set aside.
3. In small bowl stir together yogurt, butter, vanilla, and egg.
4. Add to flour mixture stirring just until moist.
5. Spoon ⅔ of batter into sprayed 8-inch round cake pan and spread evenly.
6. Top with raspberry mixture; spoon remaining batter on top.
7. Top with almonds.
8. Bake at 350 degrees F. for 40 minutes.
9. Let cool 10 minutes on rack.

Directions for icing:

1. Combine all ingredients and drizzle over cake.
2. Serve warm or at room temperature.

Yields: 8 servings.

Raspberry Scones

For a truly decadent morning meal, try these raspberry scones!

Ingredients:

2 c. all purpose flour
½ tsp. salt
2 tsp. baking powder
¼ tsp. baking soda
¼ c. butter
1 c. raspberries
⅔ c. buttermilk
1 Tbs. molasses

Directions:

1. Combine first 4 ingredients in bowl; mix well with a fork.
2. Cut in butter with pastry blender or fork until coarse crumbs are formed.
3. Add raspberries and combined buttermilk and molasses; stir well.
4. Turn dough out on floured board.
5. To avoid crushing berries, use hands to pat into ½ inch thickness.
6. Cut into triangles and arrange on greased baking sheet.
7. Bake in 450 degrees F. oven for 12 minutes, until browned.
8. Serve hot with butter.

Yields: 10 servings.

Raspberry Breakfast Bars

These breakfast bars are easy to make and so delicious.

Ingredients for crust:

- 1 c. all purpose flour
- 1 c. quick cooking rolled oats
- ⅔ c. packed brown sugar
- ¼ tsp. ground cinnamon
- ⅛ tsp. baking soda
- ½ c. butter, melted

Ingredients for filling:

- 2 c. raspberries, fresh or frozen
- 2 Tbs. sugar
- 2 Tbs. water
- 1 Tbs. lemon juice
- ½ tsp. ground cinnamon

Directions for crust:

1. In a mixing bowl stir together flour, oats, brown sugar, ¼ teaspoon cinnamon, and baking soda.
2. Stir in melted butter until thoroughly combined.
3. Set aside 1 cup of oat mixture for topping.
4. Press remaining oat mixture into ungreased 9 x 9 inch pan.
5. Bake in 350 degrees F. oven for 20 to 25 minutes.

Directions for filling:

1. In medium saucepan combine berries, sugar, water lemon juice, and ½ teaspoon cinnamon.
2. Bring to a boil, reduce heat, and simmer, uncovered, for about 8 minutes or until slightly thickened, stirring frequently. Remove from heat.
3. When crust is done, remove from oven and carefully spread filling on top of baked crust.

4. Sprinkle with reserved oat mixture, lightly pressing oat mixture into filling.
5. Bake in 350 degrees F. oven for 20 to 25 minutes more or until topping is set.
6. Cool in pan on wire rack. Cut into bars.

Yields: 18 bars.

Raspberry Breakfast Cake

This makes a great-tasting breakfast cake. Try this recipe with sour cream for a tasty addition to a company breakfast or brunch.

Ingredients:

3   eggs, beaten
1½ c. milk
¾   c. all purpose flour
⅓   c. sugar
8   oz. sour cream
¼   c. brown sugar
3   c. raspberries, sugared to taste
1   kiwi fruit for garnish
3   Tbs. butter, melted

Directions:

1. In blender, mix eggs, milk, flour, and sugar.
2. Pour melted butter into fluted quiche pan. (Regular quiche pan will work, but it's not as pretty.)
3. Pour mixture into pan and bake at 375 degrees F. for 30 minutes until edges brown and center is set.
4. Sprinkle fruit with sugar to taste.
5. Mix sour cream with brown sugar.
6. When cake is done, turn over onto serving tray.
7. Fill center with yogurt or sour cream mixture.
8. Top with fruit and garnish with sliced kiwi fruit.

Raspberry-Fig Breakfast Bar

My daughter and son love fig cookies. This makes an interesting combination of raspberry and figs for a delicious breakfast bar.

Ingredients for fig purée:

1½ c. dried figs, coarsely chopped
1   c. water
2   Tbs. honey

Ingredients for breakfast bar:

4½ c. flour
3   tsp. baking powder
3   c. brown sugar
4½ c. oats
½   c. butter, softened
1½ c. fig purée
8   oz. raspberry jam

Directions for fig purée:

1. Combine figs, water, and honey in saucepan; bring to boil.
2. Cover, reduce heat, and simmer 20 minutes until softened.
3. Pour fig mixture into food processor and purée 10 seconds until smooth.

Directions for breakfast bar:

1. Preheat oven to 250 degrees F.
2. Mix all ingredients except jam; form into crumbs.
3. Press ½ mixture into pan sprayed with nonstick oil.
4. Spread jam on crumb crust.
5. Form top layer with remaining mixture.
6. Bake 50 to 60 minutes.

Yields: 36 servings.

Raspberry French Toast

My daughter loves French toast, and this makes an enjoyable variation of the classic version.

Ingredients:

2   c. raspberries, frozen
¾   c. maple syrup
1   tsp. orange peel, grated
1   Tbs. cornstarch
2   Tbs. water
4   eggs, beaten
¾   c. milk
1   tsp. vanilla extract
¼   tsp. nutmeg
8   slices bread
4   Tbs. butter
    powdered sugar

Directions:

1. Combine raspberries, maple syrup, and orange peel in small saucepan.
2. Dissolve cornstarch in water; add to berry mixture.
3. Cook and stir until mixture comes to a boil.
4. Reduce heat and simmer 1 minute or until mixture begins to thicken.
5. Combine eggs, milk, vanilla, and nutmeg.
6. Mix well.
7. Dip each slice of bread into egg mixture.
8. Cook each slice in small amount of butter in skillet or on griddle about 2 minutes until golden.
9. Place one slice on each individual plate.
10. Spread with 3 tablespoons raspberry mixture.
11. Sprinkle lightly with powdered sugar.

Raspberry Sticky Rolls

These raspberry rolls are a nice variation to the usual sticky rolls.

Ingredients for topping:

½ c. sugar
2   Tbs. cornstarch
    reserved syrup from can of red raspberries

Ingredients for sticky rolls:

1   loaf frozen bread dough (16 oz.), thawed
    /or/ homemade rolls recipe below
2   Tbs. butter, softened
1   c. brown sugar
1   can red raspberries, drained, reserve syrup

Ingredients for homemade rolls:

½   c. water, warm
½   c. milk, warm
1   egg
⅓   c. butter, softened
⅓   c. sugar
1   tsp. salt
3¾ c. all-purpose flour
1   pkg. active dry yeast (¼ oz.)

Directions for topping:

1. In small saucepan mix together sugar and cornstarch.
2. Gradually add reserved raspberry syrup.
3. Cook and stir over medium heat until thickened.
4. Set aside to cool.
5. Pour into greased 10 x 15 pan.

Directions for homemade rolls:

1. Place water, milk, egg, ⅓ cup butter, sugar, salt, flour, and yeast in the pan of bread machine in the order recommended by manufacturer.
2. Select dough/knead, and first rise cycle; press start.
3. When cycle finishes, turn dough out onto lightly floured surface,
4. Proceed to step 1 below for sticky rolls.

Directions for sticky rolls:

1. Preheat oven to 375 degrees F.
2. On lightly floured surface, roll dough into 15 x 9 rectangle.
3. Spread butter over entire surface and sprinkle with brown sugar and raspberries.
4. Beginning on 15-inch side, roll up tightly, jellyroll style.
5. Pinch edge of dough into roll to seal well.
6. Stretch roll to make even.
7. Cut into 15 equal-sized pieces.
8. Place 3 across and 5 down over raspberry topping, keeping rolls slightly apart.
9. Let rise until double, about 35 to 45 minutes.
10. Bake until golden brown, 25 to 30 minutes.
11. Remove from oven and immediately invert pan on heatproof serving platter.
12. Let pan remain a minute or two so raspberry topping can drizzle over rolls.

Yields: 15 servings.

Did You Know? . . . .

Did you know that bread rises best in a moist, warm environment? For a perfect place to raise bread, place bread in a microwave oven or regular oven with a pan of steaming water. Do not turn oven on, but close the door.

Raspberry Pancakes

The beaten egg whites in this recipe lighten the texture of the pancakes. These pancakes will disappear quickly. Serve warm with butter and your favorite syrup.

Ingredients:

2   lg. eggs, separated, yolks in one lg. bowl, whites in another lg. bowl
2   c. plain yogurt
½   c. applesauce, unsweetened
¼   c. sugar
1   tsp. vanilla extract
2   tsp. baking soda
½   tsp. salt
1¾ c. all-purpose flour
3   lg. egg whites, added to bowl with egg white
½   tsp. vegetable oil, more if needed
2   c. raspberries

Directions:

1. Add yogurt, applesauce, sugar, and vanilla to egg yolk. Stir with rubber spatula to mix, then stir in baking soda, salt, and flour until blended.
2. Beat egg whites with electric mixer until stiff peaks form.
3. Stir ⅓ of the whites into batter until blended.
4. Gently fold in remaining whites until no white streaks remain.
5. Heat griddle over medium heat until a few drops water flicked onto surface skitter.
6. Wipe ½ teaspoon vegetable oil over cooking surface with paper towel.
7. Pour ¼ cup batter onto griddle.
8. Quickly sprinkle some berries on top, then cook 2 minutes longer or until bubbles appear on surface of pancake and undersides are golden brown.
9. Turn pancakes over with broad metal spatula and cook until tops bounce back when touched, about 2 minutes.

Raspberry Skillet Soufflé

This is a nice soufflé and makes a great breakfast dish. This is perfect for that special weekend breakfast.

Ingredients:

2	pt. raspberries, fresh
⅓	c. raspberry preserves
1	Tbs. framboise (raspberry flavored liqueur)
2	Tbs. butter, unsalted (no substitutions)
8	lg. egg whites
¼	tsp cream of tartar
¼	tsp. salt
¼	c. plus 2 Tbs. sugar, divided

Directions:

1. Preheat oven to 375 degrees F.
2. Mash 1 cup raspberries and raspberry preserves with potato masher in a bowl.
3. Stir in framboise.
4. Melt butter in deep 10 or 11 inch skillet over low heat.
5. In a large mixing bowl, beat egg whites, cream of tartar, and salt to soft peaks.
6. Gradually beat in ¼ cup sugar.
7. Beat to stiff peaks.
8. Fold raspberry mixture into whites, ⅓ at a time, just until blended.
9. Increase heat to medium low.
10. Pour mixture into skillet, gently spreading to the sides and mounding in the center.
11. Cook 2 minutes.
12. Transfer skillet to oven and bake soufflé 15 minutes until set.
13. Add remaining raspberries to bowl.
14. Toss with remaining 2 tablespoons sugar.
15. Serve soufflé immediately with berries.

Simple Stuffed French Toast

This version is easy to make and delicious, too.

Ingredients:

1   loaf French bread
2   eggs
½   c. half and half cream
2   Tbs. brandy
    raspberry preserves

Directions:

1. Heat griddle over medium heat.
2. Cut French loaf into 1-inch slices.
3. Take 2 matching slices and spread preserves on one side then close like a sandwich.
4. Repeat until whole loaf is used.
5. Beat eggs, half and half, and brandy in cake pan.
6. Dip bread in egg batter then grill until golden brown, flip over, and grill other side.
7. Cut in half on an angle and serve with sides of whipped butter and syrup.

Raspberry Waffles

Raspberries are a delicious addition to waffles. Serve them hot with homemade raspberry syrup.

Ingredients:

1½ c. flour
3   tsp. baking powder
½   tsp. salt
2   Tbs. brown sugar
1½ c. buttermilk
3   egg yolks
6   Tbs. butter, melted
3   egg whites
1   c. raspberries

Directions:

1. Sift together flour, baking powder, and salt.
2. Beat egg yolks; combine with buttermilk and melted butter.
3. Beat in flour mixture.
4. Beat egg whites until stiff, add sugar, and beat again.
5. Fold into batter and gently stir in raspberries.
6. Grease waffle irons well and preheat to very hot.
7. Prepare waffles and serve with raspberry topping.

Raspberry Puffs

Our family enjoys cream puffs and French donuts, so these were a natural. This is a great treat to enjoy for an occasional treat.

Ingredients:

1   c. water
1   c. flour
4   oz. butter
4   eggs
¾   c. fresh raspberries
½   c. powdered sugar
    pinch of salt

Directions:

1. Preheat oil to 350 degrees F.
2. In medium saucepan bring water, salt, and butter to a boil.
3. Remove pan from heat and vigorously whisk in the flour until the mixture forms a ball.
4. Whisk in eggs one at a time.
5. Fold in the raspberries.
6. Drop small balls into the oil and cook until golden brown and the batter puffs and expands.
7. Remove raspberry puffs from oil and set on paper towel.
8. Repeat for remaining batter.
9. Sprinkle with powdered sugar and serve immediately.

Raspberry Chocolate Chip Pancakes

The combination of chocolate and raspberries are great.

Ingredients:

¼	c. unsalted butter
¾	c. milk
3	Tbs. milk
1	lg. egg, beaten
1	c. flour
2	tsp. baking powder
¼	tsp. salt
1	c. raspberries
½	c. semi-sweet chocolate, chopped

Directions:

1. In saucepan over low heat, melt 2 tablespoons butter.
2. Stir in milk and heat until warm; remove pan from heat.
3. Whisk together the flour, baking powder, and salt in bowl.
4. Stir in egg and warm milk.
5. Fold in raspberries and chocolate.
6. Melt 1 tablespoon butter on griddle.
7. Place ¼ cup pancake batter on griddle; cook until bubbles appear on surface and bottom is golden brown.
8. Flip and cook on other side.
9. Repeat with remaining batter, keeping cooked pancakes warm in 200 degrees F. oven.

Yields: 6 pancakes.

Did You Know? . . . .

Did you know you can revive stale bread by placing it inside a brown paper bag, seal the bag, and moisten a portion of the outside of the bag with water? After placing it in a preheated 350-degrees F. oven for about five minutes, the bread will emerge warm and soft.

Raspberry Delights Cookbook

A Collection of Raspberry Recipes
Cookbook Delights Series – Book 14

Cakes

Table of Contents

Chocolate Raspberry Flourless Cake

Our family loves flourless cakes, and this is an intense chocolate cake with subtle raspberry flavor. It is delicious.

Ingredients for cake:

12 pieces chocolate, bittersweet (not unsweetened) /or/ semisweet, chopped
¾ c. unsalted butter (1½ sticks) cut into pieces
6 lg. eggs, separated
6 Tbs. sugar
6 Tbs. raspberry syrup
2 tsp. vanilla extract

Ingredients for glaze:

½ c. whipping cream
⅓ c. dark corn syrup
3 Tbs. raspberry maple syrup
9 oz. bittersweet or semisweet chocolate, chopped

Directions for cake:

1. Preheat oven to 350 degrees F.
2. Butter 9-inch spring form pan, line bottom with parchment or waxed paper, and butter paper.
3. Wrap outside of pan with foil.
4. Stir chocolate and butter in heavy medium saucepan over low heat until melted and smooth (or microwave at medium, stirring frequently).
5. Remove from heat; cool to lukewarm, stirring often.
6. Using electric mixer, beat egg yolks and sugar until very thick and pale, about 3 minutes.
7. Fold lukewarm chocolate mixture into yolk mixture, then vanilla extract.
8. Using clean dry beaters, beat egg whites in another large bowl until stiff peaks form. Gradually add 6 tablespoons raspberry maple syrup; continue to beat.

9. Fold egg white mixture into chocolate mixture in 3 additions; pour into prepared pan.
10. Bake cake until top is puffed and cracked, and tester inserted into center comes out with a few moist crumbs, about 45 minutes.
11. Cool cake in pan on rack. (Don't worry - the cake will fall!)
12. Gently press down on crusty top to make evenly thick cake.
13. Loosen sides of pan with small knife and remove pan sides.
14. Invert cake onto serving plate; peel off parchment paper.

Directions for glaze:

1. Bring cream, corn, and maple syrup to simmer in medium saucepan; remove from heat.
2. Add chocolate and whisk until melted and smooth.
3. Spread ½ cup glaze over top and sides of cake.
4. Freeze until almost set, about 3 minutes.
5. Pour additional ½ cup (remaining glaze for intense chocolate!) over cake. Smooth sides and top.
6. Chill until glaze is firm, about 1 hour.
7. Note: You can make cake 1 day ahead, cover with cake dome, and store at room temperature.
8. Serve with dollop of raspberry maple cream on top and garnish with chocolate shavings or chocolate leaves.

Yields: 10 servings.

Did You Know?....

Did you know that wild berries typically grow in forest clearings or fields, particularly where fire or wood-cutting has produced open space for colonization by this opportunistic colonizer of disturbed soil?

Did you know to help prevent jam from foaming during cooking, add one half teaspoon butter to the jam along with the fruit pectin before the jam boils?

Cocoa Raspberry Sweethearts

These make attractive chocolate hearts with delicious raspberry sauce.

Ingredients for cake:

⅔ c. flour
⅔ c. cocoa
½ tsp. salt
5 eggs, separated
½ tsp cream of tartar
1½ c. sugar; divided
⅔ c. water
1 tsp. vanilla extract
   powdered sugar for garnish
   raspberries, fresh, for garnish
   mint leaves, fresh, for garnish

Ingredients for raspberry sauce:

1 pkg. raspberries, frozen in light syrup
1 Tbs. cornstarch

Ingredients for chocolate sauce:

1¼ c. sugar
¾ c. cocoa
1 c. water
1 tsp. vanilla extract

Directions for cake:

1. Grease a 13 x 9 cake pan.
2. Line with wax paper or parchment paper. Set aside.
3. Sift together flour, cocoa, and salt; set aside.
4. In large bowl, beat egg whites and cream of tartar until frothy.
5. Gradually beat in ½ cup sugar, 1 tablespoon at a time, continuing to beat until stiff peaks form; set aside.

6. In large bowl, beat egg yolks and remaining sugar at high speed until very light and lemon-colored, about 6 minutes.
7. Stir in water and vanilla.
8. Sift dry ingredients over surface of yolk mixture; whisk together gently.
9. Scrape over egg whites and fold together. Spread evenly in prepared pan.
10. Bake in 375 degrees F. oven for 12 to 15 minutes, or until cake springs back when lightly touched.
11. Cool pan on rack.
12. Note: Cake can be made up to 8 hours ahead and wrapped well to prevent drying out.
13. Invert cake on cutting board; peel off paper.
14. Using heart shaped cookie cutters of various shapes, cut out hearts, leaving as little space as possible between hearts.
15. Using sieve, shake powdered sugar over hearts; arrange on serving plates.
16. Pool raspberry and chocolate sauces around the hearts.
17. Garnish with fresh raspberries and mint leaves.

Directions for raspberry sauce:

1. Purée thawed raspberries in blender until smooth.
2. Strain through sieve to remove seeds.
3. Transfer purée to saucepan; stir in cornstarch, and cook over medium heat until thickened and clear, stirring often.
4. Transfer to a storage container; cover surface with plastic wrap, place in refrigerator to chill.
5. Sauce can be made a day ahead and stored in refrigerator.

Directions for chocolate sauce:

1. In medium saucepan, whisk together sugar and cocoa.
2. Gradually whisk in 1 cup water.
3. Cook over medium heat, stirring often, until boiling.
4. Reduce heat and boil gently 4 minutes.
5. Let cool; stir in 1 teaspoon vanilla.
6. Transfer to storage container; can refrigerate several days.

Yields: 8 servings.

Fresh Berry Coffeecake

This is actually very easy to make, and it's delicious.

Ingredients for coffeecake:

2½ c. fresh raspberries
6   Tbs. brown sugar
2   c. all-purpose flour
⅔   c. sugar
1   tsp. baking powder
½   tsp. baking soda
¼   tsp. salt
1   c. sour cream
¼   c. butter, melted
3   tsp. vanilla extract
2   eggs
2½ c. pecans, toasted, chopped

Ingredients for frosting:

2   tsp. milk
½   tsp. vanilla extract
½   c. powdered sugar

Directions for coffeecake:

1. Preheat oven to 350 degrees F.
2. Spray 10-inch bundt pan with non-stick cooking spray.
3. Stir together raspberries and brown sugar; set aside.
4. In separate bowl, mix together flour, sugar, baking powder, baking soda, and salt; set aside.
5. In third bowl, cream together sour cream, butter, and 2 teaspoons vanilla.
6. Beat in eggs one at a time.
7. Stir in flour mixture just until moist.
8. Sprinkle ½ cup berries and 1 cup pecans in pan.
9. Pour in half of the batter.
10. Pour on the remaining berries and remaining cup of pecans.
11. Spread the remaining batter over berries.

12. Bake in preheated oven 35 to 40 minutes, or until a toothpick inserted into center of cake comes out clean.

Directions for frosting:

1. While cake bakes stir together in a small bowl 2 teaspoons milk, ½ teaspoon vanilla, and ½ cup powdered sugar.
2. Remove cake from pan; cool 20 minutes before frosting.

Chilled Raspberry Bavarian Cake

This is a very refreshing Bavarian-style cake.

Ingredients:

1½ Tbs. unflavored gelatin
¼   c. water, cold
2   c. milk
2   eggs, separated
¾   c. sugar
1   tsp. lemon juice
1   c. raspberries
½   c. heavy cream, whipped

Directions:

1. Soften gelatin in water 5 minutes.
2. Scald milk, add gelatin, and stir until dissolved.
3. Mix egg yolks with sugar and add hot milk gradually.
4. Cook over boiling water 3 minutes until mixture coats spoon.
5. Remove from heat and chill.
6. When mixture begins to thicken, add lemon juice and raspberries.
7. Fold in stiffly beaten egg whites and whipped cream.
8. Pour into spring form pan and chill until firm.
9. Unmold and serve in slices like cake.

Raspberry Crumb Cake

This crumb cake is easy to make and delicious. It freezes well also.

Ingredients for filling:

⅔ c. sugar
¼ c. cornstarch
¾ c. water
2 c. raspberries, fresh or frozen
1 Tbs. lemon juice

Ingredients for crust:

1 tsp. cinnamon
¼ tsp. mace
1 c. butter, cold
2 eggs
1 c. milk
1 tsp. vanilla extract

Ingredients for topping:

½ c. flour
½ c. sugar
¼ c. butter, cold
¼ c. sliced almonds

Directions for filling:

1. In saucepan, combine sugar, cornstarch, water, and raspberries.
2. Bring to boil over medium heat; boil 5 minutes until thickened, stirring constantly.
3. Remove from heat, stir in lemon juice. Cool.

Directions for crust:

1. In a bowl, combine cinnamon, mace, and cut in butter until mixture resembles coarse crumbs.
2. Beat eggs, milk, and vanilla.
3. Add to crumb mixture and mix.

4. Spread ⅔ of mixture into greased 9 x 13-inch pan.
5. Spoon raspberry filling over crust to within 1 inch of edges.
6. Top with remaining crust mixture.

Directions for topping:

1. Combine flour and sugar; cut in butter until crumbly.
2. Stir in almonds and sprinkle over top.
3. Bake at 350 degrees F. for 50 to 55 minutes until browned.

Yields: 12 to 16 servings.

Wild Raspberry Cake

This raspberry cake is simply delicious.

Ingredients:

1¾ c. flour
½ tsp. salt
1 c. sugar
1 c. raspberries
1 tsp. baking soda
½ c. milk
2 eggs, slightly beaten
¾ c. shortening
1 tsp. cinnamon

Directions:

1. Prepare 9 x 13-inch pan with butter and flour.
2. Dissolve baking soda in ½ cup milk.
3. Sift together, flour, salt, sugar, cinnamon.
4. Cut in shortening.
5. Mix in soda, eggs, and raspberries.
6. Pour into greased pan and bake at 325 degrees F. 1 hour.

Raspberry Whipped Cream Cake

This layered cake is great with raspberry filling and frosted with whipped cream.

Ingredients for cake:

4   eggs, separated
1¼ c. sifted all-purpose flour
¼   tsp. salt
1   c. sugar
2   Tbs. fresh lemon juice
2   tsp. grated lemon peel

Ingredients for raspberry filling:

3   c. boiling water
2   pkg. raspberry flavored gelatin
2   c. whipped cream
2   Tbs. raspberry jam
    sliced almonds, or coarsely chopped pistachio nuts

Ingredients for whipped cream topping:

1   c. whipping cream
2   Tbs. powdered sugar
½   tsp. vanilla extract

Directions for cake:

1. Preheat oven to 350 degrees F.
2. Sift flour with salt.
3. Beat egg whites until foamy.
4. Gradually beat in ½ cup sugar, beating after each addition.
5. Continue beating until soft peaks form.
6. In small bowl beat egg yolks on high speed until thick and lemon colored.
7. Gradually beat in the remaining sugar and beat until smooth.
8. On low speed, blend in flour mixture.
9. Add lemon juice, 2 tablespoons water, and the lemon peel, beating until just combined.

10. With wire whisk or rubber scraper, gently fold egg yolk mixture into the egg white mixture, just until blended.
11. Pour batter into 2 ungreased 8 inch cake pans.
12. Bake at 350 degrees F. for 25 minutes or until surface springs back when gently pressed with fingertip.
13. Invert the cake by hanging it between two other pans.
14. Cool completely, about 1 hour.
15. With a spatula, carefully loosen cake from the pan; remove.
16. Cut each layer in half to make four layers and frost.

Directions for filling:

1. Stir boiling water into gelatin until dissolved.
2. Cool to lukewarm and then refrigerate.
3. When mixture begins to thicken, in about 1 hour, beat until frothy.
4. Fold into whipped cream.
5. Refrigerate until firm.
6. Spread on the cake layers and reassemble the cake.
7. Frost cake with whipped cream.
8. Decorate with nuts.

Directions for whipped cream topping:

1. Beat 1 cup cream until stiff.
2. Beat in 2 tablespoons powdered sugar and ¼ teaspoon vanilla.

Did You Know? . . . .

Did you know that temperatures between 34 and 38 degrees F. are best for raspberries? But be careful not to freeze raspberries. Fresh raspberries are highly prone to freeze damage.

Raspberry White Chocolate Cream Cake

This is a delicious, moist cake with a raspberry filling and white chocolate butter cream frosting.

Ingredients for filling:

¼ c. sugar
2 Tbs. cornstarch
⅛ tsp. salt
1 c. raspberry-flavored wine
1 Tbs. butter
⅛ tsp. almond extract
2 drops red food coloring

Ingredients for cake:

3 oz. white chocolate baking bar, chopped
2¼ c. all-purpose flour
1½ c. sugar
2¼ tsp. baking powder
½ tsp. salt
1⅔ c. heavy whipping cream
3 eggs
1 tsp. almond extract

Ingredients for white chocolate frosting:

3 oz. white chocolate baking bar, chopped
3½ c. powdered sugar
5 Tbs. raspberry-flavored wine
¼ c. butter, softened
½ tsp. almond extract

Directions for filling:

1. Mix sugar, corn starch, and salt in 1½-quart saucepan.
2. Stir in wine cooler.
3. Cook over medium heat, stirring constantly, until mixture thickens and boils.

126

4. Boil and stir 1 minute; remove from heat.
5. Stir in butter, almond extract, and food coloring.
6. Cover and refrigerate until chilled.

Directions for cake:

1. Heat oven to 350 degrees F.
2. Grease and flour 2 round cake pans, 8 or 9 inches.
3. Heat white baking bar over low heat, stirring occasionally until melted.
4. Cool.
5. Mix flour, 1½ cup sugar, baking powder, and salt.
6. Reserve.
7. Beat whipping cream in chilled large bowl until stiff.
8. Reserve.
9. Beat eggs about 5 minutes until thick and lemon colored.
10. Beat in melted baking bar and 1 teaspoon almond extract.
11. Fold egg mixture into whipping cream.
12. Add flour mixture, ½ cup at a time, folding gently after each addition until blended.
13. Pour into pans.
14. Bake 8 inch rounds 35 to 40 minutes; 9-inch rounds 30 to 35 minutes.
15. Cool 10 minutes; remove from pans.
16. Cool completely on wire racks.
17. Fill layers with raspberry filling.

Directions for white chocolate frosting:

1. Heat white baking bar over low heat, stirring occasionally, until melted.
2. Cool.
3. Beat melted baking bar and remaining ingredients in medium bowl on medium speed until smooth and of spreading consistency.
4. If necessary, stir in additional wine cooler, 1 teaspoon at a time.
5. Spread over side and top of cake.

Domed Raspberry Angel Food Cake

Fresh raspberries add great flavor and moisture to this angel food cake. The cake absorbs the raspberry flavor and makes a colorful dessert dome.

Ingredients for cake:

10 egg whites
1¼ tsp. cream of tartar
1   tsp. vanilla extract
½   tsp. almond extract
½   c. sugar
1   c. cake flour
2   c. fresh raspberries

Ingredients for topping:

2   envelopes gelatin
½   c. sugar
1   can frozen raspberry juice concentrate (12 oz.), thawed
2   c. water
2   c. whipping cream, divided
1   c. fresh raspberries
1   c. flaked coconut, toasted

Directions for cake:

1. In mixing bowl, beat egg whites until frothy.
2. Beat in cream of tartar until soft peaks form.
3. Add extracts.
4. Gradually beat in sugar until stiff, scraping bowl occasionally.
5. Sift flour over beaten whites, sprinkle with berries.
6. Gently fold flour and raspberries into batter until well mixed.
7. Pour into ungreased 10-inch tube pan.

8. Bake at 325 degrees F. 40 to 45 minutes or until lightly browned and entire top appears dry.
9. Immediately invert cake pan; cool completely, about 1 hour.

Directions for domed topping:

1. Cool angel food cake completely.
2. Cut angel food cake into 1-inch cubes.
3. Set aside.
4. Mix gelatin and sugar together.
5. Stir in raspberry juice and water.
6. Bring to a boil, stirring constantly until dissolved.
7. Chill until it starts to set.
8. Whip ½ the whipping cream to stiff peaks.
9. Beat gelatin mixture on high speed of electric mixer until light.
10. Fold in whipped cream and berries.
11. Line large bowl with plastic wrap.
12. Put ⅓ of cake cubes into bowl.
13. Cover with ⅓ of the gelatin mixture, pressing in lightly.
14. Repeat layers twice more.
15. Cover and chill overnight.
16. Turn out rounded side up onto serving platter.
17. Remove plastic wrap.
18. Whip remaining cream until stiff and frost cake with the whipped cream.
19. Sprinkle toasted coconut over top.

Yields: 16 servings.

Did You Know?....

Did you know that raspberries contain significant amounts of polyphenol antioxidants, chemicals linked to promoting endothelial and cardiovascular health? Xylitol, a sugar alcohol alternative sweetener, can be extracted from raspberries.

Low Fat Cheesecake with Raspberry

This is a low fat version of a delicious raspberry sauce.

Ingredients for cheesecake:

¼   c. graham cracker crumbs
2⅛. c. cottage cheese, 2% fat
17½ oz. cream cheese - fat free
1   c. sugar
2   Tbs. cornstarch
1   tsp. vanilla extract
1   egg
2   egg whites

Ingredients for raspberry sauce:

10½ oz. frozen raspberries (1¼ c.), thawed
1   Tbs. cornstarch
½   c. jelly

Directions for cheesecake:

1. Sprinkle graham cracker crumbs evenly over bottom of lightly greased 9-inch spring form pan.
2. Purée drained cottage cheese in processor until smooth.
3. Add cream cheese and process until smooth.
4. Gradually add sugar, cornstarch, and vanilla.
5. Add egg and egg whites, one at a time, to mixture.
6. Process using on and off action until blended.
7. Pour into pan and bake at 450 degrees F. for 10 minutes.
8. Reduce to 250 degrees F. and bake 35 to 40 minutes.
9. Cool. Refrigerate overnight.
10. Serve with raspberry sauce.

Directions for raspberry sauce:

1. Place berries in sieve, crush, and discard seeds.
2. Whisk cornstarch and heated jelly into juice.
3. Cook sauce in microwave 1 to 2 minutes; refrigerate.

Raspberry Delights Cookbook

A Collection of Raspberry Recipes
Cookbook Delights Series – Book 14

Candies

Table of Contents

Chocolate Raspberry Bonbons

These are delicious bonbons. Enjoy.

Ingredients:

- 1 c. vanilla wafers, finely crushed
- 1 c. powdered sugar
- 1 c. chopped almonds, toasted
- 2 Tbs. cocoa, unsweetened
- 2 Tbs. butter
- ¼ c. raspberry preserves, seedless
- ¼ c. raspberry liqueur
- 6 oz. sweet baking chocolate, grated

Directions:

1. Combine wafer crumbs, sugar, almonds, and cocoa in mixing bowl.
2. Heat butter and raspberry preserves until butter melts.
3. Blend butter mixture into crumb mixture; add raspberry liqueur.
4. Chill for 1 hour, then shape into 1 inch balls.
5. Roll balls in grated chocolate.
6. May be stored in airtight container for up to 2 weeks.

Yields: 20 pieces.

Raspberry Divinity

Try this edition of raspberry divinity.

Ingredients:

- 3 c. sugar
- 1 sm. box raspberry gelatin
- ½ c. flaked coconut
- 2 egg whites, stiffly beaten
- ¾ c. light corn syrup

1   c. nuts, chopped
¾   c. water

Directions:

1. Combine sugar, corn syrup, and water.
2. Bring to boil, stirring constantly.
3. Reduce heat and cook to hard ball stage.
4. Combine beaten egg whites and gelatin.
5. Beat until mixture forms stiff peaks.
6. Pour hot syrup slowly into egg whites, beating until candy loses gloss and holds shape.
7. Fold in coconut and nuts (optional).
8. Pour into greased 9-inch square pan and top with rows of chopped nuts and coconut.

Raspberry Fudge Balls

This candy is easy to make, yet delicious. It will disappear quickly.

Ingredients:

8   oz. cream cheese, softened
1   c. semisweet chocolate morsels, melted
¾   c. vanilla wafer crumbs
¼   c. raspberry preserves
¾   c. almonds or pecans, toasted, finely chopped

Directions:

1. Beat cream cheese at medium speed with electric mixer until creamy.
2. Beat in melted chocolate until smooth.
3. Stir in vanilla wafer crumbs and raspberry preserves.
4. Cover and chill 1 hour.
5. Shape into 1-inch balls; roll in toasted chopped almonds or pecans, and chill.

Yields: 4 dozen candies.

Raspberry Bombs

Try this delicious and rich candy.

Ingredients:

2   c. sugar
1¾ c. cranberry-raspberry juice
¼   c. raspberry liqueur
6   oz. liquid pectin
24 oz. chocolate bits

Directions:

1. Cut two 8 x 13 inch rectangles from wax paper.
2. Line 8-inch square baking pan with one sheet, allowing ends to extend over the sides of pan. Place the second sheet over it, in the opposite direction, so the bottom of pan and the sides are completely covered.
3. Combine sugar, juice, and liqueur in saucepan. Bring to boil over medium heat, stirring to dissolve sugar. Boil and stir 3 minutes.
4. Remove from heat and stir in the pectin. Return to heat and bring to a boil, stirring. Boil and stir for 1 minute.
5. Pour into the prepared pan. Allow to sit at room temperature for at least 24 hours.
6. When jelly is firm, cut into bite-size squares.
7. Using the overhanging paper, lift jelly from pan, and place on a work surface.
8. Melt chocolate to 110 to 120 degrees F. in top of double boiler, using an instant-read thermometer to accurately measure the temperature.
9. Remove from heat and cool to 90 degrees F.
10. Return to very low heat, keeping temperature of chocolate an even 90 to 95 degrees F.
11. Place a jelly square on a fork and dip into chocolate, coating completely.
12. Transfer to another fork, letting excess chocolate drip back into pan.

13. Place on wax paper to dry.
14. Repeat with remaining jelly squares.
15. Store at room temperature or refrigerate.

Yields: 36 candies.

Raspberry Truffle Fudge

This is an easy-to-make raspberry fudge. Enjoy!

Ingredients:

3   c. semi-sweet chocolate chips
1   can sweetened condensed milk (14-oz.)
1½ tsp. vanilla extract
¼   c. heavy cream
¼   c. raspberry flavored liqueur
2   c. semi-sweet chocolate chips
    salt

Directions:

1. Spray a 9 x 9 pan with non-stick cooking spray and line with wax paper.
2. In microwave-safe bowl, combine 3 cups chocolate chips and sweetened condensed milk.
3. Heat in microwave until chocolate melts, stirring occasionally. Be careful not to let it scorch.
4. Stir in vanilla and salt. Spread into pan and cool.
5. In microwave-safe bowl, combine cream, liqueur, and 2 cups chocolate chips.
6. Heat in microwave until chocolate melts.
7. Stir until smooth and cool to lukewarm, then pour over fudge layer.
8. Refrigerate 1 hour until both layers are completely set.
9. Cut into 1 inch pieces.

Yields: 40 servings.

Raspberry English Toffee

The raspberry jam adds a pleasant addition to this version of English toffee.

Ingredients for toffee:

1   c. butter, unsalted
1⅓ c. sugar
1   Tbs. corn syrup
2   Tbs. water
1   tsp. real vanilla extract

Ingredients for topping:

1   c. white chocolate
1   Tbs. heavy whipping cream or half and half
4   Tbs. raspberry jam, seedless
⅔   c. almonds, slivered

Directions for toffee if using microwave:

1. Place butter, sugar, corn syrup, and water in microwave bowl and microwave on high 5 minutes.
2. Stir gently to blend ingredients.
3. Microwave another 3 to 6 minutes, watching carefully, and cook until color changes to rich golden brown, but is not burning.
4. Slowly add vanilla; pour onto buttered baking sheet.

Directions for toffee if using sauce pan on cook top:

1. Bring mixture to boil, stirring slowly.
2. Cook until mixture reaches 295 to 310 degrees F. on candy thermometer.
3. Slowly add vanilla extract and pour onto buttered baking sheet.
4. Allow to cool.

Directions for topping:

1. Meantime, combine white chocolate, cream, and jam.
2. Microwave on high 30 seconds. Stir.
3. Microwave another 30 to 40 seconds until mixture melts.
4. Spread over toffee.
5. Sprinkle with slivered almonds before chocolate sets.
6. Refrigerate to set.
7. Break into chunks.
8. This chocolate mixture will remain a little soft, so chilling is necessary in order to break pieces correctly.

Dark Chocolate Raspberry Truffles

Try these bittersweet raspberry truffles.

Ingredients:

⅓   c. whipping cream
8   oz. bittersweet chocolate, finely chopped
6   Tbs. butter, unsalted
¼   c. raspberry jelly, seedless
     sweetened cocoa or ground almonds

Directions:

1. In large saucepan, heat cream to a simmer.
2. Turn off heat.
3. Add chocolate and butter to hot cream and allow to melt.
4. Whisk until smooth.
5. Add jelly and mix until blended.
6. Cool to room temperature.
7. Refrigerate until firm.
8. Roll chocolate mixture into balls of any size you prefer.
9. Roll each in cocoa or nuts.
10. Transfer to paper candy cups and chill.
11. May be stored in airtight tin in refrigerator for 2 weeks, or frozen up to 1 month.

Chocolate Raspberry Truffles

You'll think you're in heaven when you try this truffle. Be careful, or you might eat the whole batch!

Ingredients:

- ¾ c. (1½ sticks) butter, unsalted
- 1 lb. semi-sweet chocolate, finely chopped
- ½ c. raspberry jam, seedless
- ¼ c. black raspberry liqueur or raspberry Chambord
- ½ c. Dutch-process cocoa powder (optional)
- 1 c. hazelnuts, roasted and finely chopped

Directions:

1. Cut butter into pieces and melt in top of double boiler or metal bowl over (but not touching) hot water.
2. Add chocolate, stirring occasionally until smooth.
3. Remove from heat; blend in raspberry jam and raspberry liqueur, until smooth.
4. Cover and freeze until firm, about 2 hours, or refrigerate until firm, 4 hours or overnight.
5. Place cocoa and hazelnuts in separate pie pans.
6. Using a melon-baller or a tablespoon, scoop 1 tablespoon of the cold chocolate mixture between your palms and roll to form a round ball.
7. Roll in desired coating and place on a sided baking sheet.
8. Repeat until all the mixture is gone.
9. Cover tightly with plastic wrap until ready to serve.
10. Remove from refrigerator 10 minutes before serving.
11. This recipe may be prepared up to 5 days ahead if truffles are covered tightly and refrigerated.
12. They may also be frozen for up to a month, double wrapped in plastic.

Yields: 37 bite-size truffles.

Raspberry Jelly Candy

This flavor goes way beyond the jelly candy you can purchase.

Ingredients:

1¾ oz. powdered fruit pectin
1   c. sugar
1   c. light corn syrup
¾   c. water
1½ tsp. raspberry extract
¼   tsp. baking soda
    red food coloring, if desired

Directions for 1st day:

1. Grease a loaf pan.
2. Stir together pectin, water, and baking soda in small pan.
3. Cook on high heat.
4. At the same time, bring the sugar and corn syrup to a rolling boil, stirring occasionally.
5. When it reaches boiling, add the pectin mixture.
6. Cook for about 1 more minute stirring constantly.
7. Remove from heat and add extract and food coloring, stirring to incorporate.
8. Pour into the prepared pan and allow to cool, loosely covered, overnight on the counter.

Directions for 2nd day:

1. Invert the pan onto platter full of sugar.
2. If you have trouble unmolding the candy, use knife to loosen from the perimeter of the pan and carefully slide your fingers underneath the candy to gently peel the candy out of the pan.
3. Press both sides of the candy into the sugar.
4. Slice the candy into ¼ inch slices, then cut each slice into ¼ inch cubes. Roll each cube in sugar. Allow to sit an additional hour before packaging or serving.

Raspberry Salt Water Taffy

My children love salt water taffy, and this version has great natural color and taste. It also makes a fun family project to pull around the family table.

Ingredients:

1   c. sugar
2   Tbs. cornstarch
¾   c. light corn syrup
¼   c. water
¼   c. raspberry juice
2   Tbs. butter
½   tsp. salt

Directions:

1. Mix sugar and cornstarch in 1½ quart saucepan.
2. Add next 4 ingredients. Cook over medium heat until mixture boils and sugar is dissolved.
3. Continue without stirring until temperature reaches 260 degrees F.
4. Remove from heat, after boiling has ceased, and stir in flavoring.
5. Pour onto greased cookie sheet. Let cool.
6. Grease hands and pull until satin-like finish.
7. Wrap in waxed paper, pieces of desired size.

Did You Know? . . . .

Did you know you can make your own egg substitute? For use in baking only, soften 1 teaspoon unflavored gelatin in 1 tablespoon cold water. Add 2 tablespoons plus 1 teaspoon boiling water and mix.

Another good egg substitute to use in baking only is 1 heaping tablespoon soy flour dissolved in 2 tablespoon water.

Raspberry Walnut Jelly Candy

This is a popular style of Northwest candy.

Ingredients:

1   pkg. frozen raspberries (10 oz.)
1   pkg. powdered pectin (1¾ oz.)
1½ tsp. baking soda
1   c. sugar
1   c. light corn syrup
1   tsp. fresh lemon juice
1   c. walnuts, chopped
    sugar (for rolling candies)

Directions:

1. In saucepan, heat raspberries to simmering, cooking to soften raspberries.
2. Force raspberries through a fine strainer to remove seeds; measure strained berries (should be ¾ cup).
3. Combine berries with pectin and baking soda in 2-quart saucepan (mixture will foam).
4. Cook 5 minutes over moderate heat, stirring constantly, until foam begins to disappear.
5. Meanwhile, combine sugar and corn syrup in second saucepan.
6. Heat to boiling, stirring occasionally, until sugar dissolves.
7. Combine syrup with cooked raspberry mixture; simmer 1 minute longer.
8. Remove from heat; stir in lemon juice and walnuts.
9. Turn onto a greased 9 x 5-inch loaf pan; let set.
10. Turn out onto a platter or board; cut into squares, and roll in sugar.
11. Let stand 1 hour longer, then roll in sugar again.

Yields: 36 candies.

Raspberry Nuggets

Fruit and nut nugget candy rolled in powdered sugar is a very popular candy in the Northwest. This candy can be made at home as a real treat. This was one of my daughter's favorite candies.

Ingredients:

1½ c. raspberry purée
2   c. sugar
2   env. gelatin, unflavored
¼   tsp. almond extract
1   c. walnuts, chopped
    powdered sugar

Directions:

1. Sprinkle gelatin over ½ cup raspberry purée and let stand.
2. Combine the rest of raspberry purée and sugar in a saucepan.
3. Bring to boil over moderate heat, stirring constantly.
4. Add the softened gelatin mixture and continue stirring.
5. Boil mixture for 15 to 20 minutes longer.
6. Stir in nuts and almond extract.
7. Pour into greased 8 x 8 inch pan.
8. Cool to room temperature, then refrigerate overnight.
9. Cut into 1 x 1 inch pieces.
10. Carefully remove them from pan and roll in powdered sugar.
11. Allow to stand 2 to 3 days before serving.

Did You Know? . . . .

Did you know that chocolate chips are not necessarily a substitute for bar chocolate, because the chips have something added to them to slow down melting?

Raspberry Fudge

This is a rich fudge recipe topped with raspberry and white chocolate. It is well worth the wait.

Ingredients:

3   c. semi-sweet chocolate chips
1   can sweetened condensed milk (14 oz.)
2   tsp. vanilla extract
⅛   tsp. salt
⅛   c. cream
½   c. seedless raspberry preserves
2   c. white chocolate chips
⅛   tsp. lemon juice
     red food coloring (optional)

Directions:

1. Line 8 x 8 pan with aluminum foil and spray foil with nonstick cooking spray.
2. Place semi-sweet chocolate chips and condensed milk in microwave-safe bowl and microwave until melted, stirring after every minute until mixture is completely smooth.
3. Add vanilla, salt, and stir until combined.
4. Pour into the prepared pan and refrigerate until this layer is mostly set, about 1 hour.
5. Once first layer is set, combine cream, white chocolate chips, and raspberry preserves in microwave-safe bowl.
6. Microwave until melted, stirring every 45 seconds, and take care the chocolate does not burn.
7. Stir until smooth, and then add lemon juice and a few drops of red food coloring, if desired.
8. Allow the raspberry-white chocolate mixture to cool to lukewarm, then pour it over the chocolate fudge layer and smooth it in an even layer using a knife or an offset spatula.
9. Return the fudge to the refrigerator to set, about 2-3 hours.
10. To serve, cut into 1-inch squares.
11. Note: For a more adult taste, ¼ cup raspberry liqueur can be substituted for the raspberry preserves in the recipe.

Yields: 64 pieces.

Chocolate Raspberry Balls

The combination of chocolate cookie crumbs and raspberries make this candy wonderfully rich.

Ingredients:

1   c. pecans
1   c. chocolate wafer cookie crumbs
1   c. powdered sugar
1½ Tbs. light corn syrup
¼   c. raspberry liqueur /or/ raspberry jam
    powdered sugar /or/ pecans, finely chopped, for rolling

Directions:

1. Grind the pecans and the chocolate wafers coarsely in a food processor and empty into a large bowl.
2. Mix in the sugar, corn syrup, and raspberry liqueur or jam very thoroughly.
3. Shape the mixture into balls the size of a quarter.
4. Roll in powdered sugar or in finely chopped pecans.
5. Keep in an airtight container in a cool place, or freeze on a baking sheet until each is firm and store in tightly sealed plastic bags.

Yields: 2 to 3 dozen.

Did You Know?....

Did you know that to make quick and easy sweet treats, all you need on hand is your favorite chocolate and some pretzels or graham crackers? Melt the chocolate (dark chocolate or white, or both!). Dip the pretzels or graham crackers into the chocolate and allow to dry on waxed paper until firm. For quicker drying time, place the waxed paper on cookie sheets and place into your refrigerator until firm. All you need next are the guests and a beautiful candy dish!

Raspberry Delights Cookbook
A Collection of Raspberry Recipes
Cookbook Delights Series – Book 14

Cookies

Table of Contents

Almond-Berry Thumbprint Cookies

These almond-raspberry cookies are wonderful!

Ingredients:

1   c. butter, softened
1   c. sugar
1   can almond filling
2   egg yolks
1   tsp. almond extract
2½ c. all-purpose flour
½   tsp. baking powder
½   tsp. salt
1   can raspberry filling

Directions:

1. Beat butter and sugar in medium bowl until light and fluffy.
2. Add almond filling, egg yolks, and almond extract; beat until blended.
3. Stir in flour, baking powder, and salt with wooden spoon to make soft dough.
4. Cover; refrigerate at least 3 hours or overnight.
5. Preheat oven to 350 degrees F.
6. Shape dough into 2-inch balls; place on ungreased baking sheets, about 1½ inch apart.
7. Press thumb into center of each ball to make indentation. Spoon ½ teaspoon raspberry filling into each indentation.
8. Bake 11 to 13 minutes until edges of cookies are golden brown.
9. Cool on baking sheets 1 minute.
10. Remove from baking sheets.
11. Cool completely on wire racks.

Yields: 5 dozen cookies.

Chocolate Berry Linzer Cookies

These cookies combine the delicious taste of spiced chocolate with raspberry jam. Enjoy.

Ingredients:

2⅓ c. flour
1   c. sugar
1   tsp. baking powder
½   tsp. cinnamon
¼   tsp. salt
¾   c. butter
½   tsp. almond extract
2   eggs
1   pkg. semi-sweet chocolate chips (12 oz.)
¾   c. raspberry jam
    powdered sugar

Directions:

1. Combine flour, baking powder, cinnamon, and salt.
2. Beat sugar and butter until creamy.
3. Add eggs and extract.
4. Beat in flour mixture.
5. Refrigerate 2 hours.
6. Roll ⅛-inch thick, and cut with 2½-inch round or heart-shaped cookie cutter.
7. Cut center out of ½ of the cookies with a smaller cookie cutter before baking.
8. Bake 8 to 10 minutes at 350 degrees F.
9. Melt chocolate chips and spread over whole cookies.
10. Top with ½ teaspoon jam in center and cover with cut-out cookie.
11. Sprinkle with powdered sugar.

Yields: 3 dozen cookies.

Oatmeal Raspberry Cookies

Oatmeal and raspberry are always great together.

Ingredients:

½ c. butter, room temperature
½ c. light brown sugar
1 c. flour
¼ tsp. baking soda
⅛ tsp. salt
1 c. rolled oats
¾ c. raspberry jam, seedless

Directions:

1. Heat oven to 350 degrees F. Butter 8-inch square pan and set aside.
2. Mix all ingredients together except the jam.
3. Press 2 cups mixture into bottom of prepared pan.
4. Spread the jam to within ¼ inch of the edge.
5. Sprinkle remaining crumb mixture over top and lightly press into the jam.
6. Bake 35 to 40 minutes and cool on wire rack before cutting into 2 x 1½ inch bars.

Yields: 2 dozen bars.

Raspberry Bar Cookies

These are easy-to-make, delicious bars that make good lunch treats. They also freeze well.

Ingredients:

¾ c. butter
1 c. brown sugar
1½ c. flour
½ tsp. salt

½ tsp. baking soda

1½ c. oats (oatmeal)

1 jar raspberry preserves (9 oz.)

Directions:

1. Cream butter and sugar.
2. Add dry ingredients.
3. Pat half of crumb mixture into 9 x 13-inch pan.
4. Spread with preserves and sprinkle with remaining crumb mixture.
5. Bake at 400 degrees F. for 25 minutes.

Raspberry Cookie Bars

These bars are very easy to make and will make a delicious snack or lunch treat.

Ingredients:

1 jar raspberry preserves (10 oz.)

1 egg

1 c. butter, soft

1 c. sugar

2¼ c. flour

1¼ c. nuts, chopped

Directions:

1. Cream egg and butter.
2. Add sugar, flour, and nuts until crumbly.
3. Save ½ of this mixture. Press remaining in 8 x 8 inch greased pan.
4. Spread jam to within ½ inch of edge.
5. Cover with remaining crumb mixture.
6. Bake at 350 degrees F. for 42 to 50 minutes until lightly browned. Cool.

Raspberry Cookie Gems

These chocolate and raspberry cookies are well named - they really are gems!

Ingredients:

1½ c. all purpose flour
1   c. butter, softened
½   c. dairy sour cream
⅓   c. raspberry preserves
3   Tbs. sugar
1   Tbs. water

Ingredients for topping:

⅔   c. semisweet chocolate pieces
1   Tbs. shortening
¼   c. finely chopped almonds

Directions:

1. Stir together flour, butter, and sour cream in a large mixing bowl, until thoroughly combined. Divide dough in half.
2. Cover and chill for 3 hours.
3. Roll each half of dough on lightly floured surface to ⅛ inch thickness.
4. Using 1¾ to 2 inch round cookie cutter, cut dough.
5. Spread about ¼ teaspoon raspberry preserves on top of half the cookies.
6. Top with remaining cookie dough.
7. Stir together sugar and 1 tablespoon water.
8. Brush over cookies.
9. Place cookies on lightly greased baking sheet.
10. Bake in 350 degrees F. oven 15 to 20 minutes until golden.
11. Remove cookies and cool on wire rack.

Directions for topping:

1. In a small heavy saucepan, melt chocolate pieces and shortening over low heat, stirring constantly.
2. Dip one side of each of the cookies into melted chocolate.
3. Place on waxed paper; sprinkle with almonds.
4. Cool until set.

Yields: 72 cookies.

Raspberry Chews

Meringue adds an elegant touch to these raspberry chews!

Ingredients:

1½ sticks butter
¾ c. sugar
2 eggs, separated
1½ c. flour
1¼ c. walnuts, chopped
1 c. raspberry jam
1¼ c. coconut, flaked

Directions:

1. Cream butter with ¼ cup sugar until fluffy.
2. Beat in egg yolks.
3. Stir in flour.
4. Spread evenly in 13 x 9 x 2 inch pan.
5. Bake at 350 degrees F. for 15 minutes.
6. Beat egg whites until foamy and double in volume.
7. Add ½ cup sugar until meringue stands in peaks.
8. Fold in nuts.
9. Spread jam and coconut over layer, then cover with meringue.
10. Bake at 350 degrees for 25 minutes.
11. Cut into squares.

Raspberry Cheesecake Cookie Bars

My family loves cheesecake and cookies, and these make a great combination.

Ingredients:

¼   c. butter, softened
¼   c. brown sugar, packed
¼   c. flour
¾   c. walnuts, ground
8   oz. cream cheese, softened
¼   c. sugar
1   egg, lightly beaten
2   Tbs. lemon juice
½   tsp. pure vanilla extract
     raspberry topping

Directions:

1. Cream butter and brown sugar.
2. Combine with flour and walnuts until mixture is crumbly.
3. Press into bottom of buttered 9 x 9 baking pan.
4. Bake at 350 degrees F. for 12 minutes.
5. Cool slightly.
6. Beat cream cheese, sugar, egg, lemon juice, and vanilla.
7. Spread evenly over crust and top with raspberry topping.
8. Return to oven and bake another 25 minutes.
9. Cool to room temperature and cut into 2-inch squares.

Yields: 16 cookies.

Did You Know? . . . .

Did you know a good, quick substitute for sweetened condensed milk? Mix 1 cup plus 2 tablespoons dry (powdered) milk and ½ cup warm water. When mixed, add ¾ cup sugar.

Raspberry Coconut Layer Cookie Bars

These are delicious and easy to make. The graham cracker, coconut, raspberry, chocolates, and walnuts make a delightful combination. Enjoy!

Ingredients:

1⅔ c. graham cracker crumbs
½   c. butter, melted
2¾   c. coconut, flaked
14   oz. sweetened condensed milk
1   c. raspberry preserves
¾   c. walnuts, chopped, toasted
½   c. semi sweet chocolate chips, melted
1½   oz. white chocolate baking bar, melted

Directions:

1. Preheat oven to 350 degrees F.
2. In medium bowl, combine graham cracker crumbs and butter.
3. Spread evenly over bottom of 9 x 13-inch pan, pressing to make crust.
4. Sprinkle coconut over crust.
5. Pour sweetened milk evenly over coconut.
6. Bake in preheated oven for 20 to 25 minutes or until lightly brown.
7. Cool.
8. Spread preserves over coconut layer.
9. Chill 3 to 4 hours.
10. Sprinkle with walnuts.
11. Drizzle dark chocolate then white chocolate over top layer to make lacey effect.
12. Chill.
13. Cut into bars.

Yields: 4 dozen bars.

Raspberry Drop Cookies

These make a great-tasting drop cookie that can be left under baked for a softer cookie or leave in the oven longer for a crisper cookie.

Ingredients:

½ c. butter
1   c. sugar
¾ c. brown sugar
1   egg, lightly beaten
¼ c. milk
2   Tbs. orange juice concentrate, thawed
3   c. flour
1   tsp. baking powder
½ tsp baking soda
1¼ c. walnuts, chopped or ground
2¾ c. frozen raspberries, thawed, rinsed, patted dry

Directions:

1. Cream butter and sugars.
2. Add egg, milk, and orange juice concentrate.
3. Sift together flour, salt, baking powder, and baking soda.
4. Combine with creamed mixture; then add nuts and raspberries.
5. Drop dough by teaspoonfuls onto greased baking sheet.
6. Bake 10 to 12 minutes.

Yields: 10 dozen cookies.

Did You Know? . . . .

Did you know cake flour can be substituted with all-purpose plain flour by removing three tablespoons per cup of flour and replacing it with corn starch or potato flour?

Raspberry Bars

These raspberry bars are delicious.

Ingredients for filling:

12 oz. frozen raspberries (3 c.), unsweetened
1 c. dates, chopped in pieces
1 c. pineapple, crushed, drained
½ c. orange juice concentrate
½ c. honey
1 tsp. fresh orange peel

Ingredients for bars:

½ c. millet flour
½ c. whole wheat flour
3 c. quick rolled oats
½ c. coconut, unsweetened shredded
1 c. orange juice plus 2-3 Tbs.
2 Tbs. canola oil
1 tsp. vanilla extract
½ tsp. salt

Directions for filling:

1. Place filling ingredients in saucepan and cook over medium low heat, stirring frequently, until thick.

Directions for bars:

1. Mix ingredients except the extra 2 to 3 tablespoons orange juice, and press half the mixture into 9 x 13 baking dish lightly sprayed with cooking spray.
2. Spread with raspberry mixture.
3. Stir in remaining 2 to 3 tablespoons orange juice with remaining oat mixture.
4. Spoon on top of fruit and press lightly.
5. Bake in 350 degrees F. oven for 30 minutes.
6. Cool and cut into 24 pieces.

Yields: 24 servings.

Red Raspberry Chocolate Bars

These bars are simple to make and so delicious.

Ingredients:

2½ c. flour
1   c. sugar
¾   c. pecans, finely chopped
1   c. butter, softened
1   egg
1   jar raspberry preserves (12 oz.)
1   pkg. chocolate chips (10 oz.)

Directions:

1. Preheat oven to 350 degrees F. and grease 13 x 9 inch pan.
2. Combine flour, sugar, nuts, butter, and egg until crumbly.
3. Set aside 1½ cups of mixture and press remaining into bottom of baking pan.
4. Spread with preserves, sprinkle with chips, then remaining crumbs.
5. Bake 40 to 45 minutes or until lightly browned.
6. Cool. Cut into bars.

Raspberry Oatmeal Bars

Oatmeal and raspberries make a great taste combination, and the coconut adds texture and flavor.

Ingredients:

1¼ c. flour
1½ c. quick oats
½   c. sugar
½   tsp. baking soda
⅓   c. butter, melted
2   tsp. pure vanilla extract
1   c. coconut, shredded
    raspberry jam

Directions:

1. Combine flour, oats, sugar, soda, butter, and vanilla to make crumb mixture.
2. Reserve 1 cup of mixture and press the rest on bottom of greased 9 x 13 baking pan.
3. Spread raspberry jam over it, then sprinkle coconut and the reserved crumb mixture over that.
4. Bake at 350 degrees F. for 25 minutes.
5. Cool completely before cutting into bars.

Yields: 2 dozen bars.

Raspberry Nut Pinwheels

These are very tasty cookies.

Ingredients:

2   c. all purpose flour
1   tsp. baking powder
1   egg
1¼ c. finely chopped nuts
½   c. butter
1   c. sugar
1   tsp. vanilla extract
1   sm. jar raspberry jam

Directions:

1. Sift flour, baking powder onto wax paper.
2. Beat butter, sugar, and egg until fluffy.
3. Stir in vanilla and add flour.
4. Roll dough between wax paper into 12 x 10 inch rectangle.
5. Remove top piece wax paper, spread raspberry jam evenly over top, and sprinkle nuts over all.
6. Firmly roll up dough, jellyroll style, removing wax paper as you roll.
7. Wrap in wax paper and refrigerate overnight.
8. Preheat oven to 375 degrees F.
9. Cut ¼-inch slices and bake 8 to 10 minutes to light golden.

Raspberry Meringue Cookie Bars

These raspberry meringue cookies are excellent!

Ingredients for bars:

1   c. butter, softened
½   c. brown sugar, firmly packed
1   egg
2   c. all-purpose flour
1   can raspberry filling

Ingredients for topping:

3   egg whites
¾   c. sugar
⅔   c. coconut, shredded
⅔   c. almonds, slivered

Directions for bars:

1. Heat oven to 325 degrees F. Grease 13 x 9 baking pan.
2. Beat butter and brown sugar in medium bowl with electric mixer at medium speed until light and fluffy.
3. Add 1 egg; beat until blended.
4. Stir in flour until well combined.
5. Pat dough evenly in prepared pan; bake 20 minutes.
6. Remove from oven; spread raspberry filling over crust.
7. Do not turn oven off.

Directions for topping:

1. Beat egg whites in medium bowl with electric mixer at high speed until soft peaks form.
2. Add sugar gradually; beat until stiff and glossy.
3. Fold coconut and almonds into beaten egg white mixture.
4. Spread over raspberry filling.
5. Return to oven and bake 20 minutes until meringue topping is lightly browned.
6. Cool completely in pan on wire rack. Cut into 48 bars.

Yields: 48 bars.

Raspberry Shortbread Bars

These are very tasty raspberry bars that can be made year round with your favorite raspberry jam.

Ingredients:

1½ c. flour
½ c. sugar
½ c. butter
¾ c. raspberry jam
2 eggs, lightly beaten
½ c. brown sugar, packed
1 tsp. pure vanilla extract
2 Tbs. flour
¼ tsp. salt
¼ tsp. baking soda
1¼ c. walnuts, chopped

Directions:

1. Combine 1½ cups flour with ½ cup sugar.
2. Cut in butter until mixture makes a fine meal.
3. Press into bottom of greased 9 x 9 inch baking pan.
4. Bake at 350 degrees F. for 20 minutes.
5. Remove from oven and allow to cool.
6. Spread raspberry jam over the crust.
7. Mix 2 tablespoons flour, salt, and baking soda.
8. Combine with eggs, brown sugar, and vanilla.
9. Gently add walnuts and spread over jam.
10. Return to oven and bake 20 minutes longer.
11. Cool in pan, dust with powdered sugar if desired, and cut into bars.

Did You Know? . . . .

Did you know that adding a little sugar or honey to your bread recipe will add flavor and moistness?

Raspberry Filled Sugar Cookies

These sugar cookies have a surprise center to enjoy. I bet you can't eat just one!

Ingredients:

1   c. sugar
1   c. butter, softened
3   Tbs. milk
1   tsp. vanilla extract
1   egg
3   c. flour
1½ tsp. baking powder
¼   tsp. salt
    raspberry jam

Directions:

1. In large bowl, combine sugar, butter, milk, vanilla, and the egg.
2. Blend well.
3. Stir in dry ingredients and mix well.
4. Chill dough.
5. Roll dough to ¼ inch thickness on floured surface.
6. Cut with 2 to 2 ½ inch round floured cookie cutter.
7. Place half of cookies on ungreased cookie sheets.
8. Place teaspoon of raspberry jam on each.
9. Top with another cookie; press edges to seal with tip of finger, or use fork.
10. Prick tops once with fork.
11. Sprinkle tops with sugar.
12. Bake at 400 degrees F. for 8 to 10 minutes or until edges are light brown.
13. Immediately remove from pans.
14. Cool completely before placing in a sealed cookie container.

Raspberry Delights Cookbook
A Collection of Raspberry Recipes
Cookbook Delights Series – Book 14

Desserts

Table of Contents

Chocolate Raspberry Cream Crepes

These chocolate crepes are excellent with the raspberry cream sauce.

Ingredients for crepes:

3	eggs
¼	c. sugar
1	c. flour
1	c. milk
1	Tbs. cocoa powder
1	Tbs. butter, melted
1	Tbs. vanilla extract

Ingredients for white sauce:

6	oz. white chocolate baking bar
5	Tbs. whipping cream
2	Tbs. light corn syrup
1½	Tbs. raspberry liqueur
½	tsp. vanilla extract

Ingredients for raspberry cream:

1	c. whipping cream
1	Tbs. raspberry liqueur
1	Tbs. sugar
2	pt. fresh raspberries
	fresh mint sprigs, for garnish

Directions for crepes:

1. Blend all ingredients for crepes in blender or food processor until smooth.
2. Heat 6-inch skillet pan over medium heat, coat with vegetable spray.
3. Pour 2 to 3 tablespoons batter in pan, swirling to form crepe. Cook 1 minute on each side or until golden.
4. Repeat with remaining batter.
5. Crepes may be stacked and freeze well.

Directions for white sauce:

1. Gently melt chocolate over low heat, stirring at intervals.
2. Set aside.

3. In small saucepan, bring cream to a boil.
4. Add corn syrup, stirring until blended.
5. Gradually add cream mixture to melted chocolate, stirring until smooth.
6. Stir in liqueur and vanilla.
7. Keep warm.

Directions for raspberry cream:

1. Whip the cream, raspberry liqueur, and sugar to form peaks.
2. Fold in ¼ of raspberries.
3. Spoon chocolate sauce over center of each dessert plate.
4. Spoon a generous 2 tablespoons raspberry cream down center of each crepe.
5. Fold 2 sides over and place seam side down on chocolate sauce, sprinkle with raspberries, and garnish with mint.
6. Serve immediately.

Yields: 14 crepes.

Raspberry Cream Cups

These raspberry cream cups are very simple and quick to make.

Ingredients:

12-14 oz. raspberries
8   oz. mascarpone cheese
⅔ c. heavy cream
4   Tbs. raspberry brandy
2   Tbs. pistachios, roughly chopped
1   Tbs. powdered sugar

Directions:

1. Whip the cream to stiff peaks.
2. Whip powdered sugar into the mascarpone cheese and then gently fold the whipped cream into the cheese.
3. Pour 1 tablespoon raspberry liqueur into each of 4 serving glasses or bowls.
4. Scoop the raspberries into the glasses and top with cream.
5. Place glasses into the fridge.
6. To serve, sprinkle with nuts and serve chilled.

Dark Chocolate Pavé with Berry Sauce

This memorable combination of dark chocolate, orange, and raspberry is perfect for the fanciest of dinner parties. It is also easy to prepare and can be made ahead.

Ingredients for pavé:

2   c. milk
6   oz. bittersweet chocolate
1   c. sugar
½   c. butter
1   c. cocoa
1   tsp. orange flavoring or 2 drops orange oil
2   tsp. unflavored gelatin
1   c. heavy whipping cream

Ingredients for raspberry sauce:

3   pkg. frozen raspberries in syrup (10 oz.), thawed
½   c. sugar
1½ Tbs. cornstarch
    juice of ½ orange

Directions for pavé:

1. Prepare 8½ x 4½ loaf pan by lining bottom and long sides with double layer of wax paper which extends over each edge of pan. Set aside.
2. In small heavy saucepan over medium-low heat, bring milk to simmering.
3. Add the bittersweet chocolate and stir occasionally until chocolate is melted and mixture is smooth.
4. Add sugar, butter, and cocoa, and whisk until completely dissolved.
5. Do no allow this mixture to boil.
6. When mixture looks smooth, strain into medium bowl.
7. Add orange flavoring and set aside to cool.
8. In small heat proof cup, sprinkle gelatin over 3 tablespoons

cold water and allow mixture to soften for 2 to 3 minutes.

9. Microwave on high for 20 seconds and allow to stand 2 minutes until granules are completely dissolved.
10. Blend into chocolate mixture and set aside.
11. Beat heavy cream in chilled bowl with chilled beaters until nearly stiff and peaks hold their shape.
12. Cool chocolate mixture to room temperature and fold in whipped cream.
13. Pour into loaf pan and freeze 6 hours or overnight.

Directions for raspberry sauce:

1. Process undrained berries and orange juice in processor or blender until smooth. Strain.
2. In small saucepan, blend sugar, cornstarch, and strained berries.
3. Bring to simmer over medium heat, stirring frequently.
4. Reduce heat and continue stirring until sauce thickens.
5. Remove from heat and allow to cool.
6. To serve, remove from freezer 20 minutes before serving.
7. Place 2 to 3 tablespoons raspberry sauce on each dessert plate.
8. Slice with clean knife dipped in warm water and place slice on each plate.
9. Garnish with thin slices orange zest and partially frozen whole frozen raspberries.
10. Pass any extra raspberry sauce around the table.

Yields: 16 servings.

Did You Know? . . . .

Did you know that even though two people use the same recipe, one often tastes a step above the other? The most important tip we can share is to use the very best chocolate, pure vanilla, heavy whipping cream, the best colorings, and the best flavorings you can find. You really can taste the difference!

Key Lime Cheesecake with Berry Sauce

Fresh Lime Cheesecake is delicious with this raspberry sauce.

Ingredients for crust:

¾ c. flour
2½ Tbs. sugar
1   egg, beaten slightly
¼ c. butter, softened
½ tsp. vanilla extract

Ingredients for filling:

24 oz. cream cheese
¾ c. sugar
5   Tbs. sour cream
5   tsp. flour
4   eggs
1   egg yolk
½ c. frozen limeade concentrate, thawed
¼ c. lime juice
1   tsp. vanilla extract
    green food coloring, optional

Ingredients for glaze:

½ c. frozen limeade concentrate, thawed
4   tsp. lime juice
1   Tbs. cornstarch
1   Tbs. honey
1   Tbs. lime peel, finely shredded
    fresh lime slices for garnish, if desired

Ingredients for sauce:

6   Tbs. sugar
¼ c. water
1   pt. red raspberries
½ tsp. lemon juice
    superfine sugar

Directions for crust:

1. In medium bowl stir flour and sugar together.
2. Add egg, butter, and vanilla.
3. Beat with mixer until well combined.

4. With generously greased fingers, press dough evenly onto bottom of greased 9-inch spring form pan.
5. Bake at 350 degrees F. for 12 to 15 minutes until lightly browned.
6. Remove from oven and set aside.

Directions for filling:

1. In large bowl combine cream cheese, sugar, sour cream, and flour; beat with mixer until smooth.
2. Add eggs and egg yolk, one at a time, beating well after each addition.
3. Beat in the limeade concentrate, lime juice, and vanilla extract.
4. Stir in green food coloring, if desired.
5. Pour cream cheese mixture over the crust and bake at 350 degrees F. for 15 minutes.
6. Lower temperature to 200 degrees F. and bake for 1 hour 10 minutes or until the center no longer looks wet and shiny.
7. Remove from oven and run knife around the inside edge of pan.

Directions for glaze:

1. In small saucepan stir together limeade concentrate, lime juice, cornstarch, honey, and lime peel.
2. Cook and stir until thickened and bubbly.
3. Cook and stir 2 minutes more.
4. Pour over cheesecake; garnish with lime slices.
5. Chill until serving time.

Directions for sauce:

1. Combine sugar and water in saucepan and heat, stirring until sugar dissolves.
2. Add berries and simmer 3 minutes.
3. Purée mixture in blender or food processor, then strain through a fine sieve into bowl.
4. Add lemon juice and superfine sugar to taste.
5. Cover and chill.
6. To serve, spoon a pool of raspberry sauce on individual dessert plates.
7. Place slice of cheesecake on sauce. Garnish with thinly sliced lime slices and whole raspberries, if desired.

Yields: 12 to 18 servings.

Key Lime Soufflé with Berry Chambord

This recipe is great for summer dinner parties. It's easy, elegant, and as written, will provide 16 sumptuous ½-cup servings. The recipe is easily halved for smaller gatherings.

Ingredients for soufflé:

2   Tbs. unflavored gelatin
⅓   c. cold water
6   eggs, separated
2   c. sugar
¾   c. strained lime juice, preferably Key Lime
3   c. whipping cream

Ingredients for sauce:

3   c. fresh /or/ 12 oz. pkg. whole frozen raspberries, thawed
4   Tbs. Chambord (raspberry liqueur)
⅓   c. sugar

Directions for soufflé:

1. In heat-proof cup, sprinkle gelatin over cold water and allow to soften 3 minutes.
2. Place cup in bowl of hot water and stir until no granules of gelatin remain. Set aside.
3. Beat egg yolks with sugar until thick, lemon-colored, and no granules of sugar remain.
4. Stir in lime juice. Set aside.
5. Whip egg whites until stiff but not dry. Set aside.
6. Whip cream. Set aside.
7. Blend dissolved gelatin and lime mixture.
8. Fold in egg whites and whipped cream, combining well.
9. Spoon into individual dessert dishes and refrigerate several hours until firm.

Directions for sauce:

1. Purée berries in blender until smooth, about 10 seconds.
2. Strain through fine sieve to remove seeds.
3. Stir in Chambord and sugar.
4. Refrigerate until ready to serve dessert.
5. To serve, remove serving dishes from refrigerator and spoon Chambord sauce over each soufflé.
6. Garnish each with several fresh raspberries and a thinly sliced lime wedge.

Yields: 16 servings.

Lemon Mousse with Raspberry Sauce

This delicious mousse can be made ahead of time and is wonderful.

Ingredients:

6   lg. eggs
6   lg. egg yolks
1½ c. sugar
1   c. lemon juice
2   Tbs. lemon peel, minced
14 Tbs. butter, cut into pieces
¾   c. whipping cream, chilled
1½ c. raspberries, fresh or frozen
2   Tbs. sugar
    mint sprigs

Directions:

1. Whisk eggs and yolks in heavy non-aluminum saucepan until foamy.
2. Whisk in 1½ cups sugar, then lemon juice.
3. Mix in peel.
4. Stir over low heat until mixture thickens to consistency of heavy custard, about 10 minutes. Do not boil.
5. Remove from heat and whisk in butter.
6. Transfer mixture to bowl and cool until very thick, stirring occasionally, about 50 minutes.
7. Whip cream in medium bowl to soft peaks.
8. Fold cream into lemon mixture, just until combined.
9. Spoon mousse into individual serving glasses.
10. Cover and refrigerate 2 hours until set.
11. Coarsely mash berries in small bowl using fork.
12. Mix in 2 tablespoons sugar.
13. Taste, adding more sugar if desired.
14. Cover and refrigerate 1 hour to release juices.
15. Can be prepared 1 day ahead.
16. Spoon sauce over center of mousse, garnish with mint sprigs.

Peach Sorbet with Berry Melba Sauce

This sorbet is refreshing after a hearty meal. The raspberry sauce is delicious with the sorbet.

Ingredients for sorbet:

29 oz. canned peaches, drained, juice reserved
1 c. sugar
⅓ c. light corn syrup
1 c. water
¼ c. lemon juice, fresh-squeezed

Ingredients for sauce:

1 pkg. whole frozen raspberries (12 oz.), thawed
1 Tbs. raspberry liqueur
⅓ c. sugar
3 c. fresh raspberries /or/ 12 oz. frozen whole raspberries, partially thawed

Directions for sorbet:

1. Drain peaches, reserving 1 cup juice.
2. Combine reserved juice, sugar, and corn syrup in small saucepan.
3. Bring to a boil, stirring constantly, until all sugar is dissolved.
4. Reduce heat and simmer 3 minutes.
5. Cool to room temperature.
6. To hasten cooling, saucepan may be placed in shallow pan of ice cold water.
7. Process drained peaches in blender or food processor until smooth, about 10 seconds.
8. Add lemon juice, water, and syrup mixture.
9. Process another 10 seconds until combined.
10. Pour into 8 inch square pan.
11. Freeze until firm enough to scoop, about 4 hours.

Directions for sauce:

1. Thaw raspberries and process in food processor or blender for 10 seconds, or until smooth.
2. Strain if desired to remove seeds.
3. Stir in liqueur and sugar.
4. Refrigerate until ready to serve.
5. Sauce is best if made ahead to allow flavors to mingle.
6. To serve, scoop and layer sorbet, raspberry melba sauce, and fresh or partially thawed raspberries in tall parfait glasses, starting with a layer of sauce on the bottom.
7. Serve promptly.

Creamy Raspberry Ice Cream

This simple recipe for raspberry ice cream is for the true raspberry lover and has the full raspberry flavor without a lot of other ingredients getting in the way.

Ingredients:

1   c. sweetened condensed milk
¼   c. water
2   c. fresh raspberries, crushed (put through food mill or sieve to remove seeds, if desired)
2   Tbs. lemon juice
½   c. heavy cream

Directions:

1. Combine condensed milk and water; add raspberries and lemon juice. Chill thoroughly.
2. Whip cream to a soft peak; fold into the chilled mixture.
3. Pour into freezer tray.
4. When mixture is half frozen, scrape away from sides and bottom, and beat until smooth but not melted.
5. Freeze until firm.

Yields: 6 servings.

Quick Frozen Raspberry Dessert

This makes a simple slush and is so refreshing.

Ingredients:

10 oz. frozen raspberries, sweetened, not thawed
3   Tbs. orange juice
1   Tbs. orange liqueur
    fresh raspberries, halved

Directions:

1. Place frozen berries (unthawed) with orange juice and liqueur in food processor.
2. If you are ready to serve, fold fresh raspberries into this and serve in glasses.
3. If you make this in advance, transfer mix to a metal bowl and freeze until ready to eat.
4. This mixture should not be rock hard. If it is, reprocess in processor, then fold into berries.
5. Add a dollop of sweetened whipped cream to the top and garnish with fresh raspberries.

Raspberry Alaskas

The raspberry in this baked Alaska is wonderful!

Ingredients:

4   lg. patty shells, homemade or frozen
4   egg whites
¼   c. sugar
¼   tsp. vanilla extract
1   c. fresh raspberries
4   scoops vanilla ice cream

Directions:

1. Bake patty shells at 450 degrees F. for 25 minutes. Cool.
2. Whip egg whites until foamy; then gradually beat in sugar.
3. Continue beating to a stiff meringue. Beat in vanilla.
4. Place patty shells on baking sheet.
5. Spoon raspberries into bottom of patty shells, top with scoop of ice cream.
6. Spread meringue over, sealing well all around, and mounding at top.
7. Bake at 450 degrees F. for 3 minutes until lightly browned.
8. Serve immediately.

Yields: 4 servings.

Huckleberry Raspberry Swirl Sherbet

This is a very colorful, light, and fruity finish to a meal.

Ingredients:

1   c. huckleberries, thawed, with juice
½   c. sugar
1   Tbs. lemon juice
½   gal. raspberry sherbet
2   drops almond extract

Directions:

1. Combine first four ingredients in saucepan.
2. Bring to boil over moderate heat, stirring.
3. Cook until berries are soft.
4. Cool and purée in blender until smooth.
5. Place in bowl and chill.
6. Soften raspberry sherbet in refrigerator about 20 minutes.
7. Place in 1 gallon plastic container; pour chilled huckleberry mixture over sherbet; and fold in to create marble effect.
8. Cover and freeze overnight until firm.

Raspberry and Coffee Tiramisu

For you coffee lovers, this raspberry and coffee tiramisu will be one of your all-time favorites.

Ingredients for ladyfingers:

½   c. all purpose flour
½   tsp. finely ground coffee (preferably espresso)
3   extra lg. eggs, separated, room temperature
5   Tbs. sugar
½   tsp. vanilla extract
    powdered sugar

Ingredients for filling:

3   Tbs. framboise eau-de-vie (clear raspberry brandy)
1   Tbs. instant espresso powder or instant coffee granules
2   pkg. cream cheese (8 oz.), room temperature
⅔   c. powdered sugar
1   basket raspberries (6 oz.) /or/ 1½ c. frozen, unsweetened, thawed, drained
¾   c. strong coffee, freshly brewed, room temperature
3   Tbs. sugar
    additional powdered sugar
    fresh mint

Ingredients for raspberry sauce:

1   pkg. frozen raspberries (10 oz.) in syrup, thawed
2   Tbs. framboise eau-de-vie

Directions for ladyfingers:

1. Preheat oven to 350 degrees F.
2. Line 2 cookie sheets with parchment.
3. Mix flour and ground coffee beans in small bowl.

4. Using electric mixer, beat egg yolks and 4 tablespoons sugar in medium bowl until thick and slowly dissolving ribbon forms when beaters are lifted, about 4 minutes.
5. Beat in vanilla.
6. Mix in dry ingredients. (Batter will be thick.)
7. Using electric mixer fitted with clean dry beaters, beat egg whites until thick and foamy.
8. Add remaining 1 tablespoon sugar and beat until whites are stiff but not dry.
9. Fold into yolk mixture in 2 additions.
10. Drop batter by rounded tablespoon (8 per sheet) onto prepared sheets, spacing evenly.
11. Sift powdered sugar thickly over rounds.
12. Bake until golden brown on edges, about 16 minutes.
13. Cool in pan on rack and then remove ladyfinger rounds from parchment. Can be prepared 1 day ahead and stored in single layer in airtight container.

Directions for filling:

1. Combine framboise and instant espresso in small bowl.
2. Stir until espresso dissolves.
3. Using electric mixer, beat cream cheese and ⅔ cup powdered sugar until light and fluffy.
4. Beat in coffee mixture.
5. Fold in 1 cup raspberries. Let stand at room temperature.
6. Combine coffee and 3 tablespoons sugar.
7. Stir until sugar dissolves.
8. Spoon 1 scant tablespoon coffee mixture over flat side of 1 ladyfinger round, then place coffee side up on plate.
9. Spread ⅓ cup filling atop round, then place flat side down on filling; sprinkle with powdered sugar.
10. Spoon raspberry sauce around desserts. Garnish with remaining raspberries and fresh mint and serve.

Directions for raspberry sauce:

1. Purée raspberries and syrup in processor.
2. Strain into small bowl to remove seeds.
3. Stir in eau-de-vie, cover, and refrigerate.
4. Can be prepared 2 days ahead.

Raspberry Bash

Rich with raspberry, cream cheese, and chocolate, these are wonderful.

Ingredients for bash:

1   batch of brownies (recipe below)
16 oz. cream cheese, softened
1   c. sugar
¼   c. all-purpose flour
1   tsp. vanilla extract
4   eggs
1   c. white chocolate pieces (6 oz.)
1   c. semisweet chocolate pieces (6 oz.)
2   c. frozen raspberries, fresh or loose-pack

Ingredients for brownie batter:

2   oz. unsweetened chocolate, chopped
2   Tbs. unsalted butter, room temperature
½   c. sugar
¾   c. all purpose flour
2   eggs, beaten
¼   c. milk, room temperature
1   tsp. vanilla extract
¼   tsp. salt
½   c. walnuts, chopped

Directions for bash:

1. Generously butter 10-inch spring form pan; set aside.
2. Spread half the brownie batter into bottom of prepared pan.
3. Set aside.
4. In large bowl, beat cream cheese, sugar, flour, and vanilla extract with electric mixer on medium speed until smooth.
5. Add eggs; beat just until mixed.
6. Spread cream cheese mixture over brownie layer.
7. Spread remaining brownie mixture over cream cheese layer.

8. Swirl with knife or spatula to marble.
9. Sprinkle with white baking pieces, chocolate pieces, and raspberries.
10. Bake in 350 degrees F. oven 1 hour 20 minutes. (Center will still jiggle slightly.)
11. Cool 30 minutes on wire rack.
12. Loosen and remove side of pan.
13. Cover and chill in refrigerator 4 hours, or up to 24 hours.
14. Let stand at room temperature 10 minutes before serving.

Directions for brownie batter:

1. Melt chocolate in double boiler. Set aside to cool.
2. With electric mixer, beat butter with sugar until pale and fluffy in large mixing bowl.
3. Add next 5 ingredients and the melted chocolate.
4. Mix thoroughly and then stir in walnuts.

Yields: 16 servings.

Raspberry Sorbet

This raspberry sorbet is delicious and refreshing to the palette. Do enjoy.

Ingredients:

1½ qt. raspberries, washed and dried
1   c. sugar
¾   c. fresh lemon juice
¼   c. crème de cassis

Directions:

1. In blender or food processor, combine all ingredients.
2. Blend until smooth.
3. Strain the purée to remove seeds and chill.
4. Place mixture in ice cream machine and freeze according to manufacturer's directions.

Raspberry Brulé

This is made with egg substitute and is quite good.

Ingredients:

1   c. raspberries
2   c. nonfat milk
2   Tbs. nonfat powdered milk
¾   c. egg substitute
⅓   c. sugar
1   tsp. vanilla extract
4   tsp. brown sugar, packed

Directions:

1. Preheat oven to 325 degrees F.
2. Gradually add powdered milk to liquid milk and mix until dissolved.
3. Add egg substitute, sugar, and vanilla, and mix well.
4. Place raspberries evenly in the bottom of six, 6 to 8-ounce custard cups and pour mixture over raspberries.
5. Place custard cups in a baking dish filled with 1 inch water for 30 to 40 minutes or until custard is set.
6. Sprinkle 1 teaspoon brown sugar over each cup.
7. Broil with tops 4 to 6 inches from heat for 2 to 3 minutes or until brown sugar is melted.
8. Serve immediately.

Yields: 6 servings.

Raspberries Romanoff

This is an elegant, easy-to-make dessert to finish a special meal.

Ingredients:

3   egg yolks
⅔   c. sugar

⅔ c. dry Marsala or cream sherry
4 c. raspberries
⅔ c. whipping cream
   raspberries, for garnish

Directions:

1. Off heat, combine egg yolks and sugar in top of double boiler; beat until thick and pale.
2. Mix in Marsala and place over simmering water.
3. Cook, stirring constantly with a wire whisk, until thick, 10 to 12 minutes.
4. Transfer egg yolk mixture to large bowl, cover, and refrigerate until ready to serve.
5. Meanwhile, rinse berries carefully; pat dry.
6. Whip cream until stiff; carefully fold into egg yolk mixture until blended, and then fold in berries.
7. Serve in stemmed dessert glasses, garnish with raspberries.

Yields: 4 to 6 servings.

Raspberry-Filled Ladyfingers

This is a quick dessert to put together for unexpected guests. Just make sure you have ladyfingers on hand.

Ingredients:

3 oz. cream cheese, softened
¼ c. raspberry jam
2 dozen ladyfingers
   powdered sugar

Directions:

1. Blend thoroughly the cream cheese and raspberry jam.
2. Split ladyfingers lengthwise, spread bottom halves with jam mixture, replace tops, and sprinkle with powdered sugar.

Huckleberry Raspberry Sorbet

Huckleberries and raspberries blend to make a great-tasting sorbet.

Ingredients:

10 oz. ripe huckleberries
10 oz. raspberries
1½ c. sugar
   juice of 2 oranges
   juice of 1 lemon

Directions:

1. Wash and hull raspberries.
2. In food processor, purée berries with orange juice, lemon juice, and sugar.
3. Strain purée and discard any seeds.
4. Pour preparation into ice cream machine and churn according to manufacturer's directions.
5. When ready, transfer to pre-chilled mould or bowl, cover with a lid or plastic film, and place in freezer.
6. Sorbet keeps well for 2 to 3 days.

Raspberry Delight

This makes a smooth, fluffy raspberry dessert.

Ingredients for filling:

1 pkg. marshmallows (10 oz.)
1 c. red frozen raspberries, thawed
½ c. raspberry juice
1 c. whipping cream

Ingredients for crust:

1 pkg. vanilla wafers or graham crackers (10 oz.), crushed
2 Tbs. butter, melted

Directions for filling:

1. Melt marshmallows in top of double boiler.
2. Add thawed raspberries and juice. Cool.
3. Whip cream and add to raspberry mixture.

Directions for crust:

1. Mix melted butter with crumbs.
2. Put ⅓ of crumbs in bottom of flat square dish.
3. Pour in raspberry mix and cover with remaining crumbs.
4. Chill in refrigerator for 12 hours.

Raspberry Frozen Yogurt

Raspberries and yogurt freeze to make a refreshing combination.

Ingredients:

3   pt. raspberries
2   Tbs. fresh lemon juice
1⅓ c. powdered sugar
1   c. yogurt, plain

Directions:

1. In food processor, purée raspberries with lemon juice.
2. To remove seeds, force purée through fine strainer into bowl.
3. Whisk in sugar and yogurt.
4. If necessary, chill until cold.
5. Pour into the canister of an ice cream maker and freeze according to the manufacturer's instructions.
6. Alternatively, freeze the mixture in a shallow metal cake pan until solid, about 6 hours.
7. Break into chunks and process in a food processor.

Raspberry Brownies

These raspberry brownies are delicious.

Ingredients:

1½ c. sugar
¾ c. cocoa powder, unsweetened
1   c. fat-free egg substitutes
1   jar raspberry preserves (10 oz.), sugar-free
1   tsp. vanilla extract
½ tsp. salt
½ tsp baking soda
¼ tsp. almond extract
1   c. flour

Directions:

1. Thoroughly coat 9 x 13-inch pan with nonstick cooking spray. Set aside.
2. With electric mixer, combine sugar and cocoa.
3. Gradually pour in egg substitutes and raspberry jam, beating on low speed until sugar is no longer grainy.
4. Add vanilla, salt, and almond extract, and beat briefly to mix.
5. Combine flour and baking soda and stir in with flexible rubber spatula.
6. Do not over mix. Turn into prepared pan.
7. Bake in preheated 325 degrees F. oven 30 to 35 minutes.
8. Brownies should be slightly under-baked but not runny in center.
9. Allow to cool and cut into 2 x 2 inch squares.

Yields: 24 servings.

Did You Know? . . . .

Did you know chocolate is moisture sensitive and absorbs odors? Keep chocolate in a cool place, but do not store in the refrigerator or freezer, as it will pick up flavors and moisture.

Peach and Raspberry Cobbler

Raspberries combine with peaches to make a delicious cobbler dessert.

Ingredients:

9   peaches (about 3 lb.)
1   c. sugar
1   tsp. sugar
2   Tbs. cornstarch
2   tsp. lemon juice
1   pt. raspberries
1½ c. flour
1½ tsp. baking powder
¾   tsp. salt
5   Tbs. butter, chilled
⅔   c. milk

Directions:

1. Heat oven to 400 degrees F.
2. Peel peaches and slice.
3. Combine with ¾ cup sugar, cornstarch, and lemon juice.
4. Gently stir in raspberries.
5. Transfer to 2-quart baking dish; cover with foil.
6. Bake until bubbling, about 30 minutes.
7. Meanwhile, combine ¼ cup sugar, flour, baking powder, and salt.
8. Cut in butter until mixture resembles coarse meal.
9. Stir milk into flour mixture until ingredients just hold together.
10. Drop 8 heaping spoonfuls of dough onto hot fruit.
11. Sprinkle remaining sugar on dough.
12. Bake, uncovered, until the biscuits have browned, about 25 minutes.
13. Serve warm right out of the oven.

Raspberry Graham Cracker Torte

These are fun to make and are delicious.

Ingredients:

1 c. fresh raspberries
½ tsp. almond extract
1 c. whipping cream, whipped, sweetened to taste
14 graham crackers (5 x 2½ in.)

Directions:

1. Place berries in food processor or blender until smooth.
2. Reserve ¼ cup, cover, and refrigerate.
3. Fold remaining berries and almond extract into whipped cream until creamy.
4. Spread 1 cracker with 2 tablespoons topping mixture.
5. Top with second cracker.
6. Place on serving plate.
7. Spread 2 tablespoons topping mixture on top cracker.
8. Repeat layers 10 times.
9. Using pancake turner, carefully turn torte onto its side so the crackers are setting on their long sides.
10. Frost top and sides with remaining topping mixture.
11. Cover and refrigerate for at least 12 hours or overnight.
12. Serve torte with the reserved berry purée.
13. Cover and refrigerate any remaining torte.

Did You Know? . . . .

Did you know that to produce a smooth, professional-looking chocolate for dipping your candies, cookies, desserts, and treats, you must keep chocolate at a constant temperature? You can purchase a griddle, or use your stove top and a frying pan. Lay two towels on the pan or griddle before placing the chocolate filled dish or plastic bowl.

Raspberry Huckleberry Cobbler

We love cobbler, and the blend of huckleberries and raspberries add a wonderful combination of flavors.

Ingredients for filling:

1   c. huckleberries
1   c. raspberries
½   c. sugar
½   c. water

Ingredients for topping:

¼   c. butter
½   c. sugar
1   c. flour
1½ tsp. baking powder
¼   tsp. salt
1   egg
1   tsp. pure vanilla extract
½   c. milk

Directions for filling:

1. Mix berries, ½ cup sugar, and water in saucepan.
2. Cook over moderate heat until berries are soft.
3. Pour into 9 x 9 baking dish.

Directions for topping:

1. Cream butter and ½ cup sugar.
2. Sift together flour, baking powder, and salt.
3. Add to creamed mixture the egg, slightly beaten, the milk, and vanilla. Beat well.
4. Spoon over berries and bake 30 minutes at 375 degrees F.
5. Serve warm with whipped cream or ice cream.

Yields: 6 servings.

Raspberries Romanov

You will love the special pastry cream flavor in this raspberry Romanov. Make this one a day ahead of time.

Ingredients for Romanov:

3   c. raspberries
½   c. orange juice, freshly squeezed, strained
4   Tbs. Cointreau or Grand Marnier
2-3   tsp. sugar
1½   c. pastry cream - recipe below

Ingredients for pastry cream:

32   oz. milk
8   oz. sugar
¼   tsp. salt
8   egg yolks
3   oz. cornstarch
½   oz. cake flour
3   oz. butter, softened
2   tsp. vanilla extract

Directions for Romanov:

1.   Prepare pastry cream below.
2.   Chill and place in refrigerator until ready to use.
3.   Place raspberries in bowl and toss very gently with the sugar, orange juice, and liqueur.
4.   Place in refrigerator for 2 to 3 hours to chill.
5.   Just before serving, pour the juice from the berries into the pastry cream and whisk to incorporate it all into the cream.
6.   To serve, divide cream among 4 dessert bowls or glasses.
7.   Top with raspberries and serve.

Directions for pastry cream:

1.   In medium sized pot, bring 24 ounces of milk and ½ the sugar to boil. Do not stir! Reserve 1 cup milk.

2. In medium-large bowl, blend together the reserved 1 cup milk with the cornstarch and cake flour.
3. Whisk until well dissolved.
4. Add yolks, salt, and remaining sugar, and whisk together thoroughly.
5. Whisking the egg mixture constantly, slowly pour in the hot milk.
6. Pour mixture back into the pot and place over medium-high heat, constantly whisking mixture until it comes to a boil.
7. Remove from heat and strain into a clean bowl.
8. Place over an ice water bath, stirring slowly until the pastry cream reaches 110 degrees F.
9. At this point, stir in chunks of softened butter and vanilla.
10. Continue to stir until cold.
11. Cover surface with plastic wrap to keep skin from forming.
12. Refrigerate.
13. For chocolate pastry cream, whisk in 2 ounces semi-sweet chocolate and 2 ounces unsweetened chocolate into the pastry cream.

Raspberry and Fig Gratin

This is so delicious after a big meal.

Ingredients:

1   c. raspberries, fresh
1   c. figs, peeled, halved
3   Tbs. brown sugar
½   c. sour cream, thinned with 2 Tbs. milk

Directions:

1. Layer raspberries in gratin dish.
2. Pour sour cream over raspberries and top with figs.
3. Sprinkle generously with brown sugar.
4. Run under broiler to brown, then serve warm.

Raspberry Surprise

This is very good and can be made a day ahead.

Ingredients:

36 ladyfingers, cut in half
1 can sliced peaches, drained (16 oz.)
1 env. unflavored gelatin
¼ c. cold water
½ c. sugar
1 bag frozen raspberries (12 oz.) thawed, puréed, strained
¾ c. whipping cream

Directions:

1. Line sides and bottom of 9-inch spring form pan with ladyfingers, overlapping if necessary, to cover completely.
2. Spread peaches in single layer over bottom; set aside.
3. In medium saucepan, sprinkle gelatin over water; let stand 1 minute.
4. Stir over low heat until gelatin is completely dissolved, about 3 minutes.
5. Stir in sugar until dissolved.
6. Remove from heat and gradually whisk in raspberry purée and cream.
7. Pour into prepared pan and chill until firm, about 4 hours.
8. Release spring form pan and serve.

Yields: 10 servings.

Raspberry Cream Crunch

This raspberry cream is delicious with pecans.

Ingredients:

2 sm. boxes raspberry gelatin
2 c. boiling water
8 oz. cream cheese

8   oz. whipping cream
1   can sweetened condensed milk (14 oz.)
5-6 c. frozen raspberries
    pecans, chopped
    additional whipping cream (optional)

Directions:

1. Whip cream cheese, whipping cream, and sweetened condensed milk together.
2. In separate bowl combine boiling water and gelatin.
3. Fold 2 mixtures together.
4. Place raspberries into bottom of a decorative glass bowl.
5. Pour mixture over raspberries. It almost instantly solidifies. Can refrigerate if not stiff enough.
6. Top with additional whipped topping and pecans.
7. To serve, pour small amount of sauce on serving plate.

Raspberry Ice Cream

There is nothing like the fresh taste of raspberries, and this raspberry ice cream is delicious.

Ingredients:

1½ qt. red raspberries, fresh or frozen (to make 2½ c.) puréed fruit
1   pt. heavy cream
¾   c. sugar
    juice of ½ lemon

Directions:

1. Purée raspberries.
2. Blend all ingredients in blender for one minute to thoroughly dissolve the sugar.
3. Pour mixture into freezer can or ice cream maker and follow manufacturer's directions to process the ice cream.
4. Store tightly covered in the freezer.

Yields: ⅓ gallon.

Raspberry Jam Bread Pudding

This is a delicious bread pudding.

Ingredients:

3   c. toasted bread cubes
4   lg. eggs (divided)
4   c. milk, scalded
1   c. sugar
¼   tsp. salt
1   tsp. vanilla extract
½   c. butter, melted
¾   c. raspberry jam

Directions:

1. Place bread cubes in 2-quart casserole dish.
2. Beat two eggs plus two egg yolks, reserving the two egg whites for the meringue.
3. Gradually beat scalded milk into eggs.
4. Beat in ½ cup sugar, salt, vanilla, and butter.
5. Pour milk mixture over the bread cubes.
6. Close to end of baking time, beat egg whites until stiff but not dry.
7. Beat in the remaining sugar, one tablespoon at a time until meringue is stiff and glossy. Set aside.
8. Bake in preheated 350 degree F. oven for 25 minutes.
9. Remove from oven and spread jam evenly over top of pudding.
10. Pile meringue over the jam, making sure to spread the meringue to edge of dish.
11. Bake another 15 minutes until meringue is set.

Did You Know? . . . .

Did you know that chocolate and water do not mix? Chocolate is oil based, and oil and water do not mix. Avoid any contact with water, including a freshly washed mold or tool - dry them first!

Raspberry Turnovers

Cream cheese, raspberry, and orange make wonderful turnovers. Your guests will love these.

Ingredients for turnovers:

1   c. flour
½   c. butter
⅛   tsp. salt
3   oz. cream cheese
1   tsp. orange peel, finely grated

Ingredients for raspberry jam filling:

1   c. raspberries, crushed
1⅓ c. sugar
¼   pkg. pectin

Ingredients for orange glaze:

½   c. powdered sugar
½   tsp. orange peel, finely grated
2-3 tsp. orange juice

Directions for turnovers:

1. Mix ingredients together in bowl.
2. Cover and refrigerate at least 1 hour.
3. Heat oven to 375 degrees F.
4. Roll dough ⅛ inch thick on lightly floured surface and cut into 2-inch circles.
5. Spoon ½ teaspoon raspberry jam on center of circle.
6.   Moisten edge with water and fold edge over.
7. Press edges with fork to seal.
8. Place 1 inch apart on ungreased cookie sheet.
9. Bake 8 to 10 minutes or until edges are light brown.
10. After cookies cool on wire rack, drizzle with orange glaze.

Directions for raspberry jam filling:

1. Mix raspberries, sugar, and pectin in saucepan.
2. Heat until mixture just comes to a boil.
3. Remove from heat and let cool.
4. Filling may be made ahead of time and kept in refrigerator.

Directions for orange glaze:

1. Mix all ingredients together until smooth and thin enough to drizzle.

White Chocolate Raspberry Cheesecake

My family loves cheesecake, and this tastes great with the white chocolate and raspberries.

Ingredients:

¾ c. graham cracker crumbs
1 Tbs. sugar
1 Tbs. butter, melted
1 c. fresh raspberries
8 oz. cream cheese, softened
⅓ c. sugar
1½ oz. white chocolate, melted
2 egg yolks
1 tsp. vanilla extract
1 tsp. grated lemon zest
½ c. sour cream
2 egg whites
raspberries for garnish

Directions:

1. Preheat oven to 325 degrees F.
2. In small bowl, combine graham cracker crumbs, sugar, and melted butter.
3. Coat 9-inch pan with graham cracker mixture into bottom and 1 inch up sides.
4. Wrap the outside of pan with a large piece of foil. Be sure the foil comes up the sides of the pan to prevent water from seeping into the crust.
5. Arrange berries in the bottom of the crust.
6. Place cream cheese in large mixer bowl and beat at medium speed until smooth.
7. Gradually add sugar and white chocolate; beat 3 minutes.
8. Add egg yolks, one at a time, beating well after each.
9. Add vanilla and lemon zest, and then stir in sour cream.
10. In separate bowl, beat egg white to stiff peaks.
11. Carefully fold egg whites into the batter.
12. Pour mixture into prepared crust and place cheese cake in a large shallow roasting pay; add hot water to pan to 1 inch.
13. Bake 45 minutes; turn off oven leaving oven door ajar by placing a long-handled spoon in the door to prop it open.
14. After 1 hour, remove cheesecake from oven and cool to room temperature.
15. Cover and refrigerate for at least 4 hours.
16. To serve, garnish with additional raspberries.

Raspberry Delights Cookbook
A Collection of Raspberry Recipes
Cookbook Delights Series – Book 14

Dressings, Sauces, and Condiments

Table of Contents

Balsamic Dressing

This is good on endive spears with bleu cheese and raspberry salad.

Ingredients:

¼   c. balsamic vinegar
¼   c. raspberry juice

Directions:

1. Mix both ingredients and ready to serve!

Yields: ½ c. dressing

Flaming Raspberry Sauce

This sauce makes a great-looking presentation for a dessert finale or special lunch.

Ingredients:

1   c. brandy
1   c. raspberries, crushed
½   c. orange juice
2   tsp. lemon juice
1   tsp. lemon rind, grated
1   tsp. sugar or honey (to taste)

Directions:

1. Mix all ingredients except brandy the night before you plan to serve. Refrigerate covered.
2. When needed, mix brandy with fruit mixture.
3. Pour over crepes and light.
4. You may want to set aside about half the mixture (without the brandy in it) to roll into the crepes.
5. You can find crepe recipes in our Desserts section.

Black Raspberry Salad Dressing

This raspberry salad dressing is delicious.

Ingredients:

½ c. olive oil
5 dash tabasco sauce
1 Tbs. black raspberry preserves
¼ c. balsamic vinegar

Directions:

1. In a small bowl, whisk all ingredients together and drizzle over salad.

Raspberry and Walnut Vinaigrette

This raspberry and walnut combination is wonderful.

Ingredients:

½ tsp. honey mustard
2 Tbs. raspberry vinegar
3 Tbs. walnut oil
3 Tbs. olive oil
1 Tbs. minced fresh tarragon
sea salt to taste

Directions:

1. In bowl, whisk together mustard, vinegar, and salt to taste.
2. Add oils in a stream, whisking.
3. Whisk until emulsified.
4. Stir in tarragon.

Yields: ½ cup.

Favorite Raspberry Sauce

This is an exceptional raspberry sauce.

Ingredients:

1   pkg. whole frozen raspberries (12 oz. or 2½ c.)
4   Tbs. Chambord or black raspberry liqueur
⅓   c. sugar

Directions:

1. Thaw raspberries, then purée in food processor or blender.
2. Strain to remove seeds.
3. Stir in liqueur and sugar.
4. Refrigerate until ready to serve.
5. Best if made 24 hours ahead.

Raspberry Compote

Serve this raspberry compote with a dollop of whipped cream or yogurt, or serve it over ice cream, over cakes, or in your breakfast cereal.

Ingredients:

¾   lb. raspberries, thawed if frozen
½   c. sugar
2   tsp. lemon juice

Directions:

1. Combine all ingredients in heavy saucepan over medium heat.
2. Cover and simmer 5 to 7 minutes or until sauce is formed.

Yields: 4 servings.

Fresh Raspberry Dessert Sauce

This makes a simple sauce to serve over your favorite ice cream or frozen yogurt.

Ingredients:

2   Tbs. cornstarch
¼   c. Chambord, Cointreau, or Port
4   c. raspberries
½   c. sugar

Directions:

1. In small saucepan, combine cornstarch and liqueur.
2. Add raspberries and sugar.
3. Stir over low heat until mixture simmers and thickens.

Yields: 2½ cups sauce.

Razz-Bourbon Barbecue Sauce

Bourbon barbecue sauce is great for poultry, beef, and pork.

Ingredients:

1   Tbs. butter
1   Tbs. olive oil
2   c. finely chopped onion
2   cloves garlic, crushed
½   c. molasses
1   c. ketchup
¼   c. raspberry jam
¼   c. red wine vinegar
1   tsp. dry mustard
¼   tsp. black pepper, freshly ground
2   Tbs. lemon juice
½   tsp. grated lemon zest
1   Tbs. soy sauce
1   Tbs. Hungarian paprika
⅓   c. bourbon whiskey

Directions:

1. In a large, heavy saucepan, melt the butter with the oil.
2. Sauté the onions until tender.
3. Add the garlic and cook 2 minutes longer.
4. Combine molasses, ketchup, vinegar, mustard, pepper, lemon juice, zest, soy sauce, paprika, and bourbon.
5. Stir into onion mixture and bring to a boil.
6. Reduce heat and simmer 30 minutes, stirring occasionally.
7. Cool and refrigerate in a covered container.

Green Peppercorn-Raspberry Sauce

This makes a delicious peppercorn-raspberry sauce.

Ingredients:

- ½ c. dry white wine
- ¾ c. all-purpose broth /or/ low-sodium chicken broth
- 2 Tbs. raspberry preserves /or/ frozen raspberry sauce
- ½ c. whipping cream
- 1 Tbs. butter
- 2 Tbs. green peppercorns in water, drained
  giblets from roasted duck /or/ from roasted goose, roughly chopped

Directions:

1. Combine wine, broth, preserves, and giblets in saucepan and bring to boil over medium heat.
2. Cook until liquid is reduced by half.
3. Add the cream and continue to cook until liquid reduces enough to coat the back of a spoon.
4. Remove from heat and whisk in the butter.
5. Strain the sauce into a sauceboat and discard the giblets.
6. Stir in the peppercorns and serve sauce with roasted bird.

Yields: 1½ cups sauce.

Raspberry Glaze

This is an ideal glaze with smoked meat: duck, pork, any game, chicken or game hen.

Ingredients:

- 1 Tbs. butter (for sautéing)
- 2 Tbs. shallots, minced
- ½ oz. brandy
- 2 oz. crème de cassis liqueur

1   tsp. raspberry jelly /or/ 1 tsp. sugar with ½ c. berries
4   oz. veal stock (may substitute beef broth)
2   oz. whole milk
    salt and pepper

Directions:

1. In large sauté pan, melt 1 ounce butter over medium high heat.
2. Add the shallots and cook until light brown.
3. Add brandy, crème de cassis liqueur, and jelly or sugar, and raspberries.
4. Reduce until almost dry.
5. Add veal or beef stock and heat until reduced by half.
6. Remove from heat and swirl in 2 ounces whole milk.
7. Adjust seasoning with salt and pepper.
8. To serve, slice and arrange cooked meat on warm platter, pour hot glaze over meat, serve immediately.

Raspberry Vinaigrette

This only takes a minute to make, and you will enjoy this raspberry vinaigrette over salad greens.

Ingredients:

3   Tbs. raspberry jam, seedless
⅔   c. vegetable oil
⅓   c. red wine vinegar
¼   tsp. salt
¼   tsp. pepper

Directions:

1. Place jam in small microwave-safe bowl and microwave uncovered on high 10 to 15 seconds until melted.
2. Pour into a jar with tight-fitting lid. Add the oil, vinegar, salt, and pepper; shake well and serve.
3. Refrigerate any remaining vinaigrette.

Hazelnut Raspberry Vinaigrette

This vinaigrette really is exceptional.

Ingredients:

½ c. fresh raspberries, puréed
1 c. raspberry vinegar
2 Tbs. sugar
3 Tbs. corn syrup
2 c. hazelnut oil
¼ c. hazelnuts, roasted and crushed

Directions:

1. Combine first 4 ingredients.
2. Slowly drizzle oil into mixture while whipping.
3. Stir in nuts to finish.

Raspberry Vinegar

This raspberry vinegar makes a great gift when placed in a decorative bottle. This vinegar makes great salad dressing using your favorite dressing recipes.

Ingredients:

2 bags whole frozen raspberries (12 oz. ea.)
1 gal. white vinegar
   sugar to taste

Directions:

1. Place frozen raspberries in large wide-mouth jar. If you don't have a wide-mouth jar, a few well-washed plastic gallon milk jugs and a funnel work very well.
2. Warm vinegar and pour over raspberries, reserving approximately ½ bag to add to gift bottles later.
3. Immediately return unused portion of raspberries to freezer to prevent thawing and freezing together.

4. Cover jar loosely and allow to stand for 8 days, shaking or stirring gently, daily.
5. Strain vinegar and funnel into gift bottles.
6. For more intense color, add a few of the reserved berries to each gift bottle.

Yields: 4 quarts.

Tapenade

Use your favorite type of olives in this easy recipe. You can leave out just about every ingredient if you don't like it, except the olives, of course.

Ingredients:

1   clove garlic, chopped
1¾ c. whole, pitted olives (kalamata, black, green, or use your favorite)
1   anchovy fillet, rinsed
2   Tbs. capers
1   tsp. chopped fresh thyme /or/ ¼ tsp. dried thyme
3   Tbs. raspberry juice
6   Tbs. olive oil
⅛   tsp. white pepper

Directions:

1. Combine garlic, olives, anchovies, capers, thyme, and raspberry juice in electric blender or food processor.
2. Slowly add olive oil while blending.
3. Blend until a paste is formed.
4. Add pepper and stir.
5. Store the spread in the refrigerator, well covered.
6. You can also make this recipe by using a mortar and pestle, or by chopping all ingredients together until very fine. The texture can be as smooth or as chunky as you like.
7. Serve with crackers or crusty French bread.
8. Can also be a sandwich spread, with roast beef and hoagie buns for a rich sandwich.

Raspberry Pecan Stuffing and Sauce

Raspberry and pecan combine for a great taste in this stuffing and sauce recipe.

Ingredients for stuffing:

4   slices bread, cubed
1   bunch green onions, chopped
1   egg, beaten
2   Tbs. raspberry vinegar
1   c. raspberries, fresh or frozen
½   c. pecans, toasted, chopped

Ingredients for sauce:

1   Tbs. olive oil
½   c. onion, chopped
½   c. raspberry vinegar
½   c. chicken stock
½   c. sour cream
1   c. raspberries, fresh or frozen

Directions for stuffing:

1. Mix all stuffing ingredients together.
2. Fill cavity of bird and roast.

Directions for sauce:

1. Heat oil in large frying pan.
2. Add onion, cook until golden.
3. Add vinegar, cook until vinegar becomes syrupy.
4. Reduce heat and whisk in stock and sour cream.
5. Add raspberries and heat 1 minute.
6. Pour over each serving.

Raspberry Fruit Salsa

This is an easy-to-make, tasty fruit salsa.

Ingredients:

2   kiwis, peeled, diced
2   Golden Delicious apples, peeled, cored, diced
8   oz. raspberries
1   lb. strawberries
2   Tbs. sugar
1   Tbs. brown sugar
3   Tbs. fruit preserves, any flavor

Directions:

1. In large bowl, thoroughly mix kiwis, Golden Delicious apples, raspberries, strawberries, sugar, brown sugar, and fruit preserves.
2. Cover and chill in the refrigerator at least 15 minutes.

Yields: 10 servings.

Raspberry Dressing for Salad

You will truly enjoy this simple blend of raspberry and orange flavors teaming up to make such a wonderful taste.

Ingredients:

1   c. raspberries
⅓   c. sugar
¼   c. orange juice

Directions:

1. Place raspberries in a blender, along with sugar and juice.
2. Process until smooth.
3. Strain and discard seeds.

Raspberry Salsa

This salsa is sweet, tart, and fresh. The raspberries are blended with the vibrant flavors of jalapeno and cilantro to create a crowd-pleasing topper for pork and other savory foods.

Ingredients:

2   c. raspberries, fresh or frozen (thawed)
¼   c. sweet onion, chopped
3   tsp jalapeno chili peppers, finely chopped
1   clove garlic, minced
¼   c. cilantro, fresh, chopped
½   tsp. sugar
3   Tbs. fresh lime juice

Directions:

1. In a medium bowl, mix together raspberries, sweet onion, jalapeno chili peppers, garlic, cilantro, sugar, and lime juice.
2. Cover and chill in the refrigerator at least 1 hour before serving.

Yields: 2½ cups.

Fruit Salsa

Like a cool breeze on a hot summer day, this flavorful fruit salsa is zesty and refreshing. Serve it with tortilla chips.

Ingredients:

1   tomato
1   orange, peeled and segmented
2   kiwis, peeled and sliced
1   red onion, coarsely chopped

1   avocado, peeled and pitted
1   bunch cilantro
2   jalapeno chili peppers
    garlic salt to taste

Directions:

1. In a food processor, place tomato, orange, kiwis, red onion, avocado, cilantro, and jalapeno chili peppers.
2. Process using pulse setting until finely chopped but not quite smooth.
3. Transfer to a medium bowl, and garnish with desired amount of garlic salt.

Yields: 4 cups.

Rummy Fruit Salsa

This delicious salsa is perfect served with grilled chicken, pork, or fish over rice.

Ingredients:

1   med. mango, peeled and finely diced
¾   c. raspberries, fresh or frozen, chopped
1   kiwi, peeled, finely diced
1   jalapeno pepper, seeded, finely chopped
2   Tbs. mint, fresh, chopped
¼   c. rum

Directions:

1. Stir together mango, raspberries, kiwi, jalapeno, mint, and rum in a glass bowl.
2. Refrigerate for 1 to 3 hours, stirring once or twice.

Yields: 6 servings.

Spicy Fruit Salsa

This is a sweet and spicy fresh fruit salsa with kiwi, raspberries, blackberries, and apples; seasoned with cayenne, hot sauce, green salsa, and lime juice. This is great as a dressing or a dip.

Ingredients:

5	kiwis, peeled and diced
1	qt. raspberries, finely chopped
1	pt. fresh blackberries, chopped
4	Granny Smith apples - peeled, cored, coarsely shredded
2	Tbs. fruit jelly, any flavor
¾	c. brown sugar
1	Tbs. cayenne pepper
3	Tbs. habanero hot sauce
1	can green salsa (7 oz.)
⅓	c. lime juice

Directions:

1. Place kiwis, raspberries, blackberries, and apples in bowl.
2. Stir in jelly, brown sugar, cayenne pepper, hot sauce, green salsa, and lime juice. Stir together.

Yields: 12 servings.

Brandied Raspberry Sauce

This is a very different adult sauce for your dinner-for-two.

Ingredients:

1	jar raspberry preserves (12 oz.)
¼	c. brandy
1	tsp. lemon juice

Directions:

1. In small saucepan, combine all ingredients.
2. Heat to just below boiling, stirring.
3. Serve hot with beignets, doughnuts, other rolls.

Raspberry Delights Cookbook
A Collection of Raspberry Recipes
Cookbook Delights Series – Book 14

Jams, Jellies, and Syrups

Table of Contents

A Basic Guide for Canning Jams, Jellies, and Syrups

1. Wash jars in hot, soapy water inside and out with brush or soft cloth.
2. Run your finger around rim of each jar, discarding any with cracks or chips.
3. Rinse well in clean, clear, hot water, using tongs to avoid burns to hands or fingers.
4. Place upside down on clean cloth to drain well.
5. Place lids in boiling water for 2 minutes to sterilize and keep hot until placing on rim of jar.
6. Immediately prior to filling each jar, immerse in very hot water with tongs to heat jar (avoids breakage of jar with hot liquid).
7. Fill jar to within 1 inch of top of rim or to level recommended in recipe.
8. Wipe rim with clean damp cloth to remove any particles of food, and check again for any chips or cracks.
9. With tongs, place lid from hot bath directly onto rim of jar.
10. Using gloves, cloth, or holders, tighten lid firmly onto jar with ring or use single formed lid in place of ring to cover inner lid. Do not tighten down too hard as it may impede sealing.
11. Place on protected surface to cool, taking care to not disturb lid and ring. A slight indentation of lid will be apparent when sealed.
12. Leave overnight until thoroughly cooled.
13. When cooled, wipe jars with damp cloth and then label and date each.
14. Store upright on shelf in cool, dark place.

Did You Know? . . . .

Did you know that if you want a larger yield of jam or jelly, you must prepare the recipe twice or as many times as necessary? Do not double the recipe since the larger quantity may not cook to the proper stage in the time suggested in the recipe. Likewise, do not cut the recipe in half.

Instant Raspberry Cordial Jam

This is so quick and easy to make, and the flavor is wonderful.

Ingredients:

12 oz. raspberry jam
1-2 Tbs. Chambord or other raspberry liqueur

Directions:

1. Stir liqueur into jam; cover, and refrigerate at least one day to allow flavors to meld.

Black Raspberry Jelly

Black raspberries make an excellent jelly.

Ingredients:

6   lb. black raspberries
7   c. sugar
1   Tbs. lemon juice, freshly squeezed
1   bottle liquid pectin (6 oz.)

Directions:

1. Wash raspberries in running water and crush thoroughly.
2. Simmer covered for 10 minutes, then place in jelly bag and extract all juice possible.
3. Measure 4 cups juice. If there is less than 4 cups, add water to make it measure 4 cups.
4. Place raspberry juice, sugar, and lemon juice in a kettle.
5. Cook over high heat until boiling, stirring constantly.
6. Immediately stir in pectin and bring to a full rolling boil.
7. Boil 1 minute, stirring constantly.
8. Remove from heat and skim off foam with spoon.
9. Ladle into hot, sterilized jars and seal immediately.

Cherry Raspberry Jam

This is a delicious jam and is good on everything from toast to biscuits.

Ingredients:

- 1   qt. (4 c.) sweet cherries
- ¼   c. orange juice
- 2   Tbs. lemon rind
- 1   Tbs. orange rind, grated
- 1½ qt. (6 c.) raspberries
- 4   c. sugar

Directions:

1. Pit and chop cherries.
2. Add juice, lemon rind, and orange rind.
3. Bring to boil and cook 10 minutes, stirring frequently.
4. Add raspberries and sugar.
5. Bring to boil stirring frequently, and cook to jam stage (about 15 minutes).
6. Remove from heat, stir, and skim for 5 minutes.
7. Pour into hot, sterile jars and seal.

Framboise Raspberry Jam

Framboise adds great flavor to this simple raspberry jam.

Ingredients:

- 4½ c. fresh raspberries
- 3   c. sugar
- ¼   c. framboise

Directions:

1. Place all ingredients in heavy saucepan over medium heat.
2. Bring to a boil, stirring occasionally.

3. When mixture comes to boil, raise heat to high and cook, stirring constantly, for 20 minutes.
4. As mixture begins to thicken, watch carefully to prevent sticking.
5. When mixture has reached a jam-like consistency, immediately remove from heat.
6. Pour into hot sterilized jars and vacuum seal (hot water bath method), or can be refrigerated up to 6 weeks.

No-Cook Apple Raspberry Jam

There is nothing like the great, flavorful combination of apples and raspberries. This hearty, no-cook jam is tasty and delicious on warm toast with butter.

Ingredients:

3   c. raspberries, fully ripe
1   c. apples, peeled, cored, finely ground
4   c. sugar
2   Tbs. fresh lemon juice
1   pouch liquid fruit pectin

Directions:

1. Thoroughly crush berries, using potato masher, and sieve half the pulp to remove some seeds, if desired.
2. Pour 1½ cups prepared berries into large bowl.
3. Add apples and sugar; mix well, and let stand 10 minutes.
4. Add lemon juice and liquid fruit pectin to bowl; stir 3 minutes. (A few sugar crystals will remain.)
5. Ladle jam into clean containers, leaving ¼ inch headspace; cover with tight fitting lids.
6. Let stand at room temperature until set (24 hours).
7. Store in freezer.
8. Jam can be stored in refrigerator for up to 3 weeks.

Yields: 4½ cups.

Mock Raspberry Fig Jam

This tastes like raspberry jam.

Ingredients:

6   c. figs, mashed
6   c. sugar
1   c. water
9   oz. raspberry gelatin

Directions:

1. Mix all ingredients and boil hard for 3 minutes.
2. Put in hot, clean jelly jars and seal.
3. Let set 6 weeks and enjoy.

Pear Raspberry Jam

Fresh raspberry and pears combine in this recipe to make a great jam.

Ingredients:

2½ lb. pears, ripe
2   c. red raspberries, fresh or frozen loose-pack, thawed
1   pkg. fruit pectin, powdered (1.75 oz.)
2   Tbs. lemon juice
¼   tsp. ground mace /or/ nutmeg
5   c. sugar

Directions:

1. Peel, core, and coarsely grind pears; measure 3 cups fruit.
2. Crush red raspberries; measure 1 cup berries.
3. In 2-quart kettle, combine ground pears, berries, pectin, lemon juice, and spice.
4. Bring to full rolling boil and then stir in sugar.

5. Boil hard stirring constantly for 1 minute, uncovered.
6. Remove from heat and skim off foam with metal spoon.
7. Ladle jam at once into hot, clean half-pint jars, leaving ¼ inch headspace.
8. Wipe jar rims and adjust lids.
9. Process in boiling water bath for 15 minutes.
10. Start timing when water boils.

Yields: 6 to 7 half-pints.

Raspberry Freezer Jam

This raspberry freezer jam tastes like it was just made today. It is so delicious; we put it on toast and muffins, on cake, ice cream, yogurt, pancakes, and waffles.

Ingredients:

2 c. raspberries, crushed (about 2-3 pt.)
4 c. sugar
1 pouch liquid pectin

Directions:

1. Wash and rinse 4 pint jars.
2. Wash, thoroughly drain, and crush raspberries, one layer at a time.
3. Sieve part of pulp to remove seeds, if desired.
4. Measure 2 cups prepared raspberries and sugar into large bowl. Mix well; let stand 10 minutes.
5. Stir in liquid pectin. Continue stirring 3 minutes.
6. Ladle jam into clean pint jar to within ½ inch of top rim.
7. Using nonmetallic utensil, remove air bubbles.
8. Wipe jar rim removing any stickiness. Cover with lids.
9. Repeat for remaining jam.
10. Let stand in refrigerator until set. Freeze within 24 hours for long term storage.
11. Store in freezer up to 1 year or in refrigerator to 3 weeks.

Yields: 4 pint jars.

Raspberry Peach Jam

Raspberries combine with peaches for a great jam.

Ingredients:

1½ pt. red raspberries, fully ripe
1½ lb. peaches, fully ripe
2   Tbs. fresh lemon juice
1   box fruit pectin
½   tsp. butter
6¼ c. sugar, measured into separate bowl

Directions:

1. Bring boiling water canner, half full with water, to simmer.
2. Wash jars and screw bands in hot soapy water; rinse with warm water.
3. Pour boiling water over flat lids in saucepan off the heat.
4. Let stand in hot water until ready to use.
5. Drain jars well.
6. Crush raspberries thoroughly, one layer at a time.
7. Strain half of the pulp to remove seeds, if desired.
8. Measure 2 cups prepared raspberries into 6 or 8 quart saucepot.
9. Peal, pit, and finely chop peaches.
10. Measure exactly 2 cups prepared peaches into saucepot with raspberries; stir until well blended.
11. Add lemon juice; mix well.
12. Stir pectin into prepared fruit mixture in saucepot.
13. Add butter to reduce foaming.
14. Bring mixture to full rolling boil (a boil that doesn't stop bubbling when stirred) on high heat, stirring constantly.
15. Stir in sugar. Return to full rolling boil and boil exactly 1 minute, stirring constantly.
16. Remove from heat. Skim off any foam with metal spoon.
17. Ladle immediately into prepared jars, filling to within ⅛ inch of tops.
18. Wipe jar rims and threads. Cover with 2-piece lids.

19. DScrew bands tightly.
20. Place jars on elevated rack in canner.
21. Lower rack into canner.
22. Water must cover jars by 1 to 2 inches. Add boiling water, if necessary.
23. Cover, bring water to gentle boil, and process 10 minutes.
24. Remove jars and place upright on towel to cool completely.
25. After jars cool, check seals by pressing middle of lid with finger. If lid springs back, lid is not sealed and refrigeration is necessary.

Yields: 7 one-cup jars.

Quick Raspberry Jelly

This jelly is quick to make, using already prepared juice. It is still delicious, and it will get you out of the kitchen in a jiffy.

Ingredients:

2   cans raspberry juice (10 oz. ea.)
¾   c. water
2   c. sugar
1   bottle liquid pectin (6 oz.)
5   half-pt. jars

Directions:

1. Combine raspberry juice, water, and sugar in heavy saucepan. Bring to boil on high, stirring constantly.
2. Stir in pectin and quickly bring to full rolling boil (Liquid will continue to boil when stirred). Boil 1 minute.
3. Remove from heat, skim off foam, pour into jars, and seal.

Did You Know? . . . .

Did you know that a light-colored, mild-flavored honey can be used in place of one-third of the sugar? Too much honey or corn syrup will mask the fruit flavor and affect gel formation.

Raspberry Rhubarb Jam

Raspberries add great flavor to this raspberry-rhubarb jam.

Ingredients:

2   qt. raspberries, fully ripe
1   lb. rhubarb, fully ripe
½   tsp. butter
7   c. sugar, measured into separate bowl

Directions:

1. Bring boiling water canner, half full with water, to simmer.
2. Wash jars and screw bands in hot soapy water; rinse with warm water.
3. Pour boiling water over flat lids in saucepan off the heat.
4. Let stand in hot water until ready to use.
5. Drain jars well.
6. Crush raspberries thoroughly, one layer at a time.
7. Finely chop unpeeled rhubarb.
8. Combine fruits; measure exactly 5 cups prepared fruit mixture into 6 to 8 quart saucepot.
9. Stir pectin into prepared fruit mixture in saucepot.
10. Add butter to reduce foaming.
11. Bring mixture to full rolling boil (a boil that doesn't stop bubbling when stirred) on high heat, stirring constantly.
12. Stir in sugar; return to full rolling boil and boil exactly 1 minute, stirring constantly.
13. Remove from heat; skim off any foam with metal spoon.
14. Ladle immediately into prepared jars, filling to within ⅛ inch of tops.
15. Wipe jar rims and threads, and cover with two-piece lids.
16. Screw bands tightly.
17. Place jars on elevated rack in canner.
18. Lower rack into canner.
19. Water must cover jars by 1 to 2 inches.
20. Add boiling water, if necessary.
21. Cover, bring water to gentle boil, and process 10 minutes.

22. Remove jars and place upright on towel to cool completely.
23. After jars cool, check seals by pressing middles of lids with finger. If lids spring back, lids are not sealed and refrigeration is necessary.

Yields: 9 one-cup jars.

Raspberry Jam with Sherry

This version of raspberry jam adds the flavor of orange and sherry for a delicious meal.

Ingredients:

½   gal. raspberries
2   pkg. fruit pectin
2   pieces orange peel (4 in. ea.)
7   c. sugar
1   c. sherry

Directions:

1. Wash and drain berries.
2. In blender, liquefy all but one cup of berries, together with orange juice.
3. Pour into 6 to 8 quart pot.
4. Add remaining whole berries and stir in fruit pectin.
5. Add orange peel and bring to a rolling boil over moderate high heat, stirring constantly.
6. Add sugar and sherry.
7. Bring to boil again and cook one minute longer.
8. Remove from heat, skim off foam, and remove orange peel.
9. Ladle into hot jars and process in hot water bath, following directions for canning on page 208.

Did You Know?....

Did you know that fresh pectin should be purchased yearly? Old pectin may result in poor gels.

Raspberry Jam

Raspberry jam is always a hit, whether it's for breakfast, lunch, or dinner.

Ingredients:

5   c. raspberries, crushed
7   c. sugar
1   pkg. pectin

Directions:

1. Mix ingredients in large saucepan.
2. Heat until mixture just comes to a boil.
3. Place into canning jars, wipe tops, and seal.

Yields: 8¾ cups.

Raspberry Syrup

Nothing is better than hot pancakes, waffles, or French toast, and homemade raspberry syrup. Adjust the sweetness to your taste.

Ingredients:

2½ c. frozen raspberries, thawed, with juice
1   c. sugar
1   c. light corn syrup

Directions:

1. Place raspberries (including juice) and sugar into a blender and process at high speed.
2. Mash and force through a sieve with potato masher.
3. Pour into saucepan and bring to boil over moderate heat.
4. Add corn syrup and cook a little while longer.
5. Pour into bottle and refrigerate.

Raspberry Delights Cookbook
A Collection of Raspberry Recipes
Cookbook Delights Series – Book 14

Main Dishes

Table of Contents

Beef Medallions with Raspberry Citrus

Beef medallions make an elegant dinner presentation. Try serving these raspberry medallions with your favorite potato, pasta, or rice.

Ingredients:

    1   c. raspberries, fresh or frozen
    6   Tbs. orange juice
    6   Tbs. lemon juice
    2   Tbs. vermouth
    2   tsp. grated orange peel
    2   tsp. lemon peel
    1   tsp. fresh ginger, minced
    3   tsp. butter
    1   lb. beef medallions
        salt and pepper to taste

Directions:

1. Combine raspberries, orange juice, lemon juice, vermouth, orange peel, lemon peel, and ginger.
2. Stir to blend and set aside.
3. Melt butter in large heavy skillet.
4. Sauté beef until brown and just cooked through.
5. Transfer veal to platter and keep warm.
6. Add raspberry mixture to skillet.
7. Cook about 2 minutes, until mixture thickens, scraping skillet periodically.
8. Spoon raspberry mixture over beef and serve.

Did You Know? . . . .

Did you know you should avoid substituting ingredients in jams and jellies? A precise balance of sugar, fruit, pectin, and acid is required for proper setting.

Black Raspberry Glazed Chicken with Wild Rice Stuffing

This dish is such a refreshing break from the every day.

Ingredients:

8   chicken breast halves, boneless, skinless, flattened
½   c. flour
½   c. butter
7   oz. long grain and wild rice blend
2   c. chicken broth
½   c. slivered almonds, toasted
½   c. black raspberry jam, seedless
2   Tbs. frozen orange juice concentrate
½   c. honey
1   tsp. orange rind, finely grated
    salt
    paprika
    garlic powder

Directions:

1. Sprinkle chicken with salt, paprika, and garlic powder. Set aside.
2. Prepare rice according to package directions, substituting broth for water.
3. Toss rice with almonds. Set aside.
4. Heat jam, orange juice concentrate, honey, and orange peel in saucepan until blended.
5. Place some rice on one breast.
6. Roll and secure with toothpicks.
7. Dust with flour.
8. Repeat with remaining breasts.
9. Melt butter in 9 x 13-inch pan and roll breasts in butter.
10. Bake 40 minutes at 325 degrees F.
11. Baste with glaze and continue baking and basting until tender, approximately 30 minutes.
12. Serve with additional rice, if desired.

Yields: 8 servings.

Chicken with Raspberry Vinegar

The raspberry vinegar is a delicious combination with chicken.

Ingredients:

6   whole chicken breasts, boned and skinned
2   Tbs. oil
6   Tbs. butter
2   Tbs. chopped shallots/onion
6   Tbs. raspberry vinegar
6   Tbs. water
    salt and pepper

Directions:

1. Bone and skin chicken breasts.
2. Lay flat and slice parallel to board into two fillets each.
3. Sprinkle each side with salt and pepper.
4. Heat oil and butter in sauce pan; sauté chicken breasts a few minutes on each side until opaque.
5. Set aside and keep warm.
6. Sprinkle shallots in pan, sauté for a few seconds, then add raspberry vinegar and 4 to 6 tablespoons water.
7. Stir well to loosen all cooking residue and cook 1 minute.
8. Return breasts to pan and cook until done, turning once.
9. Serve immediately with sauce.

Raspberry Balsamic Glazed Chicken

This is a tasty way to cook chicken.

Ingredients:

1   tsp. vegetable oil
½   c. red onion, chopped
½   tsp. dried thyme
½   tsp. salt
4   ea. chicken breast halves without skin, boned
⅓   raspberry jam
2   Tbs. balsamic vinegar
¼   tsp. pepper

Directions:

1. Heat oil in large nonstick skillet coated with cooking spray over medium-high heat until hot.
2. Add onion, sauté 5 minutes.
3. Combine thyme and ¼ teaspoon salt; sprinkle over chicken.
4. Add chicken to skillet and sauté 6 minutes on each side.
5. Remove chicken from skillet; keep warm.
6. Reduce heat to medium-low.
7. Add ¼ teaspoon salt, preserves, vinegar, and pepper, stirring constantly until preserves meld.
8. Spoon raspberry sauce over chicken.

Raspberry Grilled Lamb Chops

Raspberry and minced rosemary add excellent flavor.

Ingredients:

2   Tbs. raspberry vinegar
1   Tbs. Dijon mustard
1   Tbs. soy sauce
2   Tbs. fresh rosemary /or/ ½ tsp. dried
1   tsp. olive oil
1   clove garlic, minced
8   lamb loin chops

Directions:

1. In large shallow dish, whisk together vinegar, mustard, soy sauce, rosemary, oil, and garlic.
2. Add lamb chops in single layer, turning to coat well.
3. Cover and marinate in refrigerator for at least 2 hours or up to 8 hours, turning occasionally.
4. Discard marinade.
5. Place chops on greased grill over medium-high heat.
6. Cook about 5 minutes per side for medium-rare or to desired doneness.
7. Transfer to platter, tent with foil, let stand for 5 minutes.

Yields: 4 servings.

Crab Won Tons with Raspberry Szechwan Sauce

Our family loves wontons, and these are very good.

Ingredients for raspberry Szechwan sauce:

½   c. raspberry purée
½   c. saki or dry sherry
1   Tbs. cornstarch
½   tsp. salt
½   tsp. red pepper flakes
½   tsp. grated ginger
1   tsp. lime juice
2   cloves garlic, minced
1½ Tbs. honey

Ingredients for filling:

2-3 oz. fresh spinach, trimmed and washed
1   Tbs. butter
4   Tbs. onion, chopped finely
3   oz. cream cheese, cut into sm. chunks
2   Tbs. lemon juice
2   Tbs. dry breadcrumbs
½   lb. flaked, cooked crabmeat
    dash salt, pepper, tabasco

Ingredients for won tons:

3   dz. won ton wrappers
    vegetable oil to cover bottom of wok to ¼ inch

Directions for raspberry Szechwan sauce:

1. Mix all ingredients in saucepan. Bring to a boil over medium high heat and cook until clear and thickened.
2. The flavor of this sauce improves after standing overnight.

Directions for filling:

1. Wash spinach. With water still clinging to leaves, place in large pan over medium high heat.
2. Cook until spinach just begins to wilt and most of water has evaporated.
3. Empty onto cutting board and chop finely. Set aside.

224

4. Melt butter in sauté pan.
5. Add onion and sauté until transparent.
6. Reduce heat to low; add cream cheese.
7. When the cheese begins to soften, add lemon juice to blend.
8. Remove from heat and stir in crab, breadcrumbs, and spinach.

Directions for won tons:

1. Place 1 to 2 teaspoons filling in each wrapper and seal according to package directions.
2. Place single layer of wontons in hot oil and fry 2 to 3 minutes until golden brown.
3. Drain on paper towels and serve immediately with raspberry Szechwan sauce.

Sour Cream Soufflé with Raspberries

Try this interesting soufflé. The Parmesan cheese and the sour cream cut the sweetness and is a great contrast to the sweet raspberry.

Ingredients:

6   lg. egg yolks
½   c. sour cream
¼   c. Parmesan cheese, grated
6   egg whites, beaten stiff
3   Tbs. butter
½   c. sour cream
1   tsp. sugar
    fresh raspberries

Directions:

1. Preheat oven to 325 degrees F.
2. Beat egg yolks until thick and lemon colored; about 5 minutes.
3. Mix sour cream with sugar and Parmesan cheese.
4. Beat in ½ cup of this mixture with the egg yolks.
5. Fold in stiffly beaten egg whites.
6. Melt butter in 10-inch heavy, oven-going skillet.
7. Pour in egg mixture, leveling gently.
8. Cook over very low heat 10 minutes.
9. Carefully move to oven and bake 15 minutes until golden and puffed.
10. Cut into 4 wedges, serve with a dollop of sweetened sour cream, and top with berries.

Duck Breasts with Raspberry Sauce

This is an excellent raspberry sauce to go over duck.

Ingredients:

4   duck breast halves
2   tsp. sea salt
2   tsp. ground cinnamon
4   tsp. demerara sugar
½   c. red wine
¼   c. crème de cassis liqueur
1   tsp. cornstarch
4   oz. raspberries

Directions:

1. Preheat oven on broiler setting.
2. Using a fork, score duck breasts through the skin and fat but not all the way through to the meat.
3. Heat large heavy skillet on medium high.
4. Fry duck breasts, skin side down, until skin browns and fat runs out, about 10 minutes.
5. Remove the breasts from the pan; pour off most of the fat.
6. Return breasts to pan and fry skin side up 10 more minutes.
7. Remove breasts from pan and allow to rest on baking sheet.
8. Mix sea salt, cinnamon, and demerara sugar together and sprinkle over the skin of the duck breasts.
9. Pour most of the fat out of the frying pan.
10. Mix together the red wine, cassis, and cornstarch in small bowl.
11. Pour into the pan and simmer 3 minutes, stirring constantly, until the sauce is thickened.
12. Add raspberries and simmer for another minute until heated through.
13. Broil the duck breasts skin side up, until the sugar begins to caramelize, about 1 minute.
14. Slice the duck breasts thinly, pour a little sauce over the top; serve warm.

Grilled Game Hens with Berry Marinade

The raspberry marinade in this recipe is wonderful.

Ingredients:

6   cornish game hens, split in half
3   c. raspberries, fresh or frozen
1   c. raspberry vinegar
¾   c. olive oil
2   bay leaves
1   Tbs. dried thyme
    salt and pepper to taste

Directions:

1. One day before serving, rinse birds, pat dry, and place on shallow baking dish.
2. Combine raspberries and vinegar in saucepan, and boil 1 minute. Remove from heat.
3. Stir in oil, bay leaves, and thyme; cool to room temperature.
4. Pour the marinade over birds and sprinkle with salt and pepper.
5. Marinate overnight in refrigerator, turning occasionally.
6. Prepare hot coals for grilling.
7. Remove birds from the marinade and grill a few inches above the hot coals, basting occasionally with the marinade, until juices run clear when the thickest part of a thigh is pierced.
8. Serve immediately.

Did You Know? . . . .

Did you know that raspberries' underground root stem and crown are perennial, and canes from underground buds are biennial? Primocanes are first year canes and floricanes are canes in the second year.

Grilled Turkey Breast with Berry-Shal

This is so good on a hot summer day.

Ingredients:

4   lb. turkey breast (1 lg. breast) skinned and quartered
½   c. raspberry vinegar
2   Tbs. shallots, minced
½   c. plain yogurt
1   tsp. curry powder

Directions:

1. Place turkey breast quarters into large, shallow pan.
2. Mix together vinegar and shallots and pour over turkey.
3. Cover with plastic wrap and marinate for 8 to 10 hours in refrigerator.
4. Combine yogurt and curry powder. Set aside.
5. Prepare coals for grilling.
6. Wrap turkey breasts in aluminum foil and place on grill.
7. Cook over coals for 20 minutes, then unwrap and grill for 5 minutes more, turning once to brown lightly.
8. Spoon marinade over turkey frequently during last 5 minutes of grilling.
9. Serve with curried yogurt as a spicy sauce.

Did You Know? . . . .

Did you know you should avoid doubling jam and jelly recipes? It's easy to make mistakes in measuring, and this can result in the mixture not setting. There may not be sufficient surface area in the saucepan or enough time for liquid to evaporate.

Did you know why some bread is doughy on the bottom? This can be caused when bread is not removed from pans and allowed to cool on racks.

Pork Medallions with Port and Raspberry Sauce

This tangy yet sweet sauce perfectly complements the pork.

Ingredients:

½   c. raspberries
½   c. water
1   tsp. vegetable oil
1   lb. pork medallions
2   Tbs. minced shallots
½   c. tawny port wine
¼   c. distilled white vinegar
1   c. chicken broth
½   tsp. dried thyme
1   tsp. cornstarch
1   Tbs. water
    salt and pepper to taste

Directions:

1. Place raspberries in a small saucepan over medium low heat. Add water and stir together.
2. Bring to a simmer and let simmer for 3 minutes.
3. Drain, reserving both berries and cooking liquid. Set aside.
4. In a large skillet, heat oil over medium heat.
5. Season pork medallions with salt and pepper and add to skillet.
6. Sauté on both sides until browned and no longer pink inside, about 3 minutes per side.
7. Transfer to a platter, cover loosely and keep warm.
8. In the same skillet, add chopped shallot and cook for 30 seconds.
9. Pour in port and vinegar and bring to a boil, stirring to scrape up any brown bits on the bottom of the skillet. Boil until liquid is reduced by half, 3 to 5 minutes.
10. Add chicken stock, thyme, and reserved raspberry liquid; boil all together until reduced by half, 5 to 7 minutes.
11. In a small bowl dissolve cornstarch in 1 tablespoon water and mix together.
12. Whisk mixture into saucepan and let simmer, stirring, until sauce is slightly thickened and glossy.
13. Stir in reserved raspberries and season with salt and pepper to taste. Spoon sauce over pork and serve.

Yields: 4 servings.

Raspberry Chicken Breasts

This is another tasty and colorful chicken dish. Remember the importance of reducing the liquids in the sauce thus obtaining the full flavor of the ingredients.

Ingredients:

½   tsp. Cajun spices (or more to taste)
4   halves chicken breast, boneless, skinless
3   cloves garlic, finely chopped
1   med. onion, finely chopped
3   tsp. olive oil
½   c. red wine
2   c. raspberries
1   lemon rind, grated
¼   tsp. salt (optional)

Directions:

1. Dust chicken breasts with Cajun spices.
2. Sauté in olive oil until brown and almost cooked through, 7 to 10 minutes. If thick, cover for 3 or 4 minutes more.
3. Remove chicken breasts from pan and keep warm.
4. In same pan, sauté garlic and onion until transparent, scraping remaining bits of chicken from bottom of pan.
5. Add red wine; cook until most of the liquid is evaporated.
6. Add raspberries, lemon rind, and salt.
7. Simmer for 5 minutes. If raspberries are frozen, cook until berries are heated through.
8. Add salt and pepper to taste.
9. Let sit 5 minutes with heat off, for flavors to blend.
10. Spoon over chicken breasts and serve.

Did You Know? . . . .

Did you know how to check to see if your bread is done? Tap the crust. If it sounds hollow, it's done.

Salmon with Raspberry Horseradish

Northwest salmon, raspberry, and horseradish combine to make a piquant Northwest dish.

Ingredients:

1   lb. salmon fillet
1   pt. fresh raspberries
1   oz. horseradish, freshly grated
½   c. sugar
½   c. water
½   c. fresh basil
    juice of ½ lemon

Directions:

1. Cut salmon into six pieces (2 ounces each). Poach until just underdone or internal temperature reaches 125 degrees F.
2. Cool immediately in refrigerator.
3. Bring water to a boil and add raspberries.
4. Reduce heat and simmer just until tender.
5. Add sugar and cook for just a few more minutes.
6. Finish with lemon juice and grated horseradish.
7. Stir in basil after cooking.
8. Serve warm, pooled on a plate, with chilled salmon on top.
9. Garnish with a sprig of basil.

Did You Know? . . . .

Did you know when Lewis and Clark entered the lush Pacific watersheds in 1804, they discovered millions of salmon in the untamed wild Columbia River? At that time 15 to 20 million salmon lived in the pristine habitat of the mighty Columbia River.

Did you know that salmon returning to the Wenatchee River travel 500 miles and over 7 dams from the Pacific Ocean to get to their place of birth?

Roasted Chicken with Raspberry Sauce

This makes a delicious and colorful main dish, and the trick is to make sure you reduce the stock to concentrate the flavor.

Ingredients for marinated chicken:

2   c. port wine
¾   c. sugar, divided
¼   c. honey
4-4½ lb. chicken, wing tips removed
        salt
        ground black pepper

Ingredients for raspberry sauce:

2   Tbs. olive oil
⅓   c. diced shallots
½   c. cider vinegar
¼   c. brandy
1   c. fresh raspberries (6 oz.)
1½   tsp. fresh tarragon, chopped
2   c. chicken stock

Directions for marinated chicken:

1. In large enough pot to hold the chicken, combine wine, water, ¼ cup sugar, and honey.
2. Bring to boil.
3. Meanwhile, season poultry cavity with salt and black pepper; bind poultry; set aside.
4. When wine mixture comes to a boil, remove from heat.
5. Add poultry and let marinate at room temperature for 20 minutes, turning occasionally.
6. Preheat oven to 350 degrees F.
7. Remove poultry from marinade and place on rack in a shallow roasting pan.
8. Bake 1 hour 15 minutes until poultry is brown and reaches internal temperature of 185 degrees F.
9. Let stand at room temperature 10 minutes.

Directions for raspberry sauce:

1. In medium skillet, heat olive oil until hot.
2. Add shallots and cook 3 to 5 minutes until soft, stirring frequently.
3. Add remaining ½ cup sugar and cook over low heat, stirring constantly for 10 to 15 minutes until sugar is dark brown.
4. Stir in vinegar, brandy, raspberries, and tarragon.
5. Cook over medium high heat 5 minutes until raspberries are soft.
6. Add stock, bring to a boil, and boil until mixture is reduced by half, about 20 minutes.
7. Season to taste with salt and pepper.

Directions for serving:

1. Carve poultry, dividing between two serving plates.
2. Spoon raspberry sauce over poultry.
3. Garnish with fresh raspberries, carrot roses, etc., if desired.

Yields: 2 servings, 1½ cups sauce.

Did You Know? . . . .

Did you know yeast that is old will not rise, but yeast can be stored indefinitely in the freezer? When you buy it at the store, simply pop it in your freezer until you need it!

Did you know that if you want a shiny, brown bread crust, simply brush the crust of your dough with beaten egg whites before baking? Coating the crust with butter after baking produces a nice, soft, buttery flavored crust.

Did you know that to clean up after melting chocolate for dipping or drizzling, pour leftover chocolate onto a piece of waxed paper and let cool so you can break and re-melt later?

Trout with Raspberries

I grew up in Montana where we frequently enjoyed fresh trout. This is very easy to make grilled or baked. Feel free to use salmon with the same recipe.

Ingredients:

1	whole trout or salmon, cleaned, or center cut trout
1	c. raspberries
½	onion, chopped
2	lemons, sliced
4	tsp. butter

Directions:

1. Spread 1 teaspoon butter around center of tin foil, arrange half the lemon slices over butter and place trout on top.
2. Mix together berries and onion; stuff fish.
3. Spread butter on top of fish; arrange remaining lemon slices, fold, and seal foil.
4. Barbecue 10 minutes per inch of thickest point, turning every 5 to 10 minutes.
5. Unwrap foil, peel off skin, and remove bones.
6. Place fish on plates, spoon topping, and arrange lemon slices on top.
7. As an alternative to barbecue, substitute covered dish for foil to bake in oven at 350 degrees F. for 10 minutes per inch.

Did You Know?....

Did you know the best trout fishermen wear drab colored clothing to blend in with the scenery when they are fishing? Trout are very intelligent fish and have a keen sense of sight and smell. Loud colors, or even plain white, stand out, and the fish will be able to see you.

Raspberry Delights Cookbook

A Collection of Raspberry Recipes
Cookbook Delights Series – Book 14

Pies

Table of Contents

A Basic Recipe for Pie Crusts

This is a very good recipe for a delicious, flaky crust.

Ingredients for single crust:

1½ c. sifted all-purpose flour
½   tsp. salt
½   c. shortening
4-5 Tbs. ice water

Ingredients for double crust:

2   c. sifted all-purpose flour
1   tsp. salt
⅔   c. shortening
5-7 Tbs. ice water

Directions for single crust:

1. In large bowl stir together flour and salt.
2. Cut in shortening with pastry blender or mix with fingertips until pieces are size of coarse crumbs.
3. Sprinkle 2 tablespoons ice water over flour mixture, tossing with fork.
4. Add just enough remaining water 1 tablespoon at a time to moisten dough, tossing so dough holds together.
5. Roll pastry into 11-inch circle and wrap in plastic wrap; refrigerate for 1 hour.
6. Preheat oven to 425 degrees F.
7. Remove plastic wrap from pastry, and fit pastry into a 9-inch pie plate.
8. Fold edge under and then crimp between thumb and forefinger to make fluted crust.
9. For filled pie with an instant or cooked filling (cream-filled, custard-filled, etc.), prick crust all over with fork then bake 15 to 20 minutes until done.
10. If preparing pie with uncooked filling (such as pumpkin), do not prick crust; pour filling into unbaked pastry shell, and then bake as directed.

Directions for double crust:

1. Turn desired filling into pastry-lined pie plate; trim overhanging edge of pastry ½ inch from rim of plate.
2. Cut slits with knife in top crust for steam vents.
3. Place over filling; trim overhanging edge of pastry 1 inch from rim of plate.
4. Fold and roll top edge under lower edge, pressing on rim to seal; flute.
5. Cover fluted edge with 2- to 3-inch-wide strip of aluminum foil to prevent excessive browning.
6. Remove foil during last 15 minutes of baking.

Yields: 1 pie crust (9-inch).

A Basic Cookie or Graham Cracker Crust

This is a great crust for use with cream pies or for an unbaked pie. Use your favorite flavor of cookie to complement your filling or use graham crackers.

Ingredients:

2 c. cookie or graham cracker crumbs, finely crushed
½ c. butter, melted
⅓ c. sugar

Directions:

1. Combine crumbs, sugar, and butter.
2. Press mixture firmly against bottom and up sides of 9-inch pie plate.
3. Baking is not necessary, but if preferred crust may be baked at 400 degrees F. for 10 minutes.

Yields: 1 pie crust (9-inch).

Did You Know? . . . .

Did you know that there are four basic ingredients in pie crust? They are flour, fat, water, and salt. You can make many variations by changing your basic ingredients, as long as you maintain the ratio of three parts flour, two parts fat, and one part liquid.

Chocolate Raspberry Cheesecake Pie

This chocolate raspberry cheesecake pie is wonderful.

Ingredients for cheesecake filling:

1   chocolate pie crust (recipe below)
2   pkg. cream cheese (3 oz. ea.), softened
1   can sweetened condensed milk (14 oz.)
1   egg
1   tsp. vanilla extract
1   can raspberries, drained

Ingredients for chocolate crust:

1½ c. chocolate cookie crumbs
1   Tbs. sugar
¼   c. butter, melted

Ingredients for chocolate glaze:

2   sq. (1 oz ea.) semi-sweet baking chocolate
¼   c. whipping cream

Directions for cheesecake filling:

1. Preheat oven to 350 degrees F.
2. Beat cream cheese with mixer until fluffy.
3. Gradually beat in sweetened condensed milk until smooth.
4. Add egg and vanilla; mix well.
5. Arrange the drained raspberries in bottom of the chocolate crust.
6. Slowly pour cream cheese mixture over berries.
7. Bake 30 to 35 minutes or until center is almost set.
8. Cool for 1 hour.

Directions for chocolate crust:

1. Mix ingredients until thoroughly blended.
2. Press into 9-inch pie pan.

Directions for chocolate glaze:

1. In small saucepan, combine cream and chocolate.
2. Cook over low heat, stirring constantly, until chocolate melts and mixture thickens slightly.
3. Remove from heat, pour over cooled cheesecake, and cool for 30 minutes.
4. Refrigerate at least 2 hours.
5. Garnish with a few raspberries.
6. Store in refrigerator.

Yields: 1 pie.

Apple Raspberry Pie

This makes a delicious combination of apples and raspberries, always best served out of the oven with homemade vanilla or cinnamon ice cream.

Ingredients:

1 pie shell, unbaked double (Use your favorite recipe or follow "Pie Crust" recipe in this pie section.)
¾ c. sugar
2½ c. raspberries, fresh if possible
3 Tbs. cornstarch
5 c. apples, peeled and sliced
1 Tbs. lemon juice
2 Tbs. butter
   dash salt

Directions:

1. In large bowl, stir together sugar, cornstarch, and salt.
2. Add apples, raspberries, and lemon juice; toss to coat fruit.
3. Turn into pastry-lined, 9-inch pie pan; dot with butter.
4. Add top crust; seal, and flute edge.
5. Bake in 425 degrees F. oven until crust is browned and filling is bubbly.

Raspberry Tart

This makes a delicious and flavorful tart to enjoy.

Ingredients for tart filling:

¼ lb. butter
¼ c. almonds, shelled, ground
¼ c. caster sugar
1 tsp. distilled rose water
2 lg. eggs
1½ c. raspberries
1 baked pastry shell (9 in.), cooled (Use your favorite recipe or follow "Pie Crust" recipe in this cookbook section.)

Directions:

1. Heat oven to 400 degrees F.
2. Dice butter and soften in small saucepan over low heat.
3. Remove from heat; add sugar, ground almonds, rose water, and both lightly beaten eggs, in that order.
4. Tip the chilled berries into the pie shell, spreading evenly.
5. Pour almond mixture over fruit.
6. Bake 35 to 40 minutes until topping is golden and puffed.

Chilled Raspberry Cream Pie

This is a refreshing and attractive chilled raspberry pie.

Ingredients:

1 pie shell (9 in.), baked (Use your favorite recipe or follow "Pie Crust" recipe in this pie section.)
3 oz. cream cheese
½ c. powdered sugar
1 tsp. vanilla extract
½ pt. whipping cream
2 c. fresh raspberries

1 c. sugar
½ c. water
3 Tbs. cornstarch

Directions:

1. Mix cream cheese, powdered sugar, and vanilla together.
2. Spread cream mixture onto the bottom of pie shell.
3. In saucepan combine raspberries, sugar, water, and cornstarch.
4. Bring to a boil, stirring constantly until thickened.
5. Pour over cream mixture in pie shell.
6. Whip the cream and spread on top of cooled pie.
7. Top with fresh raspberries.

Raspberry Pie

I have raspberries growing in my yard, and I think of pie during summer time.

Ingredients:

2½ c. raspberries
½ c. brown sugar, packed
1 tsp. cornstarch
1 Tbs. butter
1 egg white
  unbaked double pastry for 9-inch pie (Use your crust recipe or follow "Pie Crust" recipe in this section.)

Directions:

1. Preheat oven to 450 degrees F. and line 9-inch pie pan with pastry, and brush with egg white.
2. Arrange berries in crust.
3. Combine sugar and cornstarch; and sprinkle over berries.
4. Dot with butter, cover with upper crust, and seal edges.
5. Bake 10 minutes, then reduce oven temperature to 400 degrees F. and continue baking for 30 minutes.

Raspberry Apricot Pie

This combination of raspberry, apricot, and almond is absolutely delicious.

Ingredients:

- 10 oz. frozen raspberries
- 32 oz. apricot halves
- ¼ c. flour
- ¾ c. sugar
- ⅛ tsp. salt
- 2 Tbs. butter
- ½ tsp. almond extract
- 2 crust pastry (Use your favorite recipe /or/ follow "Pie Crust" recipe in this cookbook section.)

Directions:

1. Defrost and drain raspberries and save ½ cup juice.
2. Place drained apricots in pie crust.
3. Spoon raspberries over apricots and pour juice over top.
4. Mix sugar, flour, and salt together and sprinkle over berries.
5. Dot with butter and sprinkle on extract.
6. Cover with top crust and sprinkle with sugar.
7. Bake at 400 degrees F. 50 to 60 minutes; watch carefully.
8. You may substitute 2½ cups fresh blackberries and 5 fresh peaches for raspberries and apricots. Increase sugar to 1 cup.

Yields: 6 to 8 servings.

Did You Know? . . . .

Did you know there are over 200 species of raspberries, and they can be grown from the Arctic to the equator? They are red, yellow, orange, purple, or black, and can be harvested from early summer through fall.

Raspberry Cheese Pie

Raspberries are also great with cream cheese and sour cream. Try this excellent variation of raspberry pie.

Ingredients for pie shell:

2 Tbs. sugar
2 c. graham cracker crumbs
½ c. butter, melted

Ingredients for filling:

2 pkg. cream cheese (8 oz.)
2 Tbs. sugar
½ c. sour cream
1 c. raspberry pie filling

Directions for pie shell:

1. Preheat oven to 350 degrees F.
2. Mix first 3 ingredients well and press them into 9-inch pie pan to form the crust.
3. Bake 6 minutes.

Directions for filling:

1. Blend until smooth the cream cheese, sour cream, and sugar.
2. Pour into pie shell.
3. Top with raspberries. Sprinkle sugar on top and bake at 350 degrees F. for 5 minutes.
4. Chill and serve.

Did You Know? . . . .

Did you know that sugar helps gel formation, adds sweetness, and acts as a preservative? Corn syrup can be substituted for half the sugar.

Raspberry Orange Chiffon Pie

Raspberries and oranges actually make a great flavorful combination. Try this interesting combination.

Ingredients:

- 3 eggs, separated
- 3 Tbs. orange juice
- 1 c. water
- ¼ c. sugar
- 1 c. water
- 1 pkg. orange flavor gelatin (3 oz.)
- 1 baked 9-inch pie shell (Use your favorite recipe /or/ follow "Pie Crust" recipe in this cookbook section.)
- 1½ tsp. orange rind, grated
- 1 pt. raspberries
  dash of salt
  sweetened whipped cream for topping

Directions:

1. Slightly beat egg yolks and combine with 1 cup water in saucepan; add ¼ cup sugar.
2. Cook and stir over low heat until mixture is slightly thickened and just comes to a boil.
3. Remove from heat.
4. Add gelatin and stir until dissolved.
5. Add ½ cup water, orange rind, and orange juice.
6. Chill until slightly thickened.
7. Beat egg whites and salt until foamy.
8. Gradually beat in ¼ cup sugar and continue beating until stiff peaks are formed.
9. Fold in thickened gelatin.
10. Blend well.
11. Fold in 1½ cup raspberries and spoon filling into pie shell.
12. Chill until firm.
13. With a toothpick, lightly mark top of pie into 6 equal wedges.

14. Fill wedges with whipped cream and remainder of raspberries; chill.
15. Cut wedges so each piece is topped with half raspberries and half topping.

Raspberry Cream Pie

This makes an easy-to-make, delicious raspberry pie.

Ingredients:

1   favorite baked pastry shell /or/ follow "Pie Crust" recipe in this cookbook section
5½ c. raspberries, fresh of frozen
¾   c. sugar
½   c. cold water
3   Tbs. lemon juice
3   Tbs. cornstarch
1   c. whipping cream
2   Tbs. sugar

Directions:

1. Prepare your favorite baked pastry shell; set aside.
2. In medium saucepan, stir together 2 cups raspberries, ¾ cup sugar, cold water, lemon juice, and cornstarch.
3. Cook and stir over medium heat until thickened and bubbly. Cook and stir for 2 minutes more.
4. Remove from heat, cool slightly.
5. Cover and refrigerate until thoroughly chilled.
6. Carefully fold 2 cups of remaining raspberries into chilled mixture. Spoon into pastry shell.
7. Cover; chill at least 2 hours or until firm.
8. To serve, in chilled, medium bowl, combine whipping cream and the 2 tablespoons sugar, beat with chilled beaters of electric mixer on medium speed until soft peaks form.
9. Serve pie with whipped cream and remaining berries.

Yields: 8 servings.

Fresh Raspberry Pie

This is a delicious pie with the great taste of raspberries.

Ingredients:

6   c. fresh raspberries
¾   c. sugar
2   Tbs. cornstarch
2-3 drops almond extract
1-2 Tbs. lemon juice
     pastry dough for 9-in. double crust (Use your favorite recipe /or/ follow "Pie Crust" recipe in this cookbook section.)

Directions:

1. In large pan combine raspberries, sugar, cornstarch, almond extract, and lemon juice.
2. Heat slowly over low heat.
3. Stir gently until juice flows and mixture begins to thicken.
4. Remove from heat and let cool.
5. Roll dough out for bottom crust; fit into 9-inch pan.
6. Pour in raspberry mixture. Dot with butter.
7. Place top pie crust dough on pie and flute edge.
8. Bake in 425 degrees F. oven 10 minutes; reduce heat to 375 degrees F. and bake until golden.
9. Needs to be covered last 10 minutes.

Did You Know? . . . .

Did you know that acid must be present in sufficient amounts for a gel to form? If natural acid is lacking, lemon juice or citrus fruit is added.

Did you know that fruit spreads made without added pectin require longer cooking and yield less product?

Raspberry Coconut Pie

This raspberry pie keeps well in your freezer for surprise guests or for your invited company.

Ingredients:

1   pastry shell, unbaked 9-inch (Use your favorite recipe /or/ follow "Pie Crust" recipe in this section.)
1   egg, well beaten
1¼ c. coconut, flaked
¼   c. walnuts, chopped
¼   c. light corn syrup
1   Tbs. flour
¼   tsp. salt
¼   c. sugar
1   pkg. frozen raspberries (10 oz.), unsweetened
⅔   c. sugar
1   c. heavy cream, whipped

Directions:

1. Make pastry shell from your own recipe and bake as directed except remove it from the oven after only 5 minutes baking, and reduce oven temperature to 375 degrees F.
2. Combine egg with the coconut, nuts, syrup, flour, salt, and the ¼ cup sugar; spread in the bottom of partly baked pastry shell.
3. Return pie to oven and bake 15 minutes. Cool thoroughly.
4. Crush frozen raspberries and combine with the ⅔ cup sugar; fold into the whipped cream.
5. Pour berry mixture over cooled coconut mixture and freeze.

Yields: 6 servings.

Did You Know? . . . .

Did you know the apoptotic process, triggered by antioxidant ellagitannin, has beneficial effects on breast, lung, esophageal, and skin cancer?

Strawberry Raspberry Festive Tart

The combination of strawberry, raspberry, and almond is impossible to resist.

Ingredients:

6   Tbs. (¾ stick) unsalted butter, softened
½   c. sugar
1   lg. egg
¾   c. blanched almonds, ground fine
1   tsp. almond extract
1   Tbs. almond flavored liqueur
1   Tbs. all-purpose flour
2   c. strawberries, hulled
2   c. raspberries, picked over and rinsed
¼   c. strawberry or raspberry jam, melted and strained
1   single unbaked pie crust (Use your favorite recipe /or/ follow "Pie Crust" recipe in this cookbook section.)

Directions:

1. Roll out dough ⅛ inch thick on lightly floured surface; fit into an 11- x 8-inch rectangular or 10- or 11-inch round tart pan with removable fluted rim.
2. Chill shell while making the frangipane.
3. In small bowl, cream together the butter and sugar, and beat in the egg, the almonds, the almond extract, the amaretto, and the flour.
4. Spread the frangipane evenly on the bottom of the shell.
5. Bake the tart in the middle of preheated 375 degrees F. oven for 20 to 25 minutes, or until the shell is pale golden.
6. If the frangipane begins to turn too brown, cover the tart loosely with a piece of foil.
7. Let the tart cool.
8. Cut the strawberries lengthwise into ⅛ inch thick slices.
9. Arrange the slices, overlapping decoratively with the raspberries in rows on the frangipane, and brush them gently with the jam.

Raspberry Delights Cookbook

A Collection of Raspberry Recipes
Cookbook Delights Series – Book 14

Preserving

Table of Contents

A Basic Guide for Canning, Dehydrating, and Freezing

1. Place empty jars in hot, soapy water. Wash well inside and out with brush or soft cloth.
2. Run your finger around rim of each jar, discarding any that are chipped or cracked.
3. Rinse in clean, clear, very hot water, being careful to use tongs to avoid burning skin or fingers.
4. Place upside down on towel or fabric to drain well.
5. Place lids in boiling water bath for 2 minutes to sterilize and keep hot until ready to place on jar rims.
6. Immediately prior to filling jars with hot food, immerse in hot bath for 1 minute to heat jars. Heating jars avoids breakage.
7. If filling with room-temperature food, you need not immerse immediately prior to filling.
8. Fill jars with food to within ½ inch of neck of jars.
9. When ladling liquid over food, fill jars to 1 inch from top rim in each jar. This leaves air allowance for sealing purposes.
10. Wipe rims of jars with damp, clean cloth to remove any particles of food and again check for chips or cracks.
11. Using tongs, place lids from hot bath directly onto jars.
12. Place rings over lids, and using cloth, gloves, or holders, tighten down firmly while hanging onto jars.
13. Do not tighten down too hard as air may become trapped in jars and prevent them from sealing.
14. For fruits, tomatoes, and pickled vegetables, place each jar into water bath canning kettle so water covers jars by at least 1 inch.
15. For vegetables, process them in a pressure canner according to manufacturer's directions.
16. Follow time recommended for food being canned.
17. Do not mix jars of food in same canning kettle as times may vary for each kind of food.
18. At end of time recommended for canning, gently lift each jar out of bath with tongs, and place on protected surface.
19. Turn lids gently to be sure they are firmly tight.
20. Place filled, ringed jars on cloth to cool gradually.
21. Do not disturb rings, lids, or jars until sealed.
22. Lids will show slight indentation when sealed.

23. When cool, wipe jars with damp cloth.
24. Label and date each jar.
25. Leave overnight until thoroughly cooled.
26. Jars may then be stored upright on shelves.

Dehydrating

1. Always begin with fresh, good quality food that is clean and inspected for damage.
2. Pretreatment is not necessary, but food that is blanched will keep its color and flavor better. Use the same blanching times as you would for freezing. Fruit, especially, responds well to pretreatment.
3. Doing some research on pretreatments may help you decide what procedure you would like to use.
4. You can marinate, salt, sweeten, or spice foods before you dehydrate them.
5. Jerky is meat that has been marinated and/or flavored by rubbing spices into it; avoid oil or grease of any kind as it will turn rancid as the food dries.
6. Vegetables and fruit can be treated the same way.
7. Slice or dice food thin and uniform so that it will dehydrate evenly. Uneven thicknesses may cause food to spoil because it did not dry as thoroughly as other parts.
8. Space food on dehydrator tray so that air can move around each piece.
9. Try not to let any piece touch another.
10. Fill your trays with all the same type of food as different foods take different amounts of time to dry.
11. You can, of course, dry different types of food at the same time, but you will have to remember to watch and remove the food that dehydrates more quickly. You can mix different foods in the same dehydrator batch, but do not mix strong vegetables like onions and garlic as other foods will absorb their taste while they are dehydrating.
12. The smaller the pieces, the faster a food will dehydrate. Thin leaves of spinach, celery, etc., will dry fastest. Remove them from the stalks before drying them or they will be overdone, losing flavor

and quality. In very warm areas, they might even scorch. If they do, they will taste just like burned food when you rehydrate them.

13. Dense food like carrots will feel very hard when they are ready. Others will be crispy. Usually, a food that is high in fructose (sugar) will be leathery when it is finished dehydrating.

14. Remember that food smells when it is in the process of drying, so outdoors or in the garage is an excellent place to dry a big batch of those onions!

15. Always test each batch to make sure it is "done."

16. You can pasteurize finished food by putting it in a slow oven (150 degrees F.) for a few minutes.

17. Let the food cool before storing.

18. Store in airtight containers to guard against moisture. Jars saved from other food work well as long as they have lids that will keep moisture out.

19. Zip-closure food storage bags work well.

20. Jars of dehydrated carrots, celery, beets, etc., may look cheerful on your countertop, but the colors and flavors will fade. Dehydrated food keeps its color and flavor best if stored in a dark, cool place.

21. Dehydrating food takes time, so do not rush it. When you are all done, you will have a dried food stash to be proud of!

Freezing

1. Wash all containers and lids in hot, soapy water using soft cloth.
2. Rinse well in clear, clean, hot water.
3. Cool and drain well.
4. Place food into container to within 1 inch of rim. This allows for expansion of food during freezing.
5. Wipe rim of container with clean damp cloth, checking for chips or breaks.
6. Be certain cover fits the container snugly to avoid leaks. Burp air from container.
7. If food is hot when placing in container, cool prior to placing in freezer.
8. Label and date each container.
9. Store upright in freezer until frozen solid.

Canned Raspberries

It's always a good idea to stock up on raspberries when they are in season to enjoy year round.

Ingredients:

1   gal. fresh raspberries
4   c. water
3   c. sugar

Directions:

1. Rinse and drain raspberries.
2. Place in sterilized pint jars.
3. In saucepan bring water and sugar to boil, over moderate high heat, stirring constantly.
4. Pour hot mixture over raspberries, leaving ⅜-inch space from the top.
5. Wipe rims, install sterilized lids, and adjust rings.
6. Process in canner, following directions.

Yields: 8 pints.

Did You Know? . . . .

Did you know if you don't grow your own raspberries, there are many berry farms in the Northwest where you can go and pick your own? You should avoid placing the picked berries in the sunshine any longer than necessary. It is better to put them in the shade of a tree or shed than in the car trunk or on the car seat.

Did you know that you should cool raspberries as soon as possible after picking? Raspberries may be kept fresh in the refrigerator for 2 or 3 days, depending upon the initial quality of the berry. After a few days in storage, however, the fruit loses its bright color and fresh flavor and tends to shrivel.

Freezing Raspberries

Raspberries are fruits that freeze incredibly well. They can be frozen whole in sugar pack, syrup pack, or unsweetened.

Ingredients:

1   qt. very ripe raspberries
¾   c. sugar

Directions for freezing in sugar pack:

1. Add ¾ cup sugar to 1 quart of raspberries.
2. Mix sugar carefully with raspberries to prevent fruit damage.
3. Fill containers leaving ½ inch headspace.
4. Seal, label, and freeze.

Directions for freezing raspberries in syrup pack:

1. Syrup pack means freezing them in cold 50% syrup.
2. Mix 1 cup sugar to 1 cup water and pour over raspberries in containers.
3. Leave ½ inch headspace in containers.
4. Seal, label, and freeze the same as with sugar pack.

Directions for freezing raspberries whole, unsweetened:

1. Wash and drain berries and place into containers.
2. Leave ½ inch headspace in containers.
3. Label containers and place in freezer.

Did You Know? . . . .

Did you know that raspberry leaf herbs have been known to reduce the delivery time for pregnant dogs and cats, have made the labor less painful, and have enriched their milk?

Mixed Fruit Preserves

You will enjoy this. The blend of cherries, apricots, and raspberries is a flavor that is divine.

Ingredients:

- 3 c. sour cherries
- 3 c. fresh apricots
- 2 c. red raspberries
- 7 c. sugar

Directions:

1. Wash and seed cherries.
2. Drop the apricots into boiling water for a few seconds; remove skins and seeds. Cut into quarters.
3. Wash the raspberries.
4. Mix the fruit and sugar together and cook quickly, until fruits are clear and tender.
5. Seal in hot jars.

Drying Raspberries

1. For drying raspberries, choose berries that are ripe, but not overly ripe.
2. Because of their seediness, raspberries have a slow drying time. Their dried texture is hard and similar to that of dried peas.
3. Before drying, wash raspberries and remove any debris.
4. Place individual raspberries on tray and dry at lowest setting.
5. For optimum results in dried raspberries, purée the fruit first and then sieve to remove seeds. This allows you to make raspberry fruit leathers or strips, which can be placed in a blender or chopper to make fruit chips.
6. Dried raspberry chips make perfect toppings for both hot and cold breakfast cereals as well as mixed in with other dried fruit snacks.

Carrot and Raspberry Preserves

Carrots and raspberries in combination make interesting preserves and are loaded with vitamins.

Ingredients:

2 lb. carrots, peeled and sliced
2 lb. raspberries
4 c. sugar
pectin

Directions:

1. Place carrots in a pot with enough water to cover.
2. Bring to a boil, cover, and cook until tender.
3. Drain, reserving ½ cup liquid.
4. Purée carrots and liquid.
5. Transfer to large pot; add raspberries, pectin, and sugar, and stir until sugar is dissolved.
6. Bring to slow boil and simmer 20 minutes.
7. Remove from heat, skim foam, and follow standard directions for canning jams and jellies found in the front part of this section of the cookbook.

Raspberry Fruit Leather

This raspberry fruit leather is a favorite way of preserving. It is so easy to take on trips, put in lunches, and we enjoy these any time for snacks.

Ingredients:

4 c. raspberry purée
¼ c. honey

Directions:

1. Purée fruit in blender.

2. For sweetening, add 1 tablespoon honey for every 1 cup of purée if desired. Or use corn syrup which prevents the formation of crystals and is best for long storage. May also substitute sugar, lemon, or orange juice. May use saccharin based sweetener. Some prefer no sweetening at all, so use your own taste-preference.
3. If using oven, line cookie sheet with freezer wrap, extending it over the edges. A very light spray of nonstick cooking oil is recommended.
4. Spread purée ¼ inch thick around the edges, ⅛ inch thick in the center.
5. Dry in the sun or the oven at 140 degrees F., or in a dehydrator at 135 degrees F. following manufacturer's directions.
6. Ready when sheet is leathery and not sticky to the touch, usually 4 to 10 hours.
7. Pull from freezer paper while still warm and roll in plastic wrap, jelly-roll fashion. If desired, use scissors to cut the roll into serving pieces.
8. Cool and then pack in airtight containers.
9. Can be stored in dark place for 30 days at room temperature, months in the refrigerator; years in the freezer.
10. Raspberry fruit leather is great alone or in combination with cranberries, strawberries, blueberries, peaches or apples. You may be even more daring and blend three fruits.
11. Orange juice is a nice liquid addition. (Although it may be necessary when using fresh fruit, it's unlikely you'll need it with thawed, frozen raspberries.)
12. For extra zing, try adding a touch of cinnamon.

Did You Know? . . . .

Did you know that many female dogs and cats that have previously experienced problems during pregnancy have subsequently had normal, easy births with the aid of raspberry leaf herbs?

Raspberry Preserves

You will have a hard time keeping these raspberry preserves in stock. They are marvelous.

Ingredients:

3   lb. raspberries to yield 4 c. crushed berries
6½ c. sugar
3   oz. liquid fruit pectin

Directions:

1. Wash jars in hot soapy water and rinse.
2. Place on a rack in the sink and pour boiling water in and over each jar. Drain.
3. Keep hot by transferring clean jars to a cookie tray and placing in a 200 degrees F. oven.
4. Prepare lids by placing in saucepan of gently boiling water.
5. Prepare raspberries by removing any stems and caps.
6. Place in a sink of cold water and stir gently with your hands for 5 seconds.
7. Lift the raspberries into a colander to drain.
8. Place raspberries in food processor and process 15 seconds or until puréed.
9. Measure the raspberries into a 6 or 8 quart pot. Stir the sugar into the berries and mix well.
10. Bring to a full rolling boil over high heat, stirring constantly.
11. Add the fruit pectin and return to a full rolling boil. Boil hard for 1 minute, stirring constantly to prevent scorching.
12. If you prefer fewer seeds in the jam, you can skim off some that float to the top with the foam.
13. Remove from heat, and skim off and discard any foam using a metal spoon.
14. Ladle the jam into a liquid measuring cup and fill the jars immediately to within ⅛ inch of tops.
15. Wipe jar rims and threads with a clean, damp cloth.
16. Remove the jar lids from the boiling water using tongs and place on a paper towel. Wipe dry.

17. Place the lids on the jars and screw on tightly.
18. Place jars on a sturdy rack in a canner or large saucepan of boiling water to cover the jars by 1 to 2 inches.
19. Place the lid on the canner and bring water back to a boil.
20. Boil 10 minutes for 8-ounce jars.
21. Remove jars from the canner and let cool.
22. Check the seals after 1 hour to make sure the lids are curving down.
23. Warning: Jars and lids are very hot. Use clean, damp dishcloths or wear padded gloves to screw the lids on the jam-filled jars.
24. Raspberry preserves are delicious used as a cake filling, in tarts, spooned over plain yogurt, ice cream, or pancakes.

Yields: 7 eight-ounce jars.

Whipped Raspberry Jam

This raspberry jam is easy to make and delicious.

Ingredients:

6 c. raspberries
6 c. sugar

Directions:

1. Mash raspberries in saucepan and stir in sugar.
2. Cook slowly until sugar dissolves.
3. Bring to a boil; boil 3 minutes, stirring constantly.
4. Remove from heat and beat with wire whip or rotary beater for 6 minutes.
5. Pour into hot jars; seal.

Yields: 5 half-pints.

Cherry and Raspberry Preserves

The cherry and raspberry flavors combine in these preserves to make a wonderful topping on cereal, pancakes, waffles, muffins, and ice cream.

Ingredients:

2   lbs. Bing cherries (4 c.)
8   c. raspberries
3½ c. sugar
2   Tbs. fresh lemon juice

Directions:

1. Stem and pit the cherries; you should have 4 cups.
2. In large bowl, stir together the cherries, raspberries, and sugar.
3. Let stand at room temperature, stirring occasionally, for 2 hours.
4. Pour the fruit into a wide, shallow, nonreactive saucepan and stir in the lemon juice.
5. Cook over moderate heat, stirring occasionally, for 30 to 40 minutes until the mixture looks thickened and glazed.
6. Remove a tablespoon of the preserves to a small saucer and chill in the freezer for 5 minutes.
7. Run your finger through the mixture; if it wrinkles, it is ready to jar.
8. If it is not ready, continue cooking for 5 more minutes and repeat the test.
9. Sterilize four 8-ounce canning jars by washing and rinsing them in the dishwasher without detergent; keep them warm in a 250 degrees F oven.
10. Pour boiling water over jar lids to soften the rubber seals.
11. Ladle hot preserves to within ½ inch of the rims of the jars.
12. Wipe the rims and seal with the hot lids and metal bands.
13. Let cool to room temperature, then refrigerate for several weeks; or to store longer, process in a water bath.

Yields: 4 eight-ounce jars.

Raspberry Delights Cookbook
A Collection of Raspberry Recipes
Cookbook Delights Series – Book 14

Salads

Table of Contents

Baby Lettuce with Raspberry Vinaigrette

Try this light salad.

Ingredients:

2   Tbs. olive oil
4   Tbs. raspberry vinegar
2   Tbs. rich vegetable stock
1   tsp. oregano, chopped
1   tsp. chives, chopped
4   c. baby lettuce leaves
1   dash black pepper; to taste

Directions:

1. Stir together oil, vinegar, and lamb stock in small bowl.
2. Add herbs as close to serving time as possible.
3. Toss with baby lettuce and serve.

Double Raspberry Salad

This is easy to make and very tasty.

Ingredients:

1   pkg. raspberry gelatin
1   c. boiling water
1   pkg. frozen raspberries
1   can whole cranberries

Directions:

1. Dissolve gelatin in boiling water.
2. Mix in raspberries and cranberries.
3. Chill until firm.

Baby Spinach and Raspberry Salad

Your guests will love this spinach and raspberry salad.

Ingredients:

¼   c. sunflower seeds
¼   c. white balsamic vinegar
1   tsp. honey
1   Tbs. parsley
1   Tbs. tarragon
1   Tbs. chives
1   Tbs. basil
1   clove garlic, minced
½   sm. shallot, minced
¼   c. canola oil
8   c. baby spinach
1   c. fresh raspberries
2   oranges, peeled, membranes removed, segmented
1   red bell pepper, cored, seeded, cut into 2-inch strips
1   med. carrot, peeled, coarsely grated
     salt and pepper to taste

Directions:

1. Heat oven to 350 degrees F.
2. Toast sunflower seeds on a cookie sheet 4 minutes.
3. Whisk together vinegar, honey, herbs, garlic, and shallot.
4. Slowly whisk in oil.
5. Season with salt and pepper; set aside.
6. In a bowl, toss spinach with 2 tablespoons vinaigrette.
7. Season with salt and pepper.
8. Toss with sunflower seeds and remaining ingredients and serve.

Yields: 4 servings.

Endive Spears with Berry Bleu Cheese

This is a delicious salad.

Ingredients for salad:

2   fresh endive spears
⅓   c. crumbled bleu cheese
     pecans or walnuts, toasted, finely chopped
     fresh raspberries

Ingredients for raspberry and balsamic dressing:

¼   c. raspberry juice
¼   c. vinegar

Directions for salad:

1. Chop bottom off endive spears.
2. Arrange leaves open faced on serving platter.
3. Fill each spear with even amount of cheese and nuts.
4. Sprinkle raspberry and balsamic dressing over plate.
5. Garnish with fresh raspberries, serve and enjoy!

Directions for raspberry and balsamic dressing:

1. Mix the raspberry juice and vinegar together and enjoy!

Raspberry Ambrosia Salad

Many people have tried different versions of ambrosia. Try this version with colorful raspberries.

Ingredients:

2   c. raspberries
¼   c. sugar
1   can pineapple, chunked, strained
16   oz. sliced peaches, strained
11   oz. mandarin oranges, strained
1   c. coconut, shredded

½ c. walnuts, chopped
3 c. cream, whipped

Directions:

1. Combine pineapple, peaches, and mandarin oranges with whipped cream.
2. Stir in walnuts and coconut.
3. Toss raspberries with sugar and fold into salad.
4. Serve chilled.

Yields: 8 to 10 servings.

Creamy Raspberry Salad

This is a unique salad that really highlights the flavor of raspberries.

Ingredients:

1 lg. raspberry gelatin
2 c. boiling water
1 c. plain yogurt
1 c. sour cream
¼ tsp. ground ginger
2 tsp. lemon rind, grated
2 c. fresh raspberries
   mint sprigs, for garnish

Directions:

1. In large bowl mix gelatin and boiling water, stirring until gelatin dissolves.
2. Smoothly combine yogurt, sour cream, ginger, lemon rind.
3. Stir into gelatin mixture until blended.
4. Refrigerate, stirring occasionally, until mixture is slightly thickened and syrupy.
5. Fold raspberries into mixture.
6. Pour into a 6-cup mold.
7. Refrigerate until firm, 4 to 6 hours.
8. Unmold onto serving plate, garnish with mint.

Raspberry Cheese Salad

This makes a colorful, molded salad to serve as a side salad.

Ingredients:

- 1   c. boiling water
- 1   pkg. raspberry flavored gelatin (3 oz.)
- ½ c. cranberry juice cocktail
- ¼ c. cold water
- 1   pkg. cream cheese (3 oz), softened
- ½ c. nuts, finely chopped
- 2½ c. raspberries
- 1   Tbs. sugar

Directions:

1. Pour boiling water on gelatin; stir until gelatin is dissolved.
2. Stir in cranberry juice and cold water.
3. Refrigerate until slightly thickened.
4. Shape cream cheese into 18 balls; roll in nuts.
5. Mix raspberries and sugar.
6. Pour ⅓ cup thickened gelatin into 6-cup ring mold.
7. Arrange cheese balls evenly in gelatin mold.
8. Spoon raspberries over cheese balls.
9. Carefully pour remaining gelatin over raspberries.
10. Refrigerate until firm; unmold.

Yields: 6 servings.

Summertime Fruit Salad

This is a very refreshing and colorful salad.

Ingredients:

- ½ c. orange juice
- ¼ c. honey
- 1   pt. basket strawberries, stemmed, halved

1 half-pt. basket raspberries
1 half-pt. basket blueberries
2 oranges, peeled and cut into sections
1 c. cantaloupe or honeydew melon balls
3 Tbs. fresh mint leaves

Directions:

1. In medium bowl whisk juice and honey, add remaining ingredients.
2. Toss gently to combine, chill for 1 hour.
3. Spoon salad into 4 individual bowls, dividing equally.

Raspberry Tossed Salad

This raspberry salad looks as festive as it sounds and is always a favorite.

Ingredients:

9 c. mixed salad greens, torn
3 c. raspberries, unsweetened fresh or frozen
2 Tbs. olive oil
2 Tbs. cider vinegar
4 tsp. sugar
⅛ tsp. salt
  dash of pepper

Directions:

1. In large salad bowl, gently combine the salad greens and 2¾ cups raspberries.
2. Mash the remaining berries and strain, reserving juice and discarding seeds.
3. In a bowl, whisk the raspberry juice, oil, vinegar, sugar, salt, and pepper.
4. Drizzle over salad, gently toss to coat.

Yields: 12 servings.

Raspberry and Chicken Salad

This is a colorful chicken salad that is great served over your favorite greens.

Ingredients:

2   c. fresh or frozen raspberries, divided (reserve ½ c. for garnish.
¼   c. sour cream
½   c. mayonnaise
1   tsp. salt
2   c. cooked chicken breasts, cubed
½   c. green onion, scallions, sliced
¾   c. celery, diagonally sliced
½   c. sweet red bell pepper, diced
    salad greens of your choice

Directions:

1. Reserve a few raspberries for garnish.
2. In medium bowl, combine sour cream, mayonnaise, salt.
3. Add remaining raspberries, the chicken, green onions, and bell pepper; mix gently.
4. Cover and refrigerate to blend flavors, at least 30 minutes.
5. Serve over endive or other greens garnished with reserved raspberries and lemon slices, if desired.

Yields: 4 servings.

Raspberry Potato Salad

Raspberries give this potato salad a refreshing flavor.

Ingredients:

¼   c. white wine vinegar
1   Tbs. olive oil
½   tsp. sugar
½   tsp. salt
½   tsp. dried basil, crushed

1/8 tsp. black pepper

4 lg. red potatoes, cooked and sliced

1 c. fresh raspberries

1/2 c. cucumber, diced

1/2 c. carrot, shredded

2 Tbs. scallions, chopped

2 Tbs. parsley

Directions:

1. Blend well the vinegar, oil, sugar, salt, basil, and pepper.
2. In large bowl, combine dressing with potatoes; mix well.
3. Stir in the raspberries, carrot, and cucumbers.
4. Sprinkle with chopped scallions and parsley.

Raspberry Spinach Salad

This is a delicious raspberry and spinach salad.

Ingredients:

2 Tbs. raspberry vinegar

3 Tbs. raspberry jam

1 Tbs. brown sugar

1/3 c. olive oil

8 c. spinach, rinsed, stemmed and torn into pieces

3/4 c. macadamia nuts, coarsely chopped /or/ toasted almond slices

1 1/4 c. fresh raspberries

1/4 c. celery hearts, finely chopped

Directions:

1. Combine vinegar and jam in blender or small bowl.
2. Add sugar and mix well.
3. Add oil in thin stream, blending well.
4. Toss spinach with 1/2 the nuts, 1/2 the raspberries, 1/2 the celery, and the dressing.
5. Top with nuts, raspberries, and celery.
6. Serve immediately

Yields: 2 servings.

Red Raspberry Salad

This salad goes beyond ordinary. It goes the extra mile and is so marvelous.

Ingredients:

2   pkg. raspberry gelatin
2   c. boiling water
2¼ c. frozen red raspberries
1½ c applesauce
¾   c. plain yogurt
⅓   c. dry milk powder
1   Tbs. sugar
½   c. whipped cream
¼   tsp. vanilla extract
1   c. miniature marshmallows

Directions:

1. Combine dry gelatin with boiling water. Mix well to dissolve gelatin. Cool 5 minutes.
2. Blend in raspberries and applesauce.
3. Pour into 9 x 13-inch dish. Refrigerate until set, about 4 hours.
4. Combine yogurt and dry milk powder in small bowl.
5. Blend in sugar, whipped cream, and vanilla.
6. Fold in marshmallows.
7. Spread mixture evenly on top of set gelatin mixture.
8. Refrigerate until ready to serve.

Yields: 8 servings.

Raspberry Cream Cheese Salad

This is a quick and easy salad to make and will become one of your favorites too.

Ingredients:

1 pkg. raspberry gelatin (3 oz.)

270

½   c. hot water
1   pkg. cream cheese (8 oz.)
¼   c. mayonnaise
1   sm. can pineapple, crushed
1   banana, diced
½   c. pecans, chopped
1   c. whipped cream, sweetened

Directions:

1. Dissolve gelatin in hot water.
2. Cream cheese with mayonnaise.
3. Stir into gelatin along with remaining ingredients.
4. Pour into square pan and chill.

Tangy Raspberry Salad

This is a very refreshing salad.

Ingredients:

2   Tbs. olive oil
⅓   c. water
¾   c. raspberry vinegar
1   Tbs. orange juice
¾   tsp. garlic, finely minced
8   c. mixed salad greens (12 oz.), torn, loosely packed
1½   c. raspberries, fresh or frozen (no sugar added)
1   Tbs. green onion with top, chopped
6   eggs, hard-cooked, quartered
     salt and pepper to taste

Directions:

1. In jar with tight-fitting lid, shake together oil, water, vinegar, orange juice, garlic, and seasonings.
2. Set aside while preparing salad or refrigerate.
3. Place salad greens in large bowl.
4. Add raspberries, onions, and eggs.
5. Shake dressing again; pour over salad and gently toss until ingredients are evenly coated with dressing.

Easy Fruit Medley

The raspberries brighten up this fruit medley, not with just color, but with flavor.

Ingredients:

¾ c. sugar
¼ c. light corn syrup
2 c. water
2 Tbs. orange juice concentrate
2 Tbs. lemonade concentrate
¼ watermelon
½ cantaloupe
½ honeydew melon
¾ lb. red and green grapes, whole
¾ lb. peaches, sliced
2 c. whole frozen blackberries
2 c. whole frozen raspberries

Directions:

1. Heat sugar, corn syrup, and water, just until sugar is dissolved.
2. Remove from heat and add orange and lemonade juice concentrates.
3. Set aside to cool.
4. Slice and seed all melons.
5. Cut into small bite-sized pieces, or use a melon baller.
6. Add whole grapes, sliced peaches.
7. Add frozen berries last, pouring flavored syrup over all.
8. Freeze in 1 quart freezer bags until ready to use.
9. Do not freeze in larger quantities, as does not thaw properly.
10. To serve, remove from freezer about 30 minutes before serving time.
11. Fruit should be slushy when served.

Yields: 10 to 12 servings.

Raspberry Delights Cookbook
A Collection of Raspberry Recipes
Cookbook Delights Series – Book 14

Side Dishes

Table of Contents

Berry Fruit Coleslaw

This recipe blends shredded cabbage with mandarin oranges, pineapples, and four kinds of juicy berries. It is delicious.

Ingredients:

1	c. mayonnaise
½	c. sugar
1	Tbs. white vinegar
1	Tbs. white horseradish (Seminole)
¼	tsp. celery seed
1	lb. shredded cabbage
½	pt. raspberries
½	pt. blueberries
½	pt. blackberries
1	pineapple, cored and cut
1	qt. strawberries
1	can mandarin oranges (15 oz.)

Directions:

1. Blend first 5 ingredients thoroughly and chill.
2. Wash berries and pat dry.
3. In bowl combine shredded cabbage, berries, pineapple, and oranges. Add coleslaw dressing. Gently stir until fruit is coated with dressing.

Yields: 6 to 8 servings.

Cran-Raspberry Gelatin

This is a delicious side dish combination of tart and sweet berries.

Ingredients:

1	pkg. frozen raspberries (10 oz.), thawed, drained, juice reserved
1	c. water
12	oz. cranberries
½	c. sugar
2	pkg. raspberry flavored gelatin (3 oz. ea.)

Directions:

1. In a saucepan, combine the reserved raspberry juice, water, cranberries, and sugar.
2. Bring to a boil over medium heat, stirring frequently, until the skins of the cranberries burst.
3. Remove from heat and add gelatin; stir until dissolved.
4. Gently fold in raspberries and pour into a square pan.
5. Refrigerate until chilled.
6. To serve, cut into 1-inch squares, and serve as individual side dishes.

Yields: 10 to 12 servings.

Sugar Snap Peas and Berries

This is a delicious, summer side dish made with your favorite berries.

Ingredients:

½   lb. sugar snap peas, trimmed
1   c. raspberries, fresh or frozen
2   Tbs. raspberry vinegar
2   Tbs. olive oil
1   pinch sugar
1   c. blueberries, fresh or frozen
2   c. mixed salad greens, torn
    salt and pepper to taste

Directions:

1. Bring pot of water to a boil and then place snap peas in pot.
2. Cook 1 to 2 minutes.
3. Drain, rinse under cold water, and set aside.
4. Place about ½ cup raspberries in a strainer over a bowl, and crush with a wooden spoon; discard pulp.
5. Mix vinegar, olive oil, sugar, salt, and pepper with the strained raspberry juice.
6. In a large bowl, gently toss the dressing with the snap peas, remaining raspberries, and blueberries.
7. Cover and chill at least 30 minutes in the refrigerator.
8. Toss with greens just before serving in side dishes.

Yields: 6 servings.

Chunky Raspberry Apple Sauce

Our family loves fresh homemade apple sauce. The addition of raspberries makes a nice variation.

Ingredients:

4	apples, peeled, cored, quartered
¾	c. raspberry juice
¼	tsp. cinnamon
6	Tbs. raspberry preserves

Directions:

1. In medium saucepan combine apples, raspberry juice, and cinnamon.
2. Bring to a boil; reduce heat, cover, and simmer 20 minutes, stirring occasionally, until apples are tender.
3. Melt preserves in a small saucepan or microwave in small bowl.
4. Strain to remove seeds. Set aside.
5. With electric mixer, beat apple mixture lightly to form a chunky sauce.
6. Stir in preserves.
7. Serve warm, or cover and refrigerate until serving time.

Yields: 3½ cups.

Honey Nut Raspberry Squash

This is a delicious side dish for you and your guests to enjoy.

Ingredients:

2	acorn squash (about 6 oz. ea.)
½	c. raspberries
¼	c. honey
2	Tbs. butter, melted

2   Tbs. nuts, chopped
2   Tbs. raisins, chopped
2   tsp. Worcestershire Sauce

Directions:

1. Cut acorn squash in half lengthwise; do not remove seeds.
2. Place cut side up in baking pan.
3. Bake at 400 degrees F. for 30 to 45 minutes until soft.
4. Remove seeds and fibers.
5. Combine honey, butter, nuts, raisins, and Worcestershire sauce.
6. Mix in raspberries; spoon into squash.
7. Bake 10 to 15 minutes more until lightly glazed.
8. Divide into 4 side dishes and serve warm.

Yields: 4 servings.

Raspberry Banana Kiwi Cocktail

Raspberries, bananas, strawberries, kiwis, and peaches make a great combination in this simple, yet great tasting fruit cocktail.

Ingredients:

1   c. raspberries
12 med. to lg. strawberries
2   med. kiwis
2   med. bananas
1½ peaches
    raspberry or strawberry soda
    lemon juice

Directions:

1. Mix all ingredients together.
2. Place in 4 individual side bowls.

Yields: 4 servings.

Raspberry Fondue

This is a wonderful fondue side dish can be served warm or cold to your guests.

Ingredients:

1   pkg. frozen raspberries (10 oz.), sweetened
1   c. apple butter
1   Tbs. red-hot candies
2   tsp. cornstarch
     assorted fresh fruit

Directions:

1. Place raspberries in a bowl, set aside to thaw.
2. Strain raspberries, reserving 1 tablespoon juice; discard seeds.
3. In small saucepan, combine strained berries, apple butter, and red-hots.
4. Cook over medium heat until candies are dissolved, stirring occasionally.
5. In a small bowl, combine cornstarch and reserved juice and mix until smooth.
6. Stir into raspberry mixture and bring to a boil; cook and stir over medium heat for 1 to 2 minutes until thickened.
7. Transfer to side dishes or mini fondue pots.
8. Note: this may be served warm or cold.

Yields: 1 cup.

Kahlua Raspberry Sides

These are absolutely wonderful.

Ingredients:

3   c. raspberries
1   pt. kahlua
¼   c. pecans, chopped, for garnish

Directions:

1. Place raspberries in a jar; cover with kahlua.
2. Set aside in refrigerate until ready to serve.
3. Serve raspberries in individual serving dishes.
4. Garnish with chopped pecans.

Raspberry Fresh Fruit Cocktail

Serve this fruit cocktail as a special chilled side dish or as a sweet treat.

Ingredients for fruit:

2   c. apple juice
1   Tbs. lemon juice
½   tsp. lemon or orange zest
2   cinnamon sticks (3 in.)
2   Red Delicious apples, cored, chopped
1½ c. fresh raspberries
1   orange, peeled, sectioned
½   c. seedless grapes

Ingredients for sauce:

1   c. sour cream
¼   c. coconut, grated
¼   c. apricot preserves
2   Tbs. dry white wine
½   c. macadamia nuts, chopped

Directions:

1. In medium saucepan, combine apple juice, lemon juice, orange or lemon zest, and cinnamon sticks.
2. Heat to a boil, then simmer uncovered 10 minutes.
3. Cool to room temperature.
4. In large serving bowl combine apples, pineapple, orange, raspberries, and grapes.
5. Remove cinnamon sticks; pour apple juice mix over fruit.
6. Combine sauce and chill.

Raspberry Ice

Make this one a day ahead of time. It is so refreshing on a hot summer day.

Ingredients:

4   c. raspberries
¾   c. sugar
1   Tbs. lemon juice
½   c. water

Directions:

1. In food processor, process raspberries until puréed.
2. Force through sieve and discard seeds.
3. Return purée to processor and blend in sugar, lemon juice, and water.
4. Place mixture in freezer-safe container and freeze.
5. To serve, break up ice and put into processor; process until slush is velvety smooth.
6. Spoon into individual serving containers, elegant glasses, or into orange or lemon shells.
7. Serve at once.

Yields: 2¾ cups.

Raspberry Parfait

My oldest daughter is a vegetarian. She frequently enjoys fruit parfaits, and they are easy to prepare.

Ingredients:

½   c. raspberries, fresh or frozen
1   c. yogurt
½   c. muesli, any variety without raisins
    whipped cream for garnish

Directions:

1. Use pretty glass parfait or dessert cups.
2. In each cup layer spoonful of muesli. then 2 spoonfuls yogurt, then top with whipped cream and raspberries.
3. Serve immediately before muesli softens.

Raspberry Sweet Potatoes

Raspberries add a wonderful new flavor to sweet potatoes.

Ingredients:

8   med. sweet potatoes
1   tsp. salt
¼   c. brown sugar, firmly packed
¼   c. butter, softened
1   pkg. frozen raspberries (10 oz.), thawed, undrained

Directions:

1. Cook sweet potatoes in boiling salted water 20 to 25 minutes or until tender.
2. Drain and let cool to touch.
3. Peel and cut in half lengthwise.
4. Arrange sweet potatoes in lightly greased 15 x 9 x 2 casserole, cut side up.
5. Combine brown sugar and butter in small bowl, mixing well.
6. Spread brown sugar mixture over cut surface of sweet potatoes.
7. Top with raspberries and juice.
8. Bake uncovered at 350 degrees F. for 25 minutes, spooning raspberries and juice over potatoes occasionally.

Yields: 8 to 10 servings.

Stuffed Bell Peppers

Stuffed bell peppers are delicious, but adding raspberry vinegar to the mix is so refreshing.

Ingredients:

4   c. cooked rice
6   tsp. olive oil
3   tsp. balsamic vinegar
3   tsp. raspberry vinegar
3   cloves garlic, minced
1   onion, chopped
1   tsp. black pepper
4   green, red, or yellow bell peppers, tops cut off, pulp removed
½   tsp. all-purpose seasoning
½   c. grated carrot
½   c. chopped celery
½   c. diced pimentos
1   c. shredded baby Swiss

Directions:

1. Combine rice with all ingredients except cheese and peppers.
2. Mix well.
3. Fill each pepper with the rice mixture.
4. Sprinkle shredded baby Swiss on top of each bell pepper.
5. Bake 15 to 20 minutes at 350 degrees F. or until hot and cheese is melted and bubbly.

Yield: 4 servings.

Peanut Croquettes with Raspberry Salsa

You probably have never tasted anything like these. Raspberry salsa is delightful combined with potatoes and peanuts.

Ingredients for croquettes:

½   pt. roasted peanuts, shelled
1   pt. mashed potatoes

1 tsp. onion juice
1 Tbs. parsley
1 egg, separated
1 tsp. salt
¼ tsp. black pepper
1 Tbs. water
1 c. bread crumbs

Ingredients for raspberry salsa:

1 Tbs. olive oil
1 sm. onion, chopped
16 oz. frozen raspberries, unsweetened
¾ c. packed brown sugar
¼ tsp. salt
¼ tsp. chili powder
1 can crushed pineapple (8 oz.), drained well
1 can green chilies (4 oz.), chopped, drained
5 sprigs cilantro, chopped
¼ tsp. grated lemon rind

Directions for croquettes:

1. Put nuts through meat grinder; add to the mashed potatoes.
2. Add the onion juice, parsley, salt, pepper, and egg yolk.
3. Mix thoroughly and form into balls the size of walnuts.
4. Beat the egg white with 1 tablespoon water.
5. Roll balls in the beaten egg white mixture, and then in bread crumbs, and fry in deep shortening.
6. Serve with raspberry salsa found in this recipe section.

Directions for raspberry salsa:

1. In 3-quart saucepan, cook onions in oil over medium heat until tender.
2. Stir in berries, brown sugar, salt, chili powder, and 2 tablespoons water; cook until berries are mushy.
3. Remove from heat.
4. Remove from heat and stir in pineapple and chilies.
5. Let cool and then refrigerate, covered.
6. Before serving, mix in cilantro and lemon rind.
7. Serve with croquettes or as a side dish with poultry or pork.

Multi-Grain Raspberry Pilaf

We have wild rice and the addition of raspberries makes this very tasty and colorful.

Ingredients:

⅔ c. wild rice
½ c. wheat berries
1 c. onion, chopped
3 cloves garlic, finely chopped
2 Tbs. butter
1 Tbs. olive oil
2½ c. chicken broth
2½ tsp dry rubbed sage
¼ tsp. ground pepper
⅓ c. brown rice
1½ c. raspberries
¾ c. almonds, slivered

Directions:

1. Rinse wild rice and wheat berries under cold running water.
2. Drain well.
3. In medium saucepan, cook onion and garlic in olive oil over medium heat for 10 minutes until tender.
4. Stir in drained wild rice and wheat berries, chicken broth, sage, and pepper.
5. Bring to a boil, reduce heat, cover, and simmer 30 minutes.
6. Stir brown rice into wild rice mixture and return to a boil.
7. Reduce heat and simmer covered for 45 minutes until grains are tender.
8. Stir raspberries and slivered almonds into hot rice mixture just before serving.

Did You Know? . . . .

Did you know that scientific reports state the efficacy of Ellagic Acid (Red raspberry extract) as a potential dietary supplement in the prevention and treatment of cancer?

Raspberry Delights Cookbook
A Collection of Raspberry Recipes
Cookbook Delights Series – Book 14

Soups

Table of Contents

Burgundy Raspberry Soup

This is a richly flavored burgundy raspberry soup.

Ingredients:

20 oz. frozen raspberries, thawed
2   c. Burgundy
2½ c. water
1   cinnamon stick (3-in.)
¼   Tbs. cornstarch
    whipping cream

Directions:

1. Combine first 5 ingredients in deep, ceramic, heatproof casserole or stainless steel saucepan. (Mixture will discolor aluminum.)
2. Bring mixture to a boil, reduce heat, and simmer 15 minutes.
3. Press raspberry mixture through a sieve, and return to casserole or saucepan; discard seeds.
4. Combine cornstarch and ¼ cup raspberry liquid; stir well.
5. Bring remaining liquid to a boil.
6. Reduce heat to low and stir in cornstarch mixture.
7. Cook, stirring constantly, until slightly thickened.
8. Chill 6 to 8 hours.
9. Drizzle whipping cream in soup and swirl in with a knife.

Yields: 6 servings.

Chilled Beet and Raspberry Soup

This is a soup you won't soon forget; it really is very good,

Ingredients:

2   c. pickled beets, sliced
1½ c. frozen raspberries

1 c. potato, cooked
2 c. water
2 tsp. pepper
1 tsp. orange zest
1 tsp. salt

Directions:

1. Purée all ingredients together.
2. Chill and serve.

Yields: 6 servings.

Mango and Raspberry Soup

Our family loves mangos and raspberries, and this is delicious, refreshing, and easy.

Ingredients:

1   pkg. frozen mango
16 oz. frozen raspberries
4   oz. brown sugar
4   Tbs. sugar
    water
    mint

Directions:

1. In a saucepan, mix and heat 4 tablespoons sugar with ½ cup plus ⅛ cup water. Leave to cool.
2. Add mango and brown sugar.
3. Pour into soup bowls or a large tureen; add raspberries and a few mint leaves.
4. Chill before serving.

Did You Know? . . . .

Did you know if your bread dough rises too long, it will become too light and will fall while baking in the oven?

Chilled Cantaloupe Raspberry Soup

Your guests will enjoy this chilled cantaloupe and raspberry soup.

Ingredients:

1   lg. ripe cantaloupe, peeled, scooped, and chopped
1½ c. sugar (varies with sweetness of the melon)
1½ pt. raspberries, puréed, strained, pips removed
¾   c. plain yogurt
¾   c. sour cream
¾   c. dry white wine
4   tsp. fresh mint leaves, washed, for garnish
½   pt. fresh raspberries, for garnish

Directions:

1. Purée the cantaloupe and sugar in small batches in food processor until smooth and sugar dissolves.
2. Transfer to bowl; whisk in yogurt, sour cream, raspberry purée, and wine.
3. Chill for 2 hours minimum, covered in the refrigerator.
4. Chill serving bowls.
5. Garnish with additional yogurt, or sour cream, whole fresh mint leaves, and fresh raspberries.

Yields: 1 quart.

Chilled Watermelon Raspberry Soup

Raspberry soup with watermelon is perfect for a hot summer day.

Ingredients:

2   c. raspberries
3   Tbs. brown sugar

2   limes, juice freshly squeezed
    watermelon, cubed
    mint, cut into ribbons as needed

Directions:

1. In bowl, gently combine raspberries and brown sugar.
2. Chill in the refrigerator for ½ hour.
3. In blender, add the watermelon and lime juice.
4. Purée until smooth.
5. Next add the raspberries and blend until smooth.
6. Place in refrigerator for 1 hour.
7. To serve, ladle into a soup bowl and garnish with a few mint ribbons.
8. Note: To add a little punch to the soup, add a little Vodka to the berries while they are chilling.

Chilled Red Raspberry Soup

This wonderful flavor is certainly not a "low calorie" version of raspberry soup. The whole family will love this deeper, more full-bodied richness, yet it is so quick to make.

Ingredients:

⅓   c. lemon juice
⅓   c. powdered sugar
⅓   c. honey
⅓   c. brown sugar, packed
1   qt. red raspberries
1   pt. heavy cream

Directions:

1. Blend until smooth.
2. Transfer to medium bowl and fold in 1 pint heavy cream, whipped stiff.

Cranberry and Raspberry Soup

Cranberries add color and flavor to this cold soup.

Ingredients:

    4   c. cranberries
    4   c. apple juice
    2   c. raspberries
    ¼   c. sugar
    2   Tbs. lemon juice
    ½   tsp. cinnamon
    2   c. cream
    2   Tbs. cornstarch

Directions:

1. Combine all ingredients.
2. Chill and serve.

Yields: 8 servings.

Cool Raspberry Soup

This raspberry soup is rich with flavor.

Ingredients:

    20 oz. raspberries, fresh or thawed frozen
    1¼ c. water
    ¼   c. white wine
    1   c. cran-raspberry juice
    ½   c. sugar
    1½ tsp. cinnamon, ground
    3   cloves, whole
    1   Tbs. lemon juice
    8   oz. yogurt, raspberry-flavored
    ½   c. sour cream

Directions:

1. In blender, purée raspberries, water, and wine.
2. Transfer to large saucepan; add cran-raspberry juice, sugar, cinnamon, and cloves.
3. Bring just to a boil over medium heat; then remove from heat, strain, and allow to cool.
4. Whisk in lemon juice and yogurt; refrigerate.
5. Serve in small bowls, topped with dollop of sour cream.

Yields: 4 to 6 servings.

Melon-Berry Swirl

You will enjoy this blend of tastes.

Ingredients:

2   lb. honeydew or canary melon meat (4 lb. melon = 3 lb. fruit)
1   tsp. frozen apple juice concentrate
¼   tsp. cinnamon, ground
⅛   tsp cloves. ground
2   tsp. lemon juice
3   Tbs. mint, fresh, minced
2   c. raspberries
2   tsp. lemon juice
⅓   c. yogurt
    fresh mint leaves for garnish

Directions:

1. Purée the first 6 ingredients; chill.
2. Purée raspberries, lemon juice, and yogurt; chill.
3. Just prior to serving, pour the melon mixture into soup bowls, filling them no more than ⅔ of the way.
4. Pour berry purée into the center of the soup bowls.
5. Create a swirling pattern by mixing the two purées using one circular motion with a spoon.
6. Garnish with fresh mint leaves.

Iced Raspberry Soup

This is a wonderful summer soup with raspberries mixing with many other flavors to make a really unique blend.

Ingredients:

2   c. fresh raspberries /or/ 2 boxes frozen raspberries
1   c. orange juice
½   c. white grape juice /or/ weak China tea
2   Tbs. red currant jelly
2   tsp. arrowroot or cornstarch
½   c. heavy cream, whipped
1   Tbs. grated orange rind
    honey to taste

Directions:

1. Combine raspberries and orange juice in blender and purée.
2. Rub through fine strainer and transfer to medium saucepan.
3. Add grape juice or tea.
4. Mix currant jelly with arrowroot or cornstarch and add to soup mixture.
5. Stir over low heat until mixture boils.
6. Add honey to taste.
7. Reduce heat to very low and simmer 10 minutes.
8. Chill thoroughly.
9. Serve in individual bowls embedded in crushed ice.
10. Garnish with float of whipped cream sprinkled with orange rind.

Yields: 4 servings.

Did You Know? . . . .

Did you know that medical studies in Europe further show that: ellagic acid reduces the occurrence of birth defects, promotes wound healing, reduces and reverses chemically induced liver fibrosis, and is helpful in the fight against heart disease?

Strawberry Raspberry Soup

This is a rich soup that would be great served in a cup at a luncheon.

Ingredients:

1   qt. fresh strawberries
3   c. fresh raspberries /or/ 12 oz. frozen raspberries, drained
½   c. apple juice, plus ⅔ c. apple juice
¼   c. sugar
2   Tbs. cornstarch
1   c. water
1   Tbs. lemon juice
½   c. nonfat yogurt
1   tsp. powdered sugar
½   tsp. vanilla extract

Directions:

1. Remove stems and cut strawberries in half.
2. Place strawberries, raspberries, ½ cup apple juice, and sugar in saucepan.
3. Let stand 15 minutes.
4. Heat over low heat until boiling.
5. Mix together the cornstarch and water, then stir into fruit mixture.
6. Boil over low heat, stirring constantly, until fruit softens and soup is clear and thickened.
7. Remove from heat and stir in lemon juice. Chill.
8. Before serving, add ⅔ cup apple juice to make soup consistency. Add more juice if needed.
9. In a small bowl combine yogurt, powdered sugar, and vanilla.
10. Serve soup in small bowls and top with a tablespoon of the yogurt mixture.

Yields: 12 servings.

Sweet Raspberry Peach Soup

This makes a delicious combination of peaches and raspberries.

Ingredients:

20 oz. frozen peaches, sliced (let thaw slightly)
⅓   c. sugar
1½ c. water
½   tsp. ground cinnamon
¼   tsp. ground nutmeg
1   Tbs. cornstarch dissolved in 3 Tbs. water
¾   c. fruity white wine
2   ripe peaches
1   c. raspberries, for garnish
    sour cream, for garnish

Directions:

1. In sauce pan, combine sugar, water, cinnamon, and nutmeg.
2. Bring to a boil and boil for 1 minute.
3. Add the cornstarch and stir until mixture thickens and boils.
4. Stir in wine and transfer mixture to a bowl.
5. Purée frozen peaches in food processor and add to a bowl.
6. Cut the fresh peaches into thin slices and add to the soup.
7. Cover and refrigerate.
8. When ready to serve, garnish soup with a dab of sour cream or whipped cream and several raspberries.

Yields: 6 servings.

Did You Know? . . . .

Did you know that scientific reports state the efficacy of Ellagic Acid (Red raspberry extract), as a potential dietary supplement in the prevention and treatment of cancer? First true studies began in early 1990. However, folklore remedies involving phytochemical extracts have been around for centuries.

Raspberry Delights Cookbook
A Collection of Raspberry Recipes
Cookbook Delights Series – Book 14

Wines and Spirits

Table of Contents

About Cooking with Alcohol

Some recipes in this cookbook contain, among other ingredients, liquors. It is for the purpose of obtaining desired flavor and achieving culinary appreciation and not to be abused in any way. In cooking and baking, alcohol evaporates and only the flavor may be enjoyed. When mixed in cold, however, such as in desserts, caution must be exercised. These recipes are intended for people who may consume small amounts of alcohol in a responsible and safe manner.

I live in Washington State and we are proud of our wine production. Washington State is rapidly gaining prestige as a premier wine producer. Do enjoy the art of wine tasting and enjoy the completeness and uniqueness of each wine. It is an art to enjoy and savor in moderation.

If consumption of even small amounts of alcoholic ingredients presents a problem, in whatever form, please substitute coffee flavor syrups, found in coffee sections of supermarkets. For example, instead of Southern Comfort liqueur, substitute with Irish Cream or Amaretto Syrup.

Karen Jean Matsko Hood

Raspberry Daiquiri

This makes a refreshing version of the daiquiri drink.

Ingredients:

1¼ oz. white rum
¾ c. raspberries
1 Tbs. simple syrup (½ water, ½ sugar)
1½ c. ice
¼ c. orange juice

Directions:

1. Blend all ingredients in blender until smooth.
2. Serve in tall glass and garnish with an orange slice and raspberry if desired.

Raspberry Fuzzy Navel

Try this fuzzy navel with a raspberry flavor.

Ingredients:

1½ oz. peach schnapps
   orange juice to taste
   raspberry juice to taste

Directions:

1. Pour peach schnapps into ice-filled Collins glass.
2. Fill with raspberry juice and orange juice; stir.
3. Adjust the amount of juices to taste.

Raspberry Brandy

This adds that wonderful raspberry flavor to brandy. Enjoy.

Ingredients:

2   pt. fresh raspberries
1   lb. sugar
   brandy

Directions:

1. Place fine, dry fruit into a stone jar.
2. Place the jar into a kettle of water.
3. Place on a hot hearth until the juice runs.
4. Strain.
5. To every pint add ½ pound of sugar, boil, and skim.
6. When cold, mix equal quantities of juice and brandy.
7. Shake well and bottle.
8. Some prefer to add more brandy.

Favorite Raspberry Sauce

This is a very good raspberry drink.

Ingredients:

1   pkg. frozen raspberries (12 oz. or 2½ c.)
4   Tbs. Chambord or black raspberry liqueur
⅓   c. sugar

Directions:

1. Thaw berries, then purée in food processor or blender.
2. Strain to remove seeds.
3. Stir in liqueur and sugar.
4. Refrigerate until ready to serve.
5. Best if made 24 hours ahead.

Raspberry Peach Sangria

This Sangria is full of flavor and makes a festive party addition.

Ingredients:

3   c. burgundy wine
½   c. orange juice
⅓   c lemon juice
⅓   c. sugar
3   Tbs. brandy
1   c. raspberries, fresh or frozen
2   peaches, quartered and sliced
12 oz. club soda /or/ sparkling mineral water
    ice

Directions:

1. In punch bowl or 2½ quart pitcher, stir together first 5 ingredients.

2. When sugar is dissolved, add berries and refrigerate 2 to 3 hours to allow flavors to mingle.
3. About 1 hour before serving, add peaches.
4. Add soda/mineral water to sangria just before serving.
5. Pour into glasses filled with ice.
6. Garnish with berries and fruit slices.

Yields: 4 to 6 servings.

Smooth Operator

This is a wonderful blend of raspberries, kahlua, and rich cream.

Ingredients for raspberry purée:

2   c. raspberries, fresh or frozen (thawed)

Ingredients for drink:

3   oz. raspberry purée
1   oz. kahlua or coffee liqueur
4   oz. vanilla ice cream (1 scoop)
1   oz. half and half cream
4   oz. ice

Directions for raspberry purée:

1. Crush 2 cups fresh or thawed berries.
2. Strain through a fine sieve.
3. Set aside.

Directions for drink:

1. Blend 3 ounces purée with all remaining ingredients.
2. Pour into a glass and serve.

Yields: 1 serving.

Raspberry Cooler

The schnapps adds flavor to this raspberry cooler.

Ingredients for raspberry purée:

2   c. raspberries, fresh or frozen (thawed)

Ingredients for drink:

2   oz. raspberry purée
1   oz. raspberry schnapps
½   oz. vodka
4   oz. ice
    splash of club soda

Directions for raspberry purée:

1. Crush 2 cups fresh or thawed berries.
2. Strain through a fine sieve.

Directions for drink:

1. Blend 2 ounces raspberry purée with all remaining ingredients.
2. Pour into glass and serve.

Yields: 1 serving.

Raspberry Eggnog

My family enjoys eggnog, and this makes a colorful drink to enjoy over the holidays or year round.

Ingredients:

2   c. raspberries
2   c. water

4   eggs
⅔   c. sugar or honey
1   Tbs. vanilla extract
1   tsp. nutmeg
2   c. heavy cream (1 pt.)
1   c. brandy or dark rum (optional)

Directions:

1. In a saucepan, mix raspberries and water.
2. Boil gently for 15 minutes.
3. Press mixture through a fine strainer.
4. Pour into a bowl and chill.
5. Beat eggs into raspberry purée until smooth.
6. Beat in sugar, vanilla, and nutmeg.
7. Gradually beat in heavy cream and brandy.
8. Chill until ready to serve.
9. Stir again before serving in punch cups.

Yields: 6 servings.

Raspberry Wine Punch

This is an easy-to-make wine punch.

Ingredients:

½   c. Raspberry Claret
1   liter ginger ale
1   bottle sauterne
1   bottle dry champagne

Directions:

1. Chill all ingredients well.
2. Mix and serve with ice ring and mint leaves.

Red Cactus

This will add a touch of Southwest to your festive gathering.

Ingredients:

1¼ c. raspberry-cranberry juice frozen concentrate
3   c. raspberries, whole, frozen
¾   c. limeade frozen concentrate
½   c. triple sec orange liqueur
¾   c. tequila, gold
4   c. crushed ice
1   lime, sliced
    sugar

Directions:

1. Combine all but last two ingredients in blender and blend until slushy, adding more ice if necessary.
2. To prepare glasses, moisten rims with lime slice and dip in plate of sugar.
3. Fill glasses and garnish with lime wheel slices.
4. Note: Look for no-alcohol version of this recipe in beverages section of this cookbook.

Yields: 4 to 6 servings.

Frozen Raspberry Margarita

This is one of the most refreshing drinks you can enjoy on a hot summer night.

Ingredients:

2   tsp. coarse salt
1   lime wedge
3   oz. white tequila
1   oz. triple sec
2   oz. lime juice
1   oz. raspberry juice
1   c. crushed ice

Directions:

1. Place salt in a saucer.
2. Rub rim of a cocktail glass with lime wedge and dip glass into salt to coat rim thoroughly.
3. Reserve lime.
4. Pour tequila, triple sec, lime juice, raspberry juice, and crushed ice into a blender.
5. Blend well at high speed.
6. Pour into cocktail glass.

Yields: 1 serving.

Creamy Raspberry Slush

You need to enjoy raspberry seeds for this one, and it is delicious. If not, you are welcome to strain the seeds out.

Ingredients:

1½ c. raspberries, fresh
1¼ c. grape juice, unsweetened white
1½ c. raspberry sherbet
¼ c. water
¼ c. red wine
1 Tbs. lemon juice
10 ice cubes
    fresh mint sprigs (optional)

Directions:

1. Combine raspberries and grape juice in electric blender.
2. Cover and process until smooth.
3. Add reserved liquid, sherbet, water, wine, and lemon juice in blender; cover, and process until smooth.
4. Add ice cubes; process until frothy.

Yields: 4 servings.

Raspberry Cheesecake

This is a wonderful blend of raspberry cream.

Ingredients:

1 Tbs. cream cheese, softened
1 oz. white Crème de Cacao
1 oz. black raspberry liqueur
2 scoops vanilla ice cream
½ c. ice

Directions:

1. Place all ingredients into blender.
2. Blend until smooth and pour into glass.

Yields: 1 serving.

Chocolate Raspberry Martini

Chocolate and raspberry are a natural hit every time you blend the two tastes together.

Ingredients:

1½ oz. raspberry vodka
½ oz. chocolate liqueur
    splash of soda

Directions:

1. Combine vodka and liqueur in a shaker with ice.
2. Shake and strain into a cocktail glass.
3. Top with a splash of soda.
4. Garnish with a fresh raspberry.

Yields: 1 serving.

Festival Information

The Annual Raspberry Festival in Cottonwood, ID
Held 1st Sunday every August.
Benefits the Historical Museum at St. Gertrude,
465 Keuterville Rd., Cottonwood, ID 83522-5183
  Family entertainment, live music, cultural demonstrations, classic car show, quilt show, tours of Monastery Chapel and the Historical Museum, fun run (10K), cake walk, arts and crafts.
Phone: 208-962-5061
www.historicalmuseumatstgertrude.com/Events/musrasfest.html

Bear Lake Raspberry Days Festival in Garden City, UT
Held 1st Thursday through Saturday every August.
  Raspberries blended, baked, and jammed. Parade, fireworks, crafts, rodeo, raspberry pancakes, and shakes.

Raspberry Day Scramble at Bear Lake West Golf Course.
Phone: 208-945-2744 | Venders Information Phone: 435-946-2901
www.bearlake.org/calendar.html

Raspberry Festival in Hopkins, MN
Held 10 days every July.
  Parade, concession stands, crafts, golf tournament, live music, 5-mile run, bike races, pageants. Festival Board of Directors: P.O. Box 504, 10921 Excelsior Blvd., Suite 116, Hopkins, MN 55343
Phone: 952-931-0878 | Fax: 952-535-8850
www.hopkinsraspberryfestival.com

Raspberry Festival in Lynden, WA
Held: 3rd weekend every July.
  Windmill hotel, shopping center, sidewalk sales, raspberry sampling, wine tasting, raspberry run/walk for cancer, rides through town in a wagon drawn by draft horses, live jazz music, berry farm tours, 3 on 3 basketball tournaments, raspberry pancake breakfast, arts and crafts, prize drawings.
Lynden Chamber of Commerce Phone: 360-354-5995
www.lynden.org

Raspberry Growers Associations and Commissions

American Farm Bureau Federation
600 Maryland Ave. SW, Suite 1000W, Washington DC 20024
Phone: 202-406-3600 - Fax: 202-406-3602
www.fb.org, www.secondharvest.org

Berry Growers Association
30 Harmony Way, Kemptville, Ont. K0G-1J0
Phone: 613-258-4587 - Fax: 613-258-9129
Email: kconsult@allstream.net

Links to Worldwide Universities, Agencies, Programs:
Northwest Berry & Grape Information Network:
Oregon State University: http://berrygrape.oregonstate.edu
University of Idaho: www.extension.uidaho.edu
Washington State University: www.gardening.wsu.edu

Oregon Raspberry and Blackberry Commission
4845 B SW Dresden Ave., Corvallis, OR 97333
Phone: 541-758-4043 - Fax: 541-758-4553
www.oregon-berries.com

Raspberry Industry Development Council
130-32160 South Fraser Way, Abbotsford, BC V2T 1W5
Phone: 604-854-8010 - Fax: 604-854-6050
http://bcraspberries.com

The North American Bramble Growers Association
1138 Rock Rest Rd., Pittsboro, NC 27312
www.raspberryblackberry.com

The Washington Red Raspberry Commission
1796 Front St., Lynden, WA 98264
Phone: 360-354-8767 - Fax: 360-354-0948
www.red-raspberry.org

USDA Links to any County Cooperative State Research, Education and
County Extension Office in the USA:
www.csrees.usda.gov/Extension

University of Idaho at Twin Falls
P.O. Box 1827, Twin Falls, ID 83303-1827
Phone: 208-736-3603 - Fax: 208-736-0843
Email: ceberl@uidaho.edu

Washington State Horticultural Association
P.O. Box 136, Wenatchee, WA 98807
Phone: 509-665-9641; Fax 509-665-8541
www.wahort.org

Washington State University
Hulbert 411, Pullman, WA, 99164-6248 USA
Phone: 509-335-2837

U.S. and Metric Measurement Charts

Here are some measurement equivalents to help you with exchanges. There was a time when many people thought the entire world would convert to the metric scale. While most of the world has, America still has not. Metric conversions in cooking are vitally important to preparing a tasty recipe. Here are simple conversion tables that should come in handy.

U.S. Measurement Equivalents

A few grains/pinch/dash, (dry) = Less than ⅛ teaspoon
A dash (liquid) = A few drops
3 teaspoons = 1 tablespoon
½ tablespoon = 1½ teaspoons
1 tablespoon = 3 teaspoons
2 tablespoons = 1 fluid ounce
4 tablespoons = ¼ cup
5⅓ tablespoons = ⅓ cup
8 tablespoons = ½ cup
8 tablespoons = 4 fluid ounces
10⅔ tablespoons = ⅔ cup
12 tablespoons = ¾ cup
16 tablespoons = 1 cup
16 tablespoons = 8 fluid ounces
⅛ cup = 2 tablespoons
¼ cup = 4 tablespoons
¼ cup = 2 fluid ounces
⅓ cup = 5 tablespoons plus 1 teaspoon
½ cup = 8 tablespoons
1 cup = 16 tablespoons
1 cup = 8 fluid ounces
1 cup = ½ pint
2 cups = 1 pint
2 pints = 1 quart
4 quarts (liquid) = 1 gallon
8 quarts (dry) = 1 peck
4 pecks (dry) = 1 bushel
1 kilogram = approximately 2 pounds
1 liter = approximately 4 cups or 1 quart

Approximate Metric Equivalents by Volume

U.S.	Metric
¼ cup	= 60 milliliters
½ cup	= 120 milliliters
1 cup	= 230 milliliters65
1¼ cups	= 300 milliliters
1½ cups	= 360 milliliters
2 cups	= 460 milliliters
2½ cups	= 600 milliliters
3 cups	= 700 milliliters
4 cups (1 quart)	= .95 liter
1.06 quarts	= 1 liter
4 quarts (1 gallon)	= 3.8 liters

Approximate Metric Equivalents by Weight

U.S.	Metric
¼ ounce	= 7 grams
½ ounce	= 14 grams
1 ounce	= 28 grams
1¼ ounces	= 35 grams
1½ ounces	= 40 grams
2½ ounces	= 70 grams
4 ounces	= 112 grams
5 ounces	= 140 grams
8 ounces	= 228 grams
10 ounces	= 280 grams
15 ounces	= 425 grams
16 ounces (1 pound)	= 454 grams

Glossary

Aerate: A synonym for sift; to pass ingredients through a fine-mesh device to break up large pieces and incorporate air into ingredients to make them lighter.

Al dente: "To the tooth," in Italian. The pasta is cooked just enough to maintain a firm, chewy texture.

Baste: To brush or spoon liquid fat or juices over meat during roasting to add flavor and prevent drying out.

Bias-slice: To slice a food crosswise at a 45-degree angle.

Bind: To thicken a sauce or hot liquid by stirring in ingredients such as eggs, flour, butter, or cream until it holds together.

Blackened: Popular Cajun-style cooking method. Seasoned foods are cooked over high heat in a super-heated heavy skillet until charred.

Blanch: To scald, as in vegetables being prepared for freezing; as in almonds so as to remove skins.

Blend: To mix or fold two or more ingredients together to obtain equal distribution throughout the mixture.

Braise: To brown meat in oil or other fat and then cook slowly in liquid. The effect of braising is to tenderize the meat.

Bread: To coat food with crumbs (usually with soft or dry bread crumbs), sometimes seasoned.

Brown: To quickly sauté, broil, or grill either at the beginning or at the end of meal preparation, often to enhance flavor, texture, or eye appeal.

Brush: To use a pastry brush to coat a food such as meat or pastry with melted butter, glaze, or other liquid.

Butterfly: To cut open a food such as pork chops down the center without cutting all the way through, and then spread apart.

Caramelization: Browning sugar over a flame, with or without the addition of some water to aid the process. The temperature range in which sugar caramelizes is approximately 320 to 360 degrees F.

Clarify: To remove impurities from butter or stock by heating the liquid, then straining or skimming it.

Coddle: A cooking method in which foods (such as eggs) are put in separate containers and placed in a pan of simmering water for slow, gentle cooking.

Confit: To slowly cook pieces of meat in their own gently rendered fat.

Core: To remove the inedible center of fruits such as pineapples.

Cream: To beat vegetable shortening, butter, or margarine, with or without sugar, until light and fluffy. This process traps in air bubbles, later used to create height in cookies and cakes.

Crimp: To create a decorative edge on a pie crust. On a double pie crust, this also seals the edges together.

Curd: A custard-like pie or tart filling flavored with juice and zest of citrus fruit, usually lemon, although lime and orange may also be used.

Curdle: To cause semisolid pieces of coagulated protein to develop in food, usually as a result of the addition of an acid substance, or the overheating of milk or egg-based sauces.

Custard: A mixture of beaten egg, milk, and possibly other ingredients such as sweet or savory flavorings, which are cooked with gentle heat, often in a water bath or double boiler. As pie filling, the custard is frequently cooked and chilled before being layered into a baked crust.

Deglaze: To add liquid to a pan in which foods have been fried or roasted, in order to dissolve the caramelized juices stuck to the bottom of the pan.

Dot: To sprinkle food with small bits of an ingredient such as butter to allow for even melting.

Dredge: To sprinkle lightly and evenly with sugar or flour. A dredger has holes pierced on the lid to sprinkle evenly.

Drippings: The liquids left in the bottom of a roasting or frying pan after meat is cooked. Drippings are generally used for gravies and sauces.

Drizzle: To pour a liquid such as a sweet glaze or melted butter in a slow, light trickle over food.

Dust: To sprinkle food lightly with spices, sugar, or flour for a light coating.

Egg Wash: A mixture of beaten eggs (yolks, whites, or whole eggs) with either milk or water. Used to coat cookies and other baked goods to give them a shine when baked.

Emulsion: A mixture of liquids, one being a fat or oil and the other being water based so that tiny globules of one are suspended in the other. This may involve the use of stabilizers, such as egg or custard. Emulsions may be temporary or permanent.

Entrée: A French term that originally referred to the first course of a meal, served after the soup and before the meat courses. In the United States, it refers to the main dish of a meal.

Fillet: To remove the bones from meat or fish for cooking.

Filter: To remove lumps, excess liquid, or impurities by passing through paper or cheesecloth.

Firm-Ball Stage: In candy making, the point where boiling syrup dropped in cold water forms a ball that is compact yet gives slightly to the touch.

Flambé: To ignite a sauce or other liquid so that it flames.

Flan: An open pie filled with sweet or savory ingredients; also, a Spanish dessert of baked custard covered with caramel.

Flute: To create a decorative scalloped or undulating edge on a pie crust or other pastry.

Fricassee: Usually a stew in which the meat is cut up, lightly cooked in butter, and then simmered in liquid until done.

Frizzle: To cook thin slices of meat in hot oil until crisp and slightly curly.

Ganache: A rich chocolate filling or coating made with chocolate, vegetable shortening, and possibly heavy cream. It can coat cakes or cookies, and be used as a filling for truffles.

Glaze: A liquid that gives an item a shiny surface. Examples are fruit jams that have been heated or chocolate thinned with melted vegetable shortening. Also, to cover a food with such a liquid.

Gratin: To bind together or combine food with a liquid such as cream, milk, béchamel sauce, or tomato sauce, in a shallow dish. The mixture is then baked until cooked and set.

Hard-Ball Stage: In candy making, the point at which syrup has cooked long enough to form a solid ball in cold water.

Hull (also husk): To remove the leafy parts of soft fruits, such as strawberries or blackberries.

Infusion: To extract flavors by soaking them in liquid heated in a covered pan. The term also refers to the liquid resulting from this process.

Jerk or Jamaican Jerk Seasoning: A dry mixture of various spices such as chilies, thyme, garlic, onions, and cinnamon or cloves used to season meats such as chicken or pork.

Julienne: To cut into long, thin strips.

Jus: The natural juices released by roasting meats.

Larding: To inset strips of fat into pieces of meat, so that the braised meat stays moist and juicy.

Marble: To gently swirl one food into another.

Marinate: To combine food with aromatic ingredients to add flavor.

Meringue: Egg whites beaten until they are stiff, then sweetened. It can be used as the topping for pies or baked as cookies.

Mull: To slowly heat cider with spices and sugar.

Parboil: To partly cook in a boiling liquid.

Peaks: The mounds made in a mixture. For example, egg white that has been whipped to stiffness. Peaks are "stiff" if they stay upright or "soft" if they curl over.

Pesto: A sauce usually made of fresh basil, garlic, olive oil, pine nuts, and cheese. The ingredients are finely chopped and then mixed, uncooked, with pasta. Generally, the term refers to any uncooked sauce made of finely chopped herbs and nuts.

Pipe: To force a semisoft food through a bag (either a pastry bag or a plastic bag with one corner cut off) to decorate food.

Pressure Cooking: To cook using steam trapped under a locked lid to produce high temperatures and achieve fast cooking time.

Purée: To mash or sieve food into a thick liquid.

Ramekin: A small baking dish used for individual servings of sweet and savory dishes.

Reduce: To cook liquids down so that some of the water evaporates.

Refresh: To pour cold water over freshly cooked vegetables to prevent further cooking and to retain color.

Roux: A cooked paste usually made from flour and butter used to thicken sauces.

Sauté: To cook foods quickly in a small amount of oil in a skillet or sauté pan over direct heat.

Scald: To heat a liquid, usually a dairy product, until it almost boils.

Sear: To seal in a meat's juices by cooking it quickly using very high heat.

Seize: To form a thick, lumpy mass when melted (usually applies to chocolate).

Sift: To remove large lumps from a dry ingredient such as flour or confectioners' sugar by passing it through a fine mesh. This process also incorporates air into the ingredients, making them lighter.

Simmer: To cook food in a liquid at a low enough temperature that small bubbles begin to break the surface.

Steam: To cook over boiling water in a covered pan, this method keeps foods' shape, texture, and nutritional value intact better than methods such as boiling.

Steep: To soak dry ingredients (tea leaves, ground coffee, herbs, spices, etc.) in liquid until the flavor is infused into the liquid.

Stewing: To brown small pieces of meat, poultry, or fish, then simmer them with vegetables or other ingredients in enough liquid to cover them, usually in a closed pot on the stove, in the oven, or with a slow cooker.

Thin: To reduce a mixture's thickness with the addition of more liquid.

Truss: To use string, skewers, or pins to hold together a food to maintain its shape while it cooks (usually applied to meat or poultry).

Unleavened: Baked goods that contain no agents to give them volume, such as baking powder, baking soda, or yeast.

Vinaigrette: A general term referring to any sauce made with vinegar, oil, and seasonings.

Zest: The thin, brightly colored outer part of the rind of citrus fruits. It contains volatile oils, used as a flavoring.

Did You Know? . . .

Did you know what to do with your leftover chocolate after dipping, drizzling, and molding is finished? You only need your imagination to find things to dip in the leftover chocolate. Pretzels, raisins, nuts, marshmallows, cookies, and dried fruits are all yummy when dipped in chocolate. You can also dip leftover candy pieces or chopped bar cookies in the chocolate. Look around your kitchen and you will be surprised at where your imagination leads you!

Did you know if you have a lot of leftover chocolate, it can be saved and re-melted next time you mold or dip chocolate?

Recipe Index of Raspberry Delights

314

315

Reader Feedback Form

Dear Reader,

We are very interested in what our readers think. Please fill in the form below and return it to:

Whispering Pine Press International, Inc.
c/o Raspberry Delights Cookbook
P.O. Box 214, Spokane Valley, WA 99037-0214
Phone: (509) 928-8700 | Fax: (509) 922-9949
Email: sales@whisperingpinepress.com
Publisher Websites: www.WhisperingPinePress.com
www.WhisperingPinePressBookstore.com
Blog: www.WhisperingPinePressBlog.com

Name: _____

Address: _____

City, St., Zip: _____

Phone/Fax: (_____) _____ / (_____) _____

Email: _____

Comments/Suggestions: _____

_____

_____

_____

_____

A great deal of care and attention has been exercised in the creation of this book. Designing a great cookbook that is original, fun, and easy to use has been a job that required many hours of diligence, creativity, and research. Although we strive to make this book completely error free, errors and discrepancies may not be completely excluded. If you come across any errors or discrepancies, please make a note of them and send them to our publishing office. We are constantly updating our manuscripts, eliminating errors, and improving quality.

Please contact us at the address above.

About the Cookbook Delights Series

The *Cookbook Delights Series* includes many different topics and themes. If you have a passion for food and wish to know more information about different foods, then this series of cookbooks will be beneficial to you. Each book features a different type of food, such as avocados, strawberries, huckleberries, salmon, vegetarian, lentils, almonds, cherries, coconuts, lemons, and many, many more.

The *Cookbook Delights Series* not only includes cookbooks about individual foods but also includes several holiday-themed cookbooks. Whatever your favorite holiday may be, chances are we have a cookbook with recipes designed with that holiday in mind. Some examples include *Halloween Delights, Thanksgiving Delights, Christmas Delights, Valentine Delights, Mother's Day Delights, St. Patrick's Day Delights,* and *Easter Delights.*

Each cookbook is designed for easy use and is organized into alphabetical sections. Over 250 recipes are included along with other interesting facts, folklore, and history of the featured food or theme. Each book comes with a beautiful full-color cover, ordering information, and a list of other upcoming books in the series.

Note cards, bookmarks, and a daily journal have been printed and are available to go along with each cookbook. You may view the entire line of cookbooks, journals, cards, posters, puzzles, and bookmarks by visiting our website at www.raspberrydelights.com, or you can email us with your questions and your comments to: sales@whisperingpinepress.com.

Please ask your local bookstore to carry these sets of books.

To order, please contact:

Whispering Pine Press International, Inc.
c/o Raspberry Delights Cookbook
P.O. Box 214, Spokane Valley, WA 99037-0214
Phone: (509) 928-8700 | Fax: (509) 922-9949
Email: sales@whisperingpinepress.com
Publisher Websites: www.WhisperingPinePress.com
www.WhisperingPinePressBookstore.com
Blog: www.WhisperingPinePressBlog.com

We Invite You to Join the
Whispering Pine Press International, Inc.,
Book Club

Whispering Pine Press International, Inc.
c/o Raspberry Delights Cookbook
P.P.O. Box 214, Spokane Valley, WA 99037-0214
Phone: (509) 928-8700 | Fax: (509) 922-9949
Email: sales@whisperingpinepress.com
Publisher Websites: www.WhisperingPinePress.com
www.WhisperingPinePressBookstore.com
Blog: www.WhisperingPinePressBlog.com

Buy 11 books and get the next one free, based on the average price of the first eleven purchased.

How the club works:

Simply use the order form below and order books from our catalog. You can buy just one at a time or all eleven at once. After the first eleven books are purchased, the next one is free. Please add shipping and handling as listed on this form. There are no purchase requirements at any time during your membership. Free book credit is based on the average price of the first eleven books purchased.

Join today. Pick your books and mail in the form today.

Yes! I want to join the Whispering Pine Press International, Inc., Book Club! Enroll me and send the books indicated below.

Title   Price

1. _____
2. _____
3. _____
4. _____
5. _____
6. _____
7. _____
8. _____
9. _____
10. _____
11. _____

Free Book Title: _____

Free Book Price: _____ Avg. Price: _____ Total Price: _____

Credit for the free book is based on the average price of the first 11 books purchased.

(Please circle one) Check | Visa | MasterCard | Discover | American Express

Credit Card #: _____ Expiration Date: _____

Name: _____

Address: _____

City: _____ State: _____ Country: _____

Zip/Postal: _____ Phone: (____) _____

Email: _____

Signature: _____

Whispering Pine Press International, Inc. Fundraising Opportunities

Fundraising cookbooks are proven moneymakers and great keepsake providers for your group. Whispering Pine Press International, Inc., offers a very special personalized cookbook fundraising program that encourages success to organizations all across the USA.

Our prices are competitive and fair. Currently, we offer a special of 100 books with many free features and excellent customer service. Any purchase you make is guaranteed first-rate.

Flexibility is not a problem. If you have special needs, we guarantee our cooperation in meeting each of them. Our goal is to create a cookbook that goes beyond your expectations. We have the confidence and a record that promises continual success.

Another great fundraising program is the *Cookbook Delights Series* Program. With cookbook orders of 50 copies or more, your organization receives a huge discount, making for a prompt and lucrative solution.

We also specialize in assisting group fundraising – Christian, community, nonprofit, and academic among them. If you are struggling for a new idea, something that will enhance your success and broaden your appeal, Whispering Pine Press International, Inc., can help.

For more information, write, phone, or fax to:

Whispering Pine Press International, Inc.
P.O. Box 214
Spokane Valley, WA 99037-0214
Phone: (509) 928-8700 | Fax: (509) 922-9949
Email: sales@whisperingpinepress.com
Publisher Websites: www.WhisperingPinePress.com
www.WhisperingPinePressBookstore.com
Blog: www.WhisperingPinePressBlog.com
Book Website: www.RaspberryDelights.com
SAN 253-200X

Personalized and/or Translated Order Form for Any Book by Whispering Pine Press International, Inc.

Dear Readers:

If you or your organization wishes to have this book or any other of our books personalized, we will gladly accommodate your needs. For instance, if you would like to change the names of the characters in a book to the names of the children in your family or Sunday school class, we would be happy to work with you on such a project. We can add more information of your choosing and customize this book especially for your family, group, or organization.

We are also offering an option of translating your book into another language. Please fill out the form below telling us exactly how you would like us to personalize your book.

Please send your request to:

Whispering Pine Press International, Inc.
P.O. Box 214, Spokane Valley, WA 99037-0214
Phone: (509) 928-8700 | Fax: (509) 922-9949
Email: sales@whisperingpinepress.com
Publisher Websites: www.WhisperingPinePress.com
www.WhisperingPinePressBookstore.com
Blog: www.WhisperingPinePressBlog.com

Person/Organization Placing Request: _____

Date: _____ Phone: (____) _____

Address: _____ Fax: (____) _____

City: _____ State: _____ Zip: _____

Language of the Book: _____

Please explain your request in detail: _____

_____

_____

_____

_____

_____

Raspberry Delights Cookbook
A Collection of Raspberry Recipes
How to Order

Get your additional copies of this book by returning an order form and your check, money order or credit card information to:

Whispering Pine Press International, Inc.
P.O. Box 214, Spokane Valley, WA 99037-0214
Phone: (509) 928-8700 | Fax: (509) 922-9949
Email: sales@whisperingpinepress.com
Publisher Websites: www.WhisperingPinePress.com
www.WhisperingPinePressBookstore.com
Blog: www.WhisperingPinePressBlog.com

Customer Name: _____

Address: _____

City, St., Zip: _____

Phone/Fax: _____

Email: _____
- -

Please send me _____ copies of _____ _____
_____ at $_____ per copy and
$4.95 for shipping and handling per book, plus $2.95 each for additional
books. Enclosed is my check, money order, or charge my account for
$_____.

☐ Check ☐ Money Order ☐ Credit Card

(*Circle One*) MasterCard | Discover | Visa | American Express
☐☐☐☐ ☐☐☐☐ ☐☐☐☐ ☐☐☐☐

Expiration Date: _____

_____
Signature

Whispering Pine Press International, Inc. Order Form

Gift-wrapping, Autographing, and Inscription

We are proud to offer personal autographing by the author. For a limited time this service is absolutely free!
Gift-wrapping is also available for $4.95 per item.

1. Sold To

Name: _____
Street/Route: _____
_____
City: _____
State: _____ Zip: _____
Country: _____
Gift message: _____
_____
Email address: _____
Daytime Phone: (_ _) _ _ _-_ _ _ _
*Necessary for verifying orders
Home Phone: (_ _) _ _ _-_ _ _ _
Fax: (_ _) _ _ _-_ _ _ _

2. Ship To

☐ Is this a new or corrected address?

☐ Alternative Shipping Address

☐ Mailing Address

Name: _____
Address: _____
_____
City: _____
State: _____ Zip: _____
Country: _____
Email address: _____

3. Items Ordered

ISBN # /Item #	Size	Color	Qty.	Title or Description	Price	Total

4. Method Of Payment

International, Inc. (No Cash or COD's)

☐ Visa ☐ MasterCard ☐ Discover ☐ American Express ☐ Check/Money Order

Please make it payable to Whispering Pine Press International, Inc. (No Cash or COD's)

Account Number   Expiration Date
                         _____ / _____
                         Month Year

☐☐☐☐ ☐☐☐☐ ☐☐☐☐ ☐☐☐☐

Signature_____
              Cardholder's signature
Printed Name_____
          Please print name of cardholder
Address of Cardholder_____

Subtotal	
Gift wrap $4.95 Each	
For delivery in WA add 8.7% sales tax.	
Shipping See chart at left	
6. Total	

5. Shipping & Handling

Continental US

US Postal Ground: For books please add $4.95 for the first book and $2.95 each for additional books.
All non-book items, add 15% of the Subtotal.
Please allow 1-4 weeks for delivery.
US Postal Air: Please add $15.00 shipping and handling.
Please allow 1-3 days for delivery.
Alaska, Hawaii, and the US Territories By Ship:
Please add 10% shipping and handling
(minimum charge $15.00).

Please
By Air: Please add 12% shipping and handling (minimum charge $15.00).
Please allow 2 –6 weeks for delivery.
International By Ship: Please add 10% shipping and handling (minimum charge $15.00).
Please allow 6-12 weeks for delivery.
By Air: Please add 12% shipping and handling (minimum charge $15.00).
Please allow 2-6 weeks for delivery.
FedEx Shipments: Add $5.00 to the above airmail charges for overnight delivery.

Shop Online:
www.whisperingpinepress.com
Fax orders to: (509) 922-9949

Whispering Pine Press International, Inc.
P.O. Box 214
Spokane Valley, WA 99037-0214 USA
Phone: (509) 928-8700 • Fax: (509) 922-9949
Email: sales@whisperingpinepress.com
Website: www.whisperingpinepress.com

About the Author and Cook

Karen Jean Matsko Hood has always enjoyed cooking, baking, and experimenting with recipes. At this time Hood is working to complete a series of cookbooks that blends her skills and experience in cooking and entertaining. Hood entertains large groups of people and especially enjoys designing creative menus with holiday, international, ethnic, and regional themes.

Hood is publishing a cookbook series entitled the *Cookbook Delights Series*, in which each cookbook emphasizes a different food ingredient or theme. The first cookbook in the series is *Apple Delights Cookbook*. Hood is working to complete another series of cookbooks titled *Hood and Matsko Family Cookbooks*, which includes many recipes handed down from her family heritage and others that have emerged from more current family traditions. She has been invited to speak on talk radio shows on various topics, and favorite recipes from her cookbooks have been prepared on local television programs.

Hood was born and raised in Great Falls, Montana. As an undergraduate, she attended the College of St. Benedict in St. Joseph, Minnesota, and St. John's University in Collegeville, Minnesota. She attended the University of Great Falls in Great Falls, Montana. Hood received a B.S. Degree in Natural Science from the College of St. Benedict and minored in both Psychology and Secondary Education. Upon her graduation, Hood and her husband taught science and math on the island of St. Croix in the U.S. Virgin Islands. Hood has completed postgraduate classes at the University of Iowa in Iowa City, Iowa. In May 2001, she completed her Master's Degree in Pastoral Ministry at Gonzaga University in Spokane, Washington. She has taken postgraduate classes at Lewis and Clark College on the North Idaho college campus in Coeur d'Alene, Idaho, and Taylor University in Fort Wayne, Indiana. Hood is working on research projects to complete her Ph.D. in Leadership Studies at Gonzaga University in Spokane, Washington.

Hood resides in Greenacres, Washington, along with her husband, sixteen children, and foster children. Her interests include writing, research, and teaching. She previously has volunteered as a court advocate in the Spokane juvenile court system for abused and neglected children. Hood is a literary advocate for youth and adults. Her hobbies include cooking, baking, collecting, photography, indoor and outdoor gardening, farming, and the cultivation of unusual flowering plants and orchids. She enjoys raising several specialty breeds of animals including Babydoll Southdown, Friesen, and Icelandic sheep, Icelandic horses, bichons frisés, cockapoos, Icelandic sheepdogs, a Newfoundland, a Rottweiler, a variety of Nubian and fainting goats, and a few rescue cats. Hood also enjoys bird-watching and finds all aspects of nature precious.

She demonstrates a passionate appreciation of the environment and a respect for all life. She also invites you to visit her websites:

www.KarenJeanMatskoHood.com
www.KarenJeanMatskoHoodBookstore.com
www.KarenJeanMatskoHoodBlog.com
www.KarensKidsBooks.com
www.KarensTeenBooks.com

www.HoodFamilyBlog.com
www.HoodFamily.com

Author's Social Media
Please Follow the Author on **Twitter**: @KarenJeanHood
Friend her on **Facebook**: Karen Jean Matsko Hood Author Fan Page
Google Plus Profile: Karen Jean Matsko Hood
Pinterest.com/KarenJMHood

www.ingramcontent.com/pod-product-compliance
Lightning Source LLC
Chambersburg PA
CBHW060247100426

42742CB00011B/1664